THE POLITICS OF INQUIRY

THE POLITICS OF INQUIRY

*Education Research and the
"Culture of Science"*

BENJAMIN BAEZ
and
DERON BOYLES

STATE UNIVERSITY OF NEW YORK PRESS

Published by
STATE UNIVERSITY OF NEW YORK PRESS, ALBANY

© 2009 State University of New York

All rights reserved

Printed in the United States of America

For information, contact
State University of New York Press, Albany, NY
www.sunypress.edu

Production, Laurie Searl
Marketing, Anne M. Valentine

Library of Congress Cataloging-in-Publication Data

Baez, Benjamin.
    The politics of inquiry : education research and the "culture of science" / Benjamin Baez
and Deron Boyles.
        p. cm.
    Includes bibliographical references and index.
    ISBN 978-0-7914-7687-1 (hardcover : alk. paper)
    ISBN 978-0-7914-7688-8 (pbk. : alk. paper)
    1. Education—Research. I. Boyles, Deron. II. Title.

LB1028.B267 2009
370.72—dc22   2008018844

10 9 8 7 6 5 4 3 2 1

CONTENTS

PREFACE

Recent federal legislation, such as the *No Child Left Behind Act* and the *Education Sciences Reform Act*, the practices of the Institute of Education Sciences (IES), reports such as *Scientific Research in Education* (SRE) from the National Research Council (NRC), and the various statements supporting or critiquing all of these, for all their real differences, have at least one thing in common: They are part of a recent discourse on the "science of education." In particular, SRE, which provides a point of departure for our arguments in this book, seeks to define what a science of education might look like. When one focuses on the text itself, that is, on what SRE actually says, one has to conclude that it is a justifiable explanation of current scientific thinking, but as such it is not particularly original or interesting. It is merely a recent manifestation of the long-standing angst over the scientificity of educational inquiry.

We will not contribute in this book to a discourse that believes itself to be offering something new about whether or not education can be scientific. Instead of focusing too much on the supposed intended meaning of SRE, which will only push us toward the tedious task of offering yet another philosophy of the science of education, we spend much of our energies, not on determining what the text means but on what makes it possible, and, in turn, what it makes possible. Our subject is, at first glance, education research, but our actual subject is much broader than that. We think SRE—indeed, the entire discourse on education science—reflects a number of distinct, but mutually constitutive, political forces or movements using science to shape what we can *think*, and, thus, what we can *become* in the so-called postmodern age. These forces or movements are, briefly, (1) the movements to professionalize educational researchers, (2) the attempts to restrict democracy via scientism, (3) the uses of academic classifications for organizing the world into social groups, (4) the imperatives of the informational society, which seek precision in order to convert the world into "data" for easy governing, and (5) the effects of transnational capitalist exchanges, which convert everything into a cost-benefit analysis and make us all complicit in ways we do not fully grasp.

Our chapters, each addressing one or more of these political forces, can be read independently of each other. Together, however, they reflect what we think is an important mode of inquiry that *SRE* and other texts seeking to establish a science for education would displace. Our mode of inquiry is interpretive and critical. Our interpretation of a text—a term we use broadly to mean anything that can be *read*, and not just actual written texts—involves two kinds of reading. The first kind of reading stays close to the text and seeks to expose its underlying logic and contradictions. The second kind of reading situates these texts within the cultural and political contexts that make them possible and of which they are representative, more or less explicitly.

This kind of reading is a highly *theoretical* practice, and as such it is also highly *practical*. What do we mean? Before saying what we mean, we must first identify our object: What is theory? Theory seems to involve hypotheses. Yet, consider a claim that could very well be made by anybody anywhere: "Bob is a busybody." If theory is nothing more than a hypothesis, then the assertion that this claim is actually a theory may very well be perfectly valid. But a "theory" seems more than simply a hypothesis, or, rather, it seems more than a simple hypothesis. Jonathan Culler provides what we think is a justifiable definition of theory. He argues that theory is a hypothesis but of a particular kind. It must involve complex relations of a systematic kind among a number of factors, and it cannot be obvious or easily confirmed or disproved.[1] This implies, then, that theory is not an "empirical" concept; it is an act of speculation, an act of interpretation, an act of reading. So, when theory is construed as a concentration of observations based on empirical "facts" by behaviorists and other positivist researchers, we can say, with Paul de Man, that such construction may in fact be a resistance to reading.[2]

Theories, at least the ones with which we are concerned, are, according to Culler, "speculative practices" whose main effect is to disrupt "common sense." Inquiry leading to theories, therefore, is "practical" to the extent it changes people's views, and makes them think differently about their objects of study and their activities in studying them. Theories, then, are not simply interpretive acts; they are "practices" with very practicable effects—they move across space and time and (re)shape the worlds they touch. Yet, in education, we seem comfortable with the idea that theory is distinct from practice, especially when we put forth the tired cliché that theory must inform practice. This distinction between theory and practice makes a certain kind of sense if its premise is correct that "theorizing" is a practice of particular actors, namely, intellectuals, academics, scientists, and so on. If such a premise is valid, then one can very well set off the practice

---

1. Jonathan Culler, *Literary Theory: A Very Short Introduction* (Oxford: Oxford University Press, 1997), 2–3.
2. Paul de Man, "The Resistance to Theory," *Yale French Studies* 63 (1982): 3–20, 15.

of theory from the world it tries to explain; that is, the world of the "commonsense," the world of the "everyday," the world of "experience," the world of "practice." We hope our book illustrates, however, that the distinction between theory and practice is not a particularly useful one, for it hides more than it tells: the world that is opposed to theory, the world theories try to explain, is greatly determined by those very theories. Theories seek to make us into some thing; they seek to determine what we can become, and as such, the practice of inquiry is a politics (thus, our title). One may resist this, and we argue for resistance at every turn in our book, but one should hardly be able to deny it.

We are saying, then, that when one reads the theories proposed by researchers, and the theories of science that seek to govern those researchers and the individuals who will become their objects, one must also attend to what those theories effect in material terms. SRE, for example, defines a science for educational inquiry, but understood as a *practice* one can ask whether it is an "offensive" or "defensive" practice. It is an "offensive" practice if it is representative of attempts to replace *mere* practitioners with scientists in the authoritative position with regard to educational "truths"; if, in other words, it seeks to authorize itself in the politics of inquiry, which is also a *politics of becoming.* It is a "defensive" practice if it is premised on a fear that such authority is being threatened by those practitioners' claims to an equally (or more) authoritative practice, or by intellectuals who question the particular authority of scientific practice, as we do in this book. Our task for this book is to read beyond SRE in order to uncover who or what supports or is supported by texts like this. This is our specific task, but the task of reading must be *democratic*—it must be a task for everyone who is affected by theories—thus, everyone. To abdicate the responsibility of reading is, in a sense, to abdicate the responsibility of becoming.

The kind of reading we offer in this book is an alternative to the kinds of work being privileged in education, which is increasingly directed toward an empiricism that will always defeat itself since, at its root, it resists reading. Our kind of reading requires *reading against a text*, so to speak, since academic texts, especially scientific ones, have an uncanny ability to hide their institutional (and thus political) bases. Reading against the text requires asking how the text represents *or* challenges the political assumptions, beliefs, values, and practices that dictate how we think and live. The world can be transformed only when it is seen differently than before. It is in this way that we offer this book to readers as a license to critique, which is the most practical thing we can offer to the field of education, and to the individuals who will be made by it. We hope that rather than ascribe to a view of inquiry premised on narrow views of science, or to the gutter utilitarianism associated with the "what works" rhetoric that is thrown about so uncritically in education, that we all do more *reading*, not only of the texts that proliferate but of the world in which such proliferation takes place.

ACKNOWLEDGMENTS

This book, though not starting out as such, took close to five years in the making, and thus we have had numerous opportunities to discuss its ideas with many individuals. Most of these opportunities took place at conferences, particularly at the American Educational Studies Association, the American Educational Research Association, the American Association for the Study of Higher Education, and the Southeast Philosophy of Education Society. As a result of our conversations with others at these conferences, both in formal presentations and informally outside the sessions, we honed our ideas. We cannot thank everyone we talked to about the ideas in this book, but we will be remiss if we do not acknowledge explicitly a few individuals.

We would like to thank Philip Kovacs, whose critique of the six principles underlying the arguments made in the National Research Council's report, *Scientific Research in Education*, so greatly influenced our own that we have included him as a co-author of chapter 2 in this book. The two anonymous reviewers of the manuscript for SUNY Press also pressed us to refine our arguments and to consider others. Yvonna Lincoln's response to a paper summarizing our arguments in chapter 4, which we presented at AERA in San Francisco, was very insightful as well as very encouraging. Ben Baez specifically thanks Gary Rhoades, not only for his comments on various aspects of the book, but also for being a good friend and an intellectual "sparring" partner.

Of course, even with such intellectual assistance, no book is possible without help of a more technical kind. Lisa Chesnel at SUNY Press has been encouraging and accommodating to our needs, particularly allowing us to keep our footnotes, and so we would like to extend our thanks to her. We also wish to thank Tony and Rahna Carusi for their help in preparing the bibliography and other technical aspects of the manuscript.

ONE

ON "EDUCATION RESEARCH"

Scientists are not content with running their own playpens in accordance
with what they regard as the rules of scientific method, they want to uni-
versalize these rules, they want them to become part of society at large
and they use every means at their disposal—argument, propaganda, pressure
tactics, intimidation, lobbying—to achieve their aims.

—Paul Feyerabend

Taking a cue from Jacques Derrida, who asked a similar question of the
university, we ask in this book: *Today, how can we not speak of education research?*[1] One of our answers to this question will be that we cannot *not* speak
of education research. Given the importance of education in our society, its
research cannot but be spoken about, and perhaps with a certain urgency.
Indeed, since the idea of "education research" came into existence, there has
been much speaking about it. The interesting thing is that such speaking is
done without a clear sense of an object. After all, what is "education"? Is it
simply training? Is it schooling? Does it specify a particular set of individual
and institutional phenomena? Does it have a "product?" Is it a service? In this
sense, adding the term *research* to *education* is not particularly problematic,
since these kinds of questions can be answered empirically. Research, we are
told, is the "empirical part of science,"[2] and it explores and discovers new
situations and relationships to understand.[3] But does not "education" also
entail particular ideals—about individuals, institutions, society, the past, the

Paul Feyerabend, *Against Method* (New York: Verso, 1975), 220.
1. Jacques Derrida, "The Principle of Reason: The University in the Eyes of its Pupils," *Graduate Faculty Philosophy Journal* 10, no. 1 (1984): 5–29, 5.
2. Andrea Vierra and Judith Pollock, *Reading Educational Research*, second ed. (Scottsdale, AZ:
Gorsuch Scarisbrick Publishers, 1992), 5.
3. David R. Krathwohl, *Methods of Educational and Social Science Research: An Integrated
Approach* (New York: Longman, 1993).

future, and so on? If so, adding the word *research* to *education* appears more troublesome. Inquiry on ideals need not be—perhaps should not be—entirely an empirical practice. Education as an ideal requires that one rethink the term *education research* as possibly incoherent, since it implies an empiricism that may be opposed to ideas and, hence, ideals. Moreover, we tend not to see educational ideals as such, that is, as *ideals*, often formulating them in notions that appear empirical, at first glance, such as "teaching," "learning," and even the idea of "the child" itself.[4]

Yet we have another response to our initial question. Also taking a cue from Derrida, in rephrasing the question in the negative, "How *can we not* speak of education research," we want to alert the reader that our real purpose is to suggest how one *should not* speak of education research. We will urge readers to reject much of the empiricism and most of the ideas that formulate the current discourse on education research. We will, of course, speak of "education research" throughout this book, but we are tempted to place the term always within quotation marks to signify that the term is to be made problematic. For now, we say simply that we will question both its empiricism and its ideas.

Education research is spoken about quite frequently, though not as if the concept was problematic, as we have just indicated. This is not to say that others have not problematized particular aspects of education research. Indeed, that is all they have done, it seems to us. While it may have always been so, it seems from reading the literature about education research that there appears today a sense in which education research is in a state of flux. It seems to be grounded predominantly in positivist theories, emphasizing often quantitative inquiries into educational phenomena, which is likely due to its roots in psychology and behaviorism.[5] One can see, however, an increase (perhaps a great one over the last thirty years or so) in constructivist understandings of reality, leading to qualitative, ethnographic, and critical inquiries into educational problems.[6]

---

4. Bernadette Baker argues that the "child" is not a natural phenomenon, but a political space for the productions of categories, distinctions, techniques, and reasonings. See Bernadette Baker, " 'Childhood' in the Emergence and Spread of U.S. Public Schools," in *Foucault's Challenge: Discourse, Knowledge, and Power in Education*, ed. Thomas S. Popkewitz and Marie Brennan (New York: Teachers College Press, 1998), 117–43, 138.

5. Ellen Condliffe Lagemann, "Contested Terrain: A History of Education Research in the United States, 1890–1990," *Educational Researcher* 26, no. 9 (1997): 5–17, 5.

6. See Harry F. Wolcott, "Ethnographic Research in Education," in *Complementary Methods for Research in Education*, second ed., ed. Richard M. Jaeger (Washington, DC: American Educational Research Association, 1988), 327–53; see also Thomas A. Schwandt, "Constructivist, Interpretivist Approaches to Human Inquiry," in *Handbook of Qualitative Research*, ed. Norman K. Denzin and Yvonna S. Lincoln (Thousand Oaks, CA: SAGE, 1994), 118–37.

The one thing about education research that can be said without offending anybody is that it privileges the empirical. In other words, education research is understood as discovering/uncovering, analyzing, reporting, and representing human experiences. Such study of human experiences, as is the case with all the studies of human phenomena, is premised on an understanding that such experience is external to the research act itself, a premise we will critique in subsequent chapters, particularly in chapter 4. For now, let us say that this empirical understanding of education research leads to critiques taking the form of polemics about (1) the methods and methodologies used by researchers,[7] (2) the so-called "paradigms" undergirding the study of human subjects,[8] and (3) the purposes to which education research should be put to use.[9] Some of these critiques, however, seem directed at something more "ethical," for lack of a better word. These other critiques, as Yvonna Lincoln suggests, destabilize the notion of the detached observer and call for a better understood (and more ethical) relationship between the researcher and the researched.[10] Here the research act is viewed as one of power, and so researchers must be concerned with questions associated with representation and voice, such as: Who speaks for whom? How does one do such speaking? and Is all this correct, ethical, and reciprocal? The concern with voice and representation leads to critiques, such as James Scheurich and Michelle Young's, asserting that much education research privileges (but unconsciously so) Western theories that devalue those of non-Western cultures.[11] Such criticisms have led to recent questions about the extent to

---

7. See, for example, Elliot W. Eisner, "The Promise and Perils of Alternative Forms of Data Representation," *Educational Researcher* 26, no. 6 (1997): 4–10; Richard E. Mayer, "What Is the Place of Science in Educational Research?" *Educational Researcher* 29, no. 6 (2000): 38–39; and Richard E.. Mayer, "Resisting the Assault on Science: The Case for Evidence-Based Reasoning in Educational Research," *Educational Researcher* 30, no. 7 (2001): 29–30; Tom Barone, "Science, Art, and the Predispositions of Educational Researchers," *Educational Researcher* 30, no. 7 (2001): 24–28.
8. See, for example, Mark A. Constas, "The Changing Nature of Educational Research and a Critique of Postmodernism," *Educational Researcher* 27, no. 2 (1998): 26–33, and "Deciphering Postmodern Educational Research," *Educational Researcher* 27, no. 9 (1998): 36–42; Egon G. Guba and Yvonna S. Lincoln, "Competing Paradigms in Qualitative Research," in *Handbook of Qualitative Research*, ed. Norman K. Denzin and Yvonna S. Lincoln (Thousand Oaks, CA: SAGE Publications, 1994), 105–17; Mayer, "What Is the Place of Science in Educational Research?"
9. George Keller, "Does Higher Education Research Need Revisions?" *The Review of Higher Education* 21, no. 3 (1998): 267–78; William G. Tierney, "On Translation: From Research Findings to Public Utility," *Theory into Practice* 39, no. 3 (2000): 185–90; John Willinsky, "The Strategic Education Research Program and the Public Value of Research," *Educational Researcher* 30, no. 1 (2001): 5–14.
10. See Yvonna S. Lincoln, "Emerging Criteria for Quality in Qualitative and Interpretive Research," *Qualitative Inquiry* 1, no. 3 (1995): 275–89.
11. See James J. Scheurich and Michelle D. Young, "Coloring Epistemologies: Are Our Research Epistemologies Racially Biased?" *Educational Researcher* 26, no. 4 (1997): 4–16.

which education research can represent "reality" (even a socially constructed one), since what is deemed "real" is a product of multiple, shifting meanings and is, therefore, necessarily partial and incomplete.[12]

In short, much of the discourse on education research relates to the empirical realm and leads one to ask questions about which methods are most appropriate in any given situation (e.g., quantitative versus qualitative), as well as, more generally, which of the so-called "paradigms" suit particular questions (e.g., positivism versus constructivism or critical theory). Yet, we can subsume the "paradigm" concerns within the methodological ones, since each is an aspect of the other. That is, "paradigms" cannot exist outside of the methodological theories that determine which questions can be asked and how.[13] However, and to repeat, what seems often spoken about education research, then, is its empiricism, which to us means also its methodology. It is in this context of debate over education research's empiricism and methodology that one can read the recent attempts at defining education research as "scientific."

The concern with whether education research is scientific is not new.[14] Ellen Lagemann points out that the formal study of education did not begin until the turn of the twentieth century, with the establishment of university schools and departments of education and the institutionalization within them of an aspiration to create a "science of education." Since then, it has elicited a continuous litany of complaints regarding its value and validity.[15] Lagemann argues that such criticisms have reflected a deep-seated American ambivalence toward education, with a tendency to rely on education to solve social problems yet discounting the costs and complexities involved in educating.[16] Lagemann appears to us to deem such ambivalence problematic, but we think that this "ambivalence" should be celebrated rather than feared and controlled. Schools are powerful instruments of normalization, and dictating what and how they do things also gives a tremendous amount of power to particular individuals and institutions.

It seems to us that the debate over whether education research can and should be scientific has reached a fevered pitch of late, a phenomenon often attributed to recent federal initiatives to define "quality" education

---

12. See Lincoln, "Emerging Criteria."
13. James Paul Gee, "It's Theories All the Way Down: A Response to Scientific Research in Education," *Teachers College Record* 107, no. 1 (2005): 10–18, 13; Thomas S. Popkewitz, "Is the National Research Council Committee's Report on Scientific Research in Education Scientific? On Trusting the Manifesto," *Qualitative Inquiry* 10, no. 1 (2004): 62–78, 66–68.
14. For two examples of such a history, see Ellen Condliffe Lagemann, *An Elusive Science: The Troubling History of Education Research* (Chicago: University of Chicago Press, 2000); Robert M. W. Travers, *How Research Has Changed American Schools: A History from 1840 to the Present* (Kalamazoo: Mythos Press, 1983).
15. Lagemann, "Contested Terrain," 5.
16. Ibid.

research via a narrow scientism.[17] We think this attribution is largely correct, but not entirely so. The concern with a "science of education" has been concomitant with the institution of education research in universities, as Lagemann points out. And even before the recent federal initiatives there was increased debate within the field about whether education research should be scientific. For example, Richard Mayer, taking exception to Elliot Eisner's argument that education research could be broadened to include studies that are not scientific,[18] argues that education research should be kept "firmly within the domain of science," since the failure to do so will slow the progress of educational theory (which "must be tested against empirical data") and would "diminish the reputation in our field."[19] (We think these remarks reflect a concern with professionalizing education researchers, a point we elaborate upon later in this chapter.) We will argue in this book that while the recent federal initiatives are largely responsible for the increased debate over the scientific nature of education research, other political forces made such federal initiatives possible, and that they continue to be at work to ensure that such a debate is not left open.

In this chapter we discuss the federal initiatives defining "good" education research as a particular kind of scientific method, and we introduce our critique of the National Research Council's (NRC) 2002 report, *Scientific Research in Education* (SRE).[20] SRE purports to explain what constitutes scientific research in education. This report is symptomatic of the social, political, and economic forces shaping educational inquiry, five of which form the primary bases of the chapters in this book: (1) the professionalization of education researchers, (2) the scientism and positivism of education research, (3) the normalization of doctoral work, (4) the institution of science in our lives, and (5) the political economy of research. Before we proceed with these arguments, we need to establish the context for the NRC's attempt to define a science of education, namely, the federal government's recent attempts to ensure "scientifically based" education research.

A "FEDERAL" SCIENCE?

Since SRE was written in the context of the federal government's attempt to create a science *for* education, it is important to give an account of such

---

17. See Patti Lather and Pamela Moss, "Introduction: Implications of the Scientific Research in Education Report for Qualitative Inquiry," *Teachers College Record* 107, no. 1 (2005): 1–3.
18. Eisner, "The Promise and Perils of Alternative Forms of Data Representation."
19. Mayer, "What Is the Place of Science in Educational Research?" 38. Mayer iterated these points in a response to Tom Barone's critique of his article; see Tom Barone, "Science, Art, and the Predispositions of Educational Researchers;" and Mayer, "Resisting the Assault on Science."
20. National Research Council, *Scientific Research in Education*, ed. Richard J. Shavelson and Lisa Towne (Washington, DC: National Academy Press, 2002). Available at http://www.nap.edu/ (Retrieved February 5, 2005).

an initiative. Federal attempts to define education research as scientific first appeared in the *Reading Excellence Act* in 1999 (REA), providing funds for "scientifically based reading research," which

> (A) means the application of rigorous, systematic, and objective procedures to obtain valid knowledge relevant to reading development, reading instruction, and reading difficulties; and (B) shall include research that (i) employs systematic, empirical methods that draw on observation or experiment; (ii) involves rigorous data analyses that are adequate to test the stated hypotheses and justify the general conclusions drawn; (iii) relies on measurements or observational methods that provide valid data across evaluators and observers and across multiple measurements and observations; and (iv) has been accepted by a peer-reviewed journal or approved by a panel of independent experts through a comparably rigorous, objective, and scientific review.[21]

REA, in essence, requires grantees to develop, select, or implement reading programs grounded in its definition of the "best science."[22] It is clear that what this legislation defines as the best science is one grounded in narrow theories of experimentalism, quantifiability, and generalization. Yet, it is important to note that while President George W. Bush's administration has intensified these efforts at establishing a science for education, the REA was passed under President Bill Clinton's term in office. This movement toward science, as we argue in more detail in chapter 4, transcends the particular political ideologies of the politicians who codify it in law.

After REA, but in line with it, draft legislation was introduced in the summer of 2000 by United States Representative Mike Castle (R-Del) that pertained to the reauthorization of the Office of Educational Research and Improvement (OERI). The proposed "Castle Bill" sought to improve education research by requiring that federal dollars be spent on "scientifically valid research" and proposed standards for "scientifically based quantitative" and "scientifically based qualitative" research.[23] The bill as such never came to fruition, but it sparked a great deal of debate about scientific education research and likely led to the establishment of the NRC committee that drafted *SRE*.

It was, however, passage of the *No Child Behind Act* of 2001 (NCLB) that brought this issue of scientific education research to a head. NCLB

---

21. Reading Excellence Act of 1999, Pub. L. No. 105–277 (1999). Available at: http://www.ed.gov/offices/OESE/REA/reading_act.pdf (Retrieved July 1, 2005).
22. Margaret Eisenhart and Lisa Towne, "Contestation and Change in National Policy on 'Scientifically Based' Education Research," *Educational Researcher* 32, no. 7 (2003): 31–38, 32.
23. Ibid., 32–33.

contains more than one hundred references to "scientifically based research," which it defines, similar to REA, as "research that involves the application of rigorous, systematic, and objective procedures to obtain reliable and valid knowledge relevant to education activities and programs." Such research

> (i) employs systematic, empirical methods that draw on observation or experiment; (ii) involves rigorous data analyses that are adequate to test the stated hypotheses and justify the general conclusions drawn; (iii) relies on measurements or observational methods that provide reliable and valid data across evaluators and observers, across multiple measurements and observations, and across studies by the same or different investigators; (iv) is evaluated using experimental or quasiexperimental designs in which individuals, entities, programs, or activities are assigned to different conditions and with appropriate controls to evaluate the effects of the condition of interest, with a preference for random-assignment experiments, or other designs to the extent that those designs contain within-condition or across-condition controls; (v) ensures that experimental studies are presented in sufficient detail and clarity to allow for replication or, at a minimum, offer the opportunity to build systematically on their findings; and (vi) has been accepted by a peer-reviewed journal or approved by a panel of independent experts through a comparably rigorous, objective, and scientific review.[24]

As with REA, the NCLB privileges scientism over scientific inquiry, establishing experimental methods as providing the best evidence of educational effectiveness. This legislation led to more legislation that explicitly sought to recreate education research within its narrow scientism, specifically the *Education Sciences Reform Act* of 2002 (ESRA).

ESRA similarly defines "scientifically based research standards" as those that "(1) apply rigorous, systematic, and objective methodology to obtain reliable and valid knowledge relevant to education activities and programs; and (2) present findings and make claims that are appropriate to and supported by the methods that have been employed." To be "rigorous, systematic, and objective," and to be deemed "reliable and valid" the research must be:

> (1) employing systematic, empirical methods that draw on observation or experiment; (2) involving data analyses that are adequate to support the general findings; (3) relying on measurement or

---

24. No Child Left Behind Act of 2001, Pub. L. No. 107-110 (2001). Available at http://www.ed.gov/policy/elsec/leg/esea02/107-110.pdf (Retrieved February 5, 2005).

observational methods that provide reliable data; (4) making claims of causal relationships only in random assignment experiments or other designs (to the extent such designs substantially eliminate plausible competing explanations for the obtained results); (5) ensuring that studies and methods are presented in sufficient detail and clarity to allow for replication or, at a minimum, to offer the opportunity to build systematically on the findings of the research; (6) obtaining acceptance by a peer-reviewed journal or approval by a panel of independent experts through a comparably rigorous, objective, and scientific review; and (7) using research designs and methods appropriate to the research question posed.[25]

ESRA further defines "scientifically valid education evaluation" as that which

(a) adheres to the highest possible standards of quality with respect to research design and statistical analysis; (b) provides an adequate description of the programs evaluated and, to the extent possible, examines the relationship between program implementation and program impacts; (c) provides an analysis of the results achieved by the program with respect to its projected effects; (d) employs experimental designs using random assignment, when feasible, and other research methodologies that allow for the strongest possible causal inferences when random assignment is not feasible; and (e) may study program implementation through a combination of scientifically valid and reliable methods.[26]

The ESRA is important for a number of reasons. First, it defines scientific research narrowly as experimental in nature. Second, it was the first explicit attempt to establish a science for education research, unlike the REA and the NCLB, which arguably were concerned with larger educational issues.[27] Third, ESRA replaced OERI with the Institute of Education Sciences (IES), which is in charge of funding education research, and it does so via a narrow vision of science.

The IES was officially established in 2002 by President George W. Bush. President Bush also appointed Grover J. Whitehurst, who was the assistant secretary of OERI, as the director of IES for a six-year term. IES

---

25. The Education Sciences Reform Act of 2002, Pub. L. No. 107-279 (2002): 4. Available at http://www.ed.gov/policy/rschstat/leg/PL107-279.pdf (Retrieved February 5, 2005).
26. Ibid.
27. We found it more than a little hypocritical that the federal government under George W. Bush insisted upon science in education while it sought to impose its religious, "faith-based," and arguably antiscientific views of the world seemingly everywhere else.

is composed of the National Center for Education Research, the National Center for Education Statistics, and the National Center for Education Evaluation and Regional Assistance. Its purported mission is to provide and expand knowledge on the condition of education, to promote practices that improve academic achievement, and to monitor the effectiveness of federal and other education programs. Its goal is to transform education "into an evidence-based field in which decision makers routinely seek out the best available research and data before adopting programs or practices that will affect significant numbers of students."[28]

Whitehurst's *Statement of Research Methods* on the IES Web site is important to this discussion, so it is worth quoting at length:

> The methods supported by the Institute vary with the question being addressed. They include methods for producing sound descriptive summaries, including surveys, observational data, and administrative records; methods appropriate for isolating possible relationships such as multivariate analysis; and methods designed to address questions concerning the effectiveness of particular policies or practices, including single-subject, quasi-experimental, and experimental approaches. *We strongly prefer, as do policy makers and the public, randomized field trials when the question is the effectiveness of mature programs and practices.* Such trials virtually always include the collection of process data that can provide insight into why an *intervention* does or does not work and that allow an examination of the relationship between implementation and outcomes. However, randomized trials are only a part of our portfolio. A substantial portion of our funding goes to upstream work in which researchers are developing new programs or identifying promising practices, using methods appropriate for those investigations. We also invest in the *development and validation of measurement and assessment tools*. All of the Institute's research programs are embedded in practice, requiring both the selection of topics that are *highly relevant* to practitioners and the conduct of research in authentic education delivery settings. The Institute aims to transform education into an *evidence-based* field. We are devoted to establishing the *rigorous and relevant* research base and the effective dissemination strategies that are a prerequisite to that goal.[29]

---

28. Institute of Education Sciences, *About the Institute of Education Sciences* (Washington, DC: Institute of Education Sciences, n.d.). Available at http://www.ed.gov/about/offices/list/ies/index.html (Retrieved June 25, 2005).
29. Grover J. Whitehurst, *Statement on Research Methods* (Washington, DC: Institute of Education Sciences, n.d.), emphasis added. Available at http://www.ed.gov/about/offices/list/ies/statement042104.html (Retrieved June 25, 2005).

We are not sure to which "public" Whitehurst's statement refers and are inclined to think that the reference is meaningless, since, we dare say, much of the public does not give this any thought at all. Regardless, the "we strongly prefer" makes it clear that the IES will privilege randomized field trials in the projects it will fund. This statement also mentions particular quantitative methods by name ("surveys," "multivariate analysis," "single-subject," "quasi-experimental," and "experimental"), indicating that these too will be given privileged consideration. It also seems to privilege studies on the "effectiveness" of programs, "interventions," and "development and validation of measurement and assessment tools." All these studies tend to be positivist. What it leaves out by name and by implication (e.g., qualitative and other interpretive approaches) is not considered "highly relevant" to practitioners, and it will not support the IES's goal of making education an "evidence-field" or constitute the kind of "rigorous and relevant research" that will further that goal.

This movement toward privileging narrow methods was made clear in a report written by the Coalition for Evidence-Based Policy and commissioned by the IES.[30] This report purports to give practitioners the "tools to distinguish interventions supported by scientifically-rigorous evidence from those which are not."[31] It supposedly gives educators a guide for determining a study's effectiveness, giving ratings to studies according to the strength of their evidence and designs. Some studies will have "strong" evidence of effectiveness; others will have "possible" evidence; and some will not have "meaningful" evidence. The report privileges the randomized controlled trial, which, when well designed and implemented, is considered the "gold standard" for evaluating an intervention's effectiveness in fields such as medicine, welfare and employment policy, and psychology, and thus will constitute "strong" evidence of an intervention's effectiveness.[32]

Such narrow scientism is the kind of logic that supports the projects of the What Works Clearinghouse (WWC), which is controlled by the IES but was actually commissioned by the now defunct OERI. The WWC claims to provide "the public with a central and trusted source of scientific evidence of what works in education." It aims to promote informed education decisions through a set of easily accessible databases and user-friendly reports that provide "education consumers" with ongoing, high quality review of the effectiveness of replicable educational interventions that seek to improve

---

30. Coalition for Evidence-Based Policy, *Identifying and Implementing Educational Practices Supported by Rigorous Evidence: A User Friendly Guide* (Washington, DC: Institute for Education Sciences, 2003). Available at http://www.ed.gov/rschstat/research/pubs/rigorousevid/rigorousevid. pdf (Retrieved June 25, 2005).
31. Ibid., iii.
32. Ibid., 1.

student outcomes.[33] WWC has selected a series of topics for which it will provide systematic review, including interventions seeking to improve middle school and elementary school mathematic achievement, beginning reading, character education, high school dropout, English language learning, pre-school children's school readiness, reductions of delinquent behavior, adult literacy, and peer-assisted learning in reading, math, and science.[34] It rates the intervention after determining the causal validity of each study. Studies will receive one of three ratings: (1) "Meets Evidence Standards," which will be assigned to "randomized controlled trials" that "do not have problems with randomization, attrition, or disruption, and regression discontinuity designs that do not have problems with attrition or disruption"; (2) "Meets Evidence Standards with Reservations," which will be assigned to "strong quasi-experimental studies that have comparison groups and meet other WWC Evidence Standards, as well as randomized trials with randomization, attrition, or disruption problems and regression discontinuity designs with attrition or disruption problems"; and (3) "Does Not Meet Evidence Standards," which will be assigned to "studies that provide insufficient evidence of causal validity or are not relevant to the topic being reviewed."[35]

In addition to the narrow scientism that undergirds these policies, projects, and reports, what is also disturbing to us as education professors who must "prepare" future educators and researchers is the gutter utilitarianism associated with these projects. The notion that what counts as valuable research is "what works" reduces education to the least common denominator and will promote more, rather than less, "faddishness,"[36] as few educators will give any program the longevity that it may require to "prove" its effectiveness. Moreover, the presumptiveness of telling educators how to do their jobs reinforces the re-skilling (or re-professionalizing) of the field and, as a result, might mean fewer and fewer qualified teachers at a time when teacher shortages abound. The IES might help educators make better decisions by leaving them alone, rather than legitimate what will become an increased amount of "interventions" into their lives. Students

33. What Works Clearinghouse, *Who We Are* (Washington, DC: Institute for Education Sciences, n.d.). Available at: http:www.whatworks.ed.gov/whoweare/overview.html (Retrieved April 18, 2005).
34. What Works Clearinghouse, *Topics* (Washington, DC: Institute for Education Sciences, n.d.). Available at: http:www.whatworks.ed.gov/topics/current_topics.html (Retrieved April 18, 2005).
35. What Works Clearinghouse, *Review Process* (Washington, DC: Institute for Education Sciences, n.d.). Available at: http:www.whatworks.ed.gov/reviewprocess/standards.html (Retrieved April 18, 2005).
36. Because it has purportedly lacked scientificity, education research is seen as moving "from fad to fad." See Robert E. Slavin, "Evidence-Based Education Policies: Transforming Educational Practice and Research," *Educational Researcher* 31, no. 7 (2002): 15–21, 15.

and teachers are now mere widgets, to be manipulated and controlled by a slew of researchers seeking money and prestige from IES grants. Students and teachers will indeed become "oil wells,"[37] to be drilled and discarded if they do not produce as expected, regardless of the environmental impact of this search and discard mentality.

Thus, in the name of utility, the federal government now seeks to create a science for education research. Yet it must be stressed that this is not the first time the federal government has become interested in educational research; indeed, such involvement, in small or in large part, has coincided with the history of public education. And while the role of the federal government in education research has changed, it is a role it nevertheless has always had.[38] But there can be little question that these federal initiatives seek to promote scientism and utilitarianism at the expense of inquiry. The IES unabashedly privileges randomized trials in education, which are now defined as the "gold standard" of science. Many education researchers have little problem with this, since this is the logic of much of quantitative research. These education researchers *want* this intervention into their research by the federal government, an intervention that, ironically, is itself not subject to a randomized field trial or to a "what works" logic. For example, Robert Slavin, who is also on the board of directors of the Coalition for Evidence-Based Policy, argues that because of these federal initiatives education research is "on the brink of a scientific revolution that has the potential to transform policy, practice, and research," and so at the "dawn of the 21st century, education is finally being dragged, kicking and screaming, into the 20th century."[39] The federal movements toward defining valuable education research as experimental are good, Slavin argues, because they "create the kind of progressive, systematic improvement over time that has characterized successful parts of our economy and society throughout the 20th century, in fields such as medicine, agriculture, transportation, and technology." Education has failed to do this in Slavin's view, and so has simply "moved from fad to fad."[40] For Slavin, only rigorous experiments evaluating replicable programs and practices can ensure confidence in

---

37. This is an analogy that SRE makes, paradoxically, to counter the simplistic logic of the "what works" mentality. Its logic being that as with oil wells, some projects will not produce effective results right away, and there will need to be much "drilling" before any such results come to fruition. The studies themselves are less important than the process of continually searching for good results. We discuss further the use of the oil well as an analogy for education research later in the chapter.

38. Maris A. Vinovskis, "The Changing Role of the Federal Government in Educational Research," *History of Education Quarterly* 36, no. 2 (1996): 111–28.

39. Slavin, "Evidence-Based Education Policies," 15.

40. Ibid., 16.

education research by policy makers and educators, although he does allow that there still is a need for correlational, descriptive, and other disciplined inquiry in education.[41]

We agree with those who claim that the move to define education research as scientific in such a narrow way is highly problematic. Such a move toward scientism may also represent a kind of fundamentalism that threatens to turn education research solely into the large, randomized-sample, experimental design studies created on the clinical model—a model that promises to be another "gold standard" for producing scientific knowledge.[42] What is interesting about this so-called "gold standard" that clinical trials are deemed to be is that federal initiatives assume in them rigor, reliability, and validity, and yet clinical trials may be sites of contested meaning, practices, and ethics.[43] Matthew Weinstein points out that while such trials are deemed emblematic of science, truth, and certainty, narratives of participants in clinical trials reveal different stories, ones of unruly participants who try to control the violence they feel foisted onto their bodies.[44]

Yet, the federal government's recent movement toward making education research scientific, even in such a narrow way, provides the context in which SRE is to be read and understood. Indeed, the NRC's report apparently had an impact on the ESRA.[45] This report, as we have indicated, provides for us the point of departure for our concerns with education research. In chapter 2, we conduct a more extensive critique of the report, arguing that it is internally incoherent. In the next section, however, we summarize the salient features of the report and highlight a few of the critiques of the report in the literature.

---

41. David Olson's response to Slavin's article points out how problematic experiments are in education research, especially given that what counts as "treatment" is difficult to define, and causality is impossible to achieve in education. See David R. Olson, "The Triumph of Hope Over Experience in the Search for 'What Works': A Response to Slavin," *Educational Researcher* 33, no. 1 (2004): 24–26. Slavin's response to Olson's article simply reiterates that we need reliable studies that we can give to practitioners and policy makers, and that while difficult, there are no better options to experimental methods for comparing alternative programs or policies. See Robert E. Slavin, "Education Research Can and Must Address 'What Works' Questions," *Educational Researcher* 33, no. 1 (2004): 27–28. As we discuss later, we find these debates over whether experiments are possible in education to be beside the point about the federal intrusion into the education research arena in such an aggressive way.

42. Yvonna S. Lincoln and Gaile S. Cannella, "Dangerous Discourses: Methodological Conservatism and Governmental Regimes of Truth," *Qualitative Inquiry* 10, no. 1 (2004): 5–14, 7.

43. Matthew Weinstein, "Randomized Design and the Myth of Certain Knowledge: Guinea Pig Narratives and Cultural Critique," *Qualitative Inquiry* 10, no. 2 (2004): 246–60, 247.

44. Ibid., 255.

45. Eisenhart and Towne, "Contestation and Change in National Policy," 35.

THE NRC AND *SRE*

The National Research Council, as we said, is the operating arm of the National Academy of Sciences (NAS), which was established by President Abraham Lincoln in 1863 and is now an honorific society of distinguished scholars engaged in scientific and engineering research and, according to its self-proclamations, is "dedicated to the furtherance of science and technology and to their use for the general welfare." The NAS eventually expanded to include the NRC in 1916, the National Academy of Engineering in 1964, and the Institute of Medicine in 1970. Since 1863, "the nation's leaders have often turned to the National Academies for advice on the scientific and technological issues that frequently pervade policy decisions." The NAS's membership is comprised of approximately two thousand members and three hundred fifty foreign associates; members and foreign associates are elected in recognition for their distinguished and continuing achievements in original research, and such election is considered one of the highest honors that can be accorded a scientist or engineer. To conduct its work, the NAS enlists scientists, engineers, and other experts who volunteer their time to study specific concerns.[46]

The NRC is the operating arm of the NAS. Its purpose is to further public knowledge and advise the federal government on engineering, science, and technology.[47] The NRC was commissioned by the United States Department of Education (DOE) to write *SRE*.[48] At the invitation of the DOE's National Educational Research Policy and Priorities Board in the fall of 2000, the NRC assembled the Committee on Scientific Principles for Education Research (the "committee") to address the question of what constitutes scientific research in education.[49] Its charge was to review and synthesize recent literature on the "science and practice of scientific research in education and consider how to support high quality science in a federal education research agency."[50] The committee then translated this charge into three questions that organized its study: (1) What are the principles of scientific quality in education research? (2) How can a federal research agency promote and protect scientific quality in the education research it supports? (3) How can research-based knowledge in education accumulate?[51]

---

46. National Academy of Sciences, *About the NAS* (n.d.). Available at http://www.nasonline. org/site/PageServer?pagename=ABOUT_main_page (Retrieved June 25, 2005).

47. National Academy of Science, *The National Research Council* (n.d.). Available at http://www. nationalacademies.org/nrc/ (Retrieved June 25, 2005).

48. In accordance with its mission of disseminating knowledge of science and technology, the NAS makes available free of charge the reports of its committees, including *SRE*. These reports are available at http://www.nap.edu/ (Retrieved February 5, 2005).

49. *SRE* is the fifth report by the NRC concerning education research since 1958. See *SRE*, 21.

50. Ibid., 22.

51. Ibid., 22–24.

According to Bruce Albers, president of the National Academy of Sciences, *SRE* "offers *a* comprehensive perspective of 'scientifically-based' education research for the policy communities who are increasingly interested in its utilization for improving education policy and practice."[52] Other than making the "policy communities" its target audience, rather than the people who will be most affected by the research the report advocates (i.e., students, teachers, administrators, parents, etc.), this statement is innocuous enough, since it appears to say only that the report seeks to provide *a* perspective on "scientifically-based" education research. It may have been written with that intention, but this report must be viewed in light of the federal government's attempt to create a science for education. The DOE, which commissioned the report, was restructuring itself to emphasize "scientific-based research" because the "field of education operates largely on the basis of ideology and professional consensus . . . and is incapable of the cumulative progress that follows from the application of scientific method."[53] (We do think the NRC report seeks to counter such a de-professionalizing view of education researchers.) The committee's explanation of what legitimately can be called "scientific education research," therefore, is not merely an academic exercise—it is not merely *a* perspective on what counts as scientific research. It will be part of the material practices that have and will continue to shape the course of education research, and thus of education itself, for the foreseeable future. Moreover, its understanding of scientific research in education was to be a way of countering what the committee accepted, uncritically, as the "prevailing view [that] the findings from education research studies are of low quality and are endlessly contested—the result of which is that no consensus emerges about anything."[54] This report, then, sought to legitimize education research, and since such research is deemed the empirical knowledge of education, the report would legitimize education itself. What is says, then, is not to be taken lightly.

The committee appears to challenge the recent federal initiatives to dictate experimentalism (i.e., privileging randomized field trials) and gutter utilitarianism (i.e., defining good research only as "what works") as emblematic of the scientific method. One of the assumptions it seeks to dispel was that "although science is often perceived as embodying a concise, unified view of research, the history of scientific inquiry attests to the fact there is no one method or process that unambiguously defines science."[55] For the committee, it is the questions that drive the methods, not the other way around, as the committee suggests is what the federal initiatives presuppose. Thus, the

52. Ibid., vii. Emphasis added.
53. U.S. Department of Education, *Strategic Plan 2002–2007* (Washington, DC: U.S. Department of Education, 2002), 59. Available at: http://www.ed.gov/about/reports/strat/plan2002-07/plan.pdf (Retrieved October 20, 2003).
54. *SRE*, 28.
55. Ibid., 24.

committee purports to take an "inclusive view" of science in education, one that would also include, apparently, qualitative approaches to understanding education phenomena. Indeed, the committee claims that quantitative and qualitative research are "epistemologically quite similar."[56] Scientific research in any discipline and irrespective to methods, the report indicates, is

> a continual process of rigorous reasoning supported by a dynamic interplay among methods, theories, and findings. It builds understandings in the form of models or theories that can be tested. Advances in scientific knowledge are achieved by the self-regulating norms of the scientific community over time, not, as sometimes believed, by the mechanistic application of a particular scientific method to a static set of questions.[57]

What constitutes scientific inquiry, the committee indicates, is not attention to particular methods, but adherence to six fundamental principles, which it summarizes briefly in this sentence: "To be scientific, the design must allow direct, empirical investigation of an important question, account for the context in which the study is carried out, align with a conceptual framework, reflect careful and thorough reasoning, and disclose results to encourage debate in the scientific community."[58] We will critique these principles in greater detail in chapter 2, but we will say here that, contrary to the committee's claims, what constitutes science may indeed be its *methods*. If we are to follow Charles Sanders Peirce, we must grant that what allows science to be an effective way of settling opinions about the world is that it permits the kind of reasoning that allows us to perceive these "things as they are." And it does this because it follows a particular *method* that does not rely on our feelings and intentions but itself involves the application of the method.[59]

Furthermore, the supposed rejection of a definition of science in terms of particular methods does not mean that the committee defined science very broadly at all. It appears that it has at first glance when it states that scientific research can contribute to understanding and improving education, "especially when integrated with *other* approaches to studying human endeavors."[60] Thus, according to the committee, historical, philosophical, and literary scholarship can and should inform important questions of purpose and direction in education. What belies the committees claim is that these "other approaches" are indeed *other*, that is, *not* scientific. We think

56. Ibid., 19.
57. Ibid., 2.
58. Ibid., 6.
59. Charles S. Peirce, "The Fixation of Belief," *Popular Science Monthly* 12 (November 1877): 1–15. Available at http://www.peirce.org/writings/p107.html (Retrieved February 7, 2005).
60. SRE, 26. Emphasis added.

the committee can distinguish science from "nonscience" only because it must rely upon particular methods. Its principles, if understood broadly, would support a broad understanding of science, but its claims that there are "other" important approaches sheds doubt on the committee's claim that it is the principles, not the methods, that dictates what science can be. In addition, the assumption that methods should be determined by the questions implies that methods and theories are simply technical matters, but such things do not arise from nowhere; they are formed within intellectual traditions in which those theories work. That is, techniques become determinate of science.[61]

One of the significant critiques of SRE in the literature relates to the committee's understanding that "it is possible to describe the physical and social world scientifically so that, for example, multiple observers can agree on what they see."[62] The committee does acknowledge that because education is "highly value laden" and involves a "diverse array of people and political forces that significantly shapes it character," scientific inquiry must pay attention to physical, social, cultural, economic, and historical contexts, so that its "theories and findings may generalize to other times, places, and populations."[63] The committee nonetheless rejects "postmodernism," which, it argues, claims that "science can never generate objective or trustworthy knowledge."[64] Yet this is the kind of universalism that the so-called postmodern critiques of the report problematize. Postmodern schools of thought, as Elizabeth Adams St. Pierre points out, do not assert that there is no reality, objectivity, or rationality, but rather that such concepts are situated rather than universal because they are understood differently within different epistemologies.[65] St. Pierre thus rejects SRE's claim that quantitative and qualitative research are "epistemologically quite similar."[66]

The committee also purports to reject "narrow tenets of behaviorism/positivism" as viewing human nature too simplistically.[67] Despite this claim, as we elaborate in great detail in chapter 2, the committee does not reject "narrow tenets of behaviorism/positivism." Only by adhering to "narrow tenets of behaviorism/positivism" can the committee make the claim that

> [a]s in other fields that have such a public character, social ideals inevitably influence the research that is done, the way it is framed

---

61. Popkewitz, "On Trusting the Manifesto," 66–68.
62. Ibid.
63. Ibid., 5.
64. Ibid., 25.
65. Elizabeth Adams St. Pierre, " 'Science' Rejects Postmodernism," *Educational Researcher* 31, no. 8 (2002): 25–27, 25.
66. *SRE*, 19.
67. Ibid., 25.

and conducted, and the policies and practices that are based on research findings. And decisions about education are sometimes instituted with no scientific basis at all, but rather are derived directly from ideology or deeply held beliefs about social justice or the good of society in general.[68]

What postmodern, critical, and other interpretive analyses often try to do is to expose the discursive, ideological, and historical nature of claims to knowledge, which "narrow tenets of behaviorism/positivism" fail to recognize. Furthermore, as Thomas Popkewitz explains, the argument that science can be defined by principles rather than methods, and that quantitative and qualitative research are epistemologically similar, suggest an idea of a unified science across the natural, social, and educational arenas. That SRE seeks to distinguish science from nonscience is reminiscent of the Logical Positivists, who sought to eliminate metaphysical arguments in favor of a position that all knowledge fits into a single conceptual framework that explains science. This unity searches for consensus and certainty, which in turn are produced through the norms of professional communities.[69] (We will discuss the report's role in the professionalization of education researchers in the next section.) Indeed, the committee's claim that it is possible to describe education "scientifically" is itself possible only because of its adherence to behaviorism and positivism, since much of what we call "education" today is deeply rooted in behaviorist and positivist assumptions.[70]

There has been quite a bit of concern over SRE, and a number of important journals have dedicated special issues to it.[71] One of the reasons for this attention to SRE is, as we stated, that it is part of an attempt to define education research in particular ways, which not only will dictate what research will be funded but also will normalize and homogenize the field. Another related reason for the attention given to this report is that it reflects a long-standing anxiety over knowledge, its production, and who

---

68. Ibid., 17.
69. Popkewitz, "On Trusting the Manifesto," 64.
70. Margaret Eisenhart argued that SRE defends a conception of science in the sense of postpositivism, not positivism, and this is important because the former accommodates both patterned behavior and human intentionality. See Margaret Eisenhart, "Science Plus: A Response to the Responses to Scientific Research in Education," *Teachers College Record* 107, no. 1 (2005): 52–58. We will have occasion to return to this logic a few more times in this book. Before then, and to be clear, we are not arguing that science can only be understood positivistically. We are arguing that science has been narrowly focused on positivist assumptions when applied to education.
71. SRE has been the focus of entire issues of *Educational Researcher* 31, no. 8 (2002); *Qualitative Inquiry* 10, no. 1 (2004); *Educational Theory* 55, no. 3 (2005); and *Teachers College Record* 107, no. 1 (2005). See, also, Gert Biesta, "Why 'What Works' Won't Work: Evidence-Based Practice and the Democratic Deficit in Educational Research," *Educational Theory* 57, no. 1 (2007): 1–22.

is authorized to speak it. Three members of the committee, Michael Feuer, Lisa Towne, and Richard Shavelson (who chaired the committee), almost said as much, explaining that nurturing and reinforcing a "scientific culture of educational research is a critical task for promoting better research," and that such culture is a "set of norms and practices and an ethos of honesty, openness, and continuous reflection."[72] It has been the "failure of the [education research] field to develop such a community and to forge consensus on such matters as research quality and coordination of perspectives that has contributed to an environment in which members of Congress are compelled to impose them."[73] Such arguments reflect a concern with professionalism, and are not simply iterations of philosophies of science, a point we discuss in the following section. Rather than condemn the ignorance and arrogance of such legislators, many education researchers instead have tried to accommodate them. We critique throughout this book the imposition of such a "culture" and how it is to be established,[74] but suffice it to say here that developing such a culture will dictate what counts as knowledge, how it is to be produced, and who is authorized to speak it. The privileged "knowers" will no longer be "mere" educators but the newly professionalized education scientists.

In addition to those we have already mentioned, there have been various other critiques of SRE. We do not wish to reiterate many of these critiques here, as we discuss many of these critiques in the next chapter,[75] but we do want to highlight a few of them in order to set up the arguments we make in this book. We start by noting that there has been a tendency in these critiques to bend over backward not to appear to be dismissing experimental designs.[76] We take a controversial view and argue *against* experimental designs in schools. With St. Pierre we ask:

> Why and to what end has the circle been drawn so narrowly around science? What "outcomes" are possible in such a structure? Who

---

72. Michael J. Feuer, Lisa Towne, and Richard J. Shavelson, "Scientific Culture and Educational Research," *Educational Researcher* 31, no. 8 (2002): 4–14, 4.

73. Ibid., 9.

74. The NRC established another committee to issue another report on how to promote scientific research in education. This report offered recommendations for promoting scientific quality in education, building an educational scientific knowledge base, and enhancing the professional development of education researchers. See National Research Council, *Advancing Scientific Research in Education*, ed.. Lisa Towne, Lauress L. Wise, and Tina M. Waters (Washington, DC: The National Academies Press, 2005). Available at http://www.nap.edu/ (Retrieved February 5, 2005). We discuss this report in greater detail in chapter 3.

75. For critiques of the NRC report, see the entire issues of *Educational Researcher* 31, no. 8 (2002); *Qualitative Inquiry* 10, no. 1 (2004); *Educational Theory* 55, no. 3 (2005); and *Teachers College Record* 107, no. 1 (2005).

76. See, for example, Joseph A. Maxwell, "Reemergent Scientism, Postmodernism, and Dialogue Across Differences," *Qualitative Inquiry* 10, no. 1 (2004): 35–41, 36; Weinstein, "Randomized Design and the Myth of Certain Knowledge," 257.

benefits? What happens to children in classrooms when we assume that the random assignment of subjects will produce true knowledge, that outcomes can be controlled and predicted, and that the reality of one classroom can be generalized to another?[77]

Yes, indeed, what happens to children when they become *useful* for experiments? Not only do such experimental designs reflect a scientism and positivism that limits inquiry and thought, the consequences of "experimenting" on children in the ways federal initiatives, SRE, and other similar reports advocate reflect a high degree of disregard for them, and impose on them an institutionalized violence that even institutional review boards cannot prevent. In fact, institutional review boards will be more than complicit here since they will grant *imprimatur* to such violence in approving these experiments. These experiments do not seem to regard children as human beings but rather as products or data—merely material "human resources" to be mined or laboratory animals on which to "experiment."

We should consider experimental designs hazardous to children rather than reifying the designs as laudable hallmarks of education research. To be sure, SRE rejects such narrow scientism, especially when linked to a "what works" logic. Not all scientific research will pan out, it argues, as, "Research is like oil exploration—there are, on average, many dry holes for every successful well."[78] This is an interesting, if odd, analogy. It implies that a particular line of research should not be deemed a failure through the short-term, "what works" kind of thinking that supports federal projects such as the What Works Clearinghouse. But there is something problematic in the analogy. As though drilling for oil is a worthy enterprise itself, the analogy seems to suggest that research projects are to be treated like "oil wells." Some may "strike it rich," but many, many others will yield nothing. Missing are questions about the impact such projects have. Will they mirror the devastating impact of actual drilling on the environment? Would this devastation even matter if we find through such constant searching for "knowledge" the solutions to the problems we have already determined they have? This is part of the problem of privileging research over people. The NRC committee positions the research enterprise *over* the individuals it affects, giving considerable power to the scientists *over* the individuals they purport to be studying and helping. As Karl Hostetler argues, the debates about education research

> have raised ethical questions about how researchers should understand and work with the human beings they study. The danger is

---

77. Elizabeth Adams St. Pierre, "Refusing Alternatives: A Science of Contestation," *Qualitative Inquiry* 10, no. 1 (2004): 130–39, 134.
78. SRE, 25.

that the debate can be limited to methodology. It would be like debating how we should research the effectiveness of thumb-screws as a means of torture.[79]

But having gotten this out of the way, we can now proceed to a few of the critiques of SRE. The bulk of the critiques seem concerned with the report's implication that quantitative methods are more likely to be deemed scientific than those that are not. Some critics of the report have taken exception to this implication, suggesting that qualitative research can be scientific.[80] We find such critiques tiresome and beside the point, as they actually wind up supporting the view that there is a distinction between science and nonscience, premised, at root, on methodological grounds. Indeed, when Frederick Erickson and Kris Gutierrez critiqued SRE's implication that science is about certainty by claiming that "*Real* science is not about certainty but uncertainty,"[81] their claim makes sense only upon accepting the existence of a "real" science, which is intelligible only upon the recognition of an "unreal" science, or a nonscience. We reject that such a distinction has any meaning in itself; its meaning is determined solely by an institutional context that establishes science, and the scientist, as the arbiter of truths. Another related critique is that the distinction between science and nonscience is problematic, but that qualitative researchers must nevertheless be more active and convincing to "stakeholders" and policy makers about the ways in which qualitative research and evaluation can contribute to a more complex understanding of pressing human problems.[82] We think that these kinds of critiques are, in essence, more sophisticated versions of the "what works" rhetoric.

More interesting to us are critiques that suggest that SRE is part of a larger strategy to impose scientism in education research. Such critiques indicate that the label "scientific research" is actually code for randomized experiments,[83] which implicates the NRC in an evidence-based social engineering scheme for education.[84] It seems to us the case that the NRC report,

79. Karl Hostetler, "What is 'Good' Education Research?" *Educational Researcher* 34, no. 5 (August/September 2005): 16–21, 16.
80. See, for example, Joseph A. Maxwell, "Causal Explanation, Qualitative Research, and Scientific Inquiry in Education," *Educational Researcher* 33, no. 4 (2004): 3–11.
81. Frederick Erickson and Kris Gutierrez, "Culture, Rigor, and Science in Educational Research," *Educational Researcher* 31, no. 8 (2002): 21–24, 22. Emphasis added.
82. See, for example, Kathleen deMarrais, "Elegant Communications: Sharing Qualitative Research With Communities, Colleagues, and Critics," *Qualitative Inquiry* 10, no. 2 (2004): 281–97, 282.
83. David C. Berliner, "Educational Research: The Hardest Science of All," *Educational Researcher* 31, no. 8 (2002): 18–20; Kenneth R. Howe, "A Critique of Experimentalism," *Qualitative Inquiry* 10, no. 1 (2004): 42–61, 46–48.
84. Erickson and Gutierrez, "Culture, Rigor, and Science," 23.

when read within the context of the recent federal initiatives to emphasize "evidence-based" research, constitutes what Patti Lather argues is a backlash against the proliferation of the approaches of the past twenty years or so out of cultural studies, feminist methodology, radical environmentalism, ethnic studies, and social studies of science—a "backlash where in the guise of objectivity and good science, 'colonial, Western, masculine, white and other biases' are smuggled in."[85] Similarly, others suggest that the report is part and parcel of a conservative strategy to return us to elitist Western notions of high modernism that would reinscribe narrow forms of experimentalism as the "gold standard" for judging legitimacy and quality.[86] This strategy takes the form of claims that discredit difference and control its interpretation, and thus it creates an "integrated intellectual, political, public network of power that would challenge discourses and institutions that would otherwise arguably foster diversity of thought and being."[87]

We believe such critiques are largely correct, especially if the report is viewed from a particular perspective. The assumption of most critiques is that SRE, like the federal initiatives, advocates scientism by privileging the experimental design. But SRE does seem to reject the narrow scientism of the federal government's policies and practices; it does explain that science is not defined by methods but by certain fundamental principles. Still, there is a legitimate concern that it does actually privilege the replication of quantitative studies, particularly those purporting to provide "causal effects," and situates interpretive and qualitative studies as preliminary and supplementary to the former.[88] So while we will take the committee at its word that it is not intending to advocate particular methods, we still argue in chapter 2 that it nonetheless advocates scientism, since "science" as defined by the committee is fundamentally only a method.

Margaret Eisenhart, who was a member of the NRC committee, defends SRE from many of these critiques. She grants that the report paid little attention to how qualitative research can contribute to the study of education, but explains that the report, for all its problems, seeks to counter long-standing low opinions of education research, a particularly important task given that the federal government has the purse strings. Furthermore, Eisenhart argues, SRE describes scientific research in a postpositivistic sense and is an answer only for particular kinds of questions, those for which

---

85. Patti Lather, "This IS Your Father's Paradigm: Government Intrusion and the Case of Qualitative Research in Education," *Qualitative Inquiry* 10, no. 1 (2004): 15–34, 16.
86. Gaile S. Cannella and Yvonna S. Lincoln, "Dangerous Discourses II: Comprehending and Countering the Redeployment of Discourses (and Resources) in the Generation of Liberatory Inquiry," *Qualitative Inquiry* 10, no. 2 (2004): 165–74, 165.
87. Yvonna S. Lincoln and Gaile S. Cannella, "Qualitative Research, Power, and the Radical Right," *Qualitative Inquiry* 10, no. 2 (2004): 175–201, 182–83.
88. See Lather and Moss, "Introduction: Implications of the Scientific Research," 2.

empirical evidence is crucial and can be gathered. Scientific research is not, she claims, appropriate for "moral questions that can be answered by philosophers, critical theorists, and others outside the purview of science."[89] Such a distinction between the so-called moral versus "scientific" questions is prima facie flawed. Scientific questions *are* moral questions. To seclude science from the arena of morals or, as Eisenhart suggests, to pass questions of morals to philosophers and others, means sidestepping the very issues we are raising about the good or right conduct regarding children, teachers, and others in education. In other words, Eisenhart appears to champion "science" as above questions of good or right action.

The problem is that in the process of side-stepping the issue, Eisenhart fails to realize that she is engaging in what Imre Lakatos identifies as a radical shift in morality. In the context of science, Lakatos points out, debates have changed the landscape of morality. To his chagrin, "a new school of dogmatists accepted the *new moral facts* and devised *new moral standards* in light of which their morality—a new morality—could be seen."[90] The irony here is that Lakatos is a staunch supporter of rationality, science, and method, and his chagrin is that relativism in moral codes is undermining the rigor and precision of logic. The real point, it seems to us, is the role SRE plays in establishing "new moral standards" for education research. The project of furthering "science" is primarily a battle over who gets to decide what "right action" in research is and how it is valued. Thus, Eisenhart fails to see the report, and her stance toward it, as ethical projects. But the authors of the report are engaged in ethical projects, even as they say they are staying above such concerns. That is not only impossible but problematic as an argument, for in arguing that scientific questions are not ethical ones, we are easily led to hand over to the scientists the question of what kind of society we want to live in.

Science has a way of blinding us to the fact that as an ethical project we all must participate in it, even if it has carved out for itself the right to say who can speak its language. Furthermore, in seeking to carve out who can speak its language and how, the NRC is engaging in a long-standing struggle over professionalism, an issue that has been ignored in the critiques of the report but which we take up next.

A QUESTION OF PROFESSIONALISM?

When we argue that the NRC's report reflects a struggle over professionalism, we mean to engage in a sociological inquiry into how the professions

---

89. Eisenhart, "Science Plus."
90. Imre Lakatos, "The Intellectuals' Betrayal of Reason," in *For and Against Method*, ed., Imre Lakatos, Paul Feyerabend, and Matteo Motterlini (Chicago: The University of Chicago Press, 1999), 398.

are constituted; that is, we seek to understand who gets the (very power-ful) privilege of the term. This inquiry provides a key to understanding our society, for as Everett Hughes points out, to understand what professions mean in our society is to note the ways in which occupations try to change themselves to emulate them, to become, that is, "professionalized."[91] Seeking professional status seems a uniquely U.S. phenomenon.[92] So reading the NRC report, and all the critiques associated with it, perhaps even including ours, via an understanding of professionalism sheds light on one of the significant sources of power in our society.

What allows an occupation the name of "profession" differs among professions and over time, but, according to Magali Larson, there appear to be three common dimensions associated with professions. First, there should be a "cognitive" dimension centered around a body of (esoteric) knowledge and techniques upon which the professionals rely in their work, and such knowledge must also ground the training necessary to master such knowledge and skills. Second, there should be a "normative" dimension that covers the service orientation of professionals and their particular ethical codes, justify-ing as well the privilege of self-regulation granted to the professions. Finally, there should be an "evaluative" dimension implicitly comparing professions to other occupations and, especially, underscoring the professions' singular characteristics of autonomy and prestige.[93] Laurence Veysey argues against such definitions and posits that the notion of the "professions" amounts to nothing more than a series of rather random occupations that have histori-cally been called that in our culture, and which have been conferred high social status on their practitioners while demanding some kind of extended training (usually) in universities.[94]

Perhaps Veysey is correct in general, but with regard to our problematic it seems clear to us that any attempt to define what constitutes scientific research in education is an attempt to establish cognitive, normative, and evaluative dimensions legitimating educational researchers as professionals. The NRC's principles, for example, seek to define the knowledge and tech-niques necessary for making education research scientific (cognitive); they seek to legitimate such knowledge for informing educational policy and im-proving educational practice (normative); and they create parameters around

91. Everett C. Hughes, "Professions," in *The Professions in America*, ed. Kenneth S. Lynn (Boston: Houghton Mifflin, 1965), 1–14, 4.

92. Nathan O. Hatch, "Introduction: The Professions in a Democratic Culture," in *The Pro-fessions in American History*, ed. Nathan O. Hatch (Notre Dame: University of Notre Dame Press, 1988), 1–13, 4.

93. Magali Sarfatti Larson, *The Rise of Professionalism: A Sociological Analysis* (Berkeley: Uni-versity of California Press, 1977), x.

94. Laurence Veysey, "Higher Education as a Profession: Changes and Continuities," in *The Professions in American History*, ed. Nathan O. Hatch (Notre Dame: University of Notre Dame Press, 1988), 15–32, 17–18.

what is scientific in educational inquiry and what is not (evaluative). In a sense, then, the NRC principles are not simple definitions, but *practices* of legitimation and control in the struggles over professionalism. Understood this way, and especially in light of the NRC's rejection of the gutter utilitarianism of the federal government's "what works" logic, the NRC is seeking to establish professional autonomy for educational researchers, and giving to the scientific community the authority to legitimate their claims.

What we find particularly interesting, and even paradoxical, in such practices of legitimation, intended to ensure professional prestige and autonomy for education researchers, is that such autonomy comes at the expense of their becoming "useful" to the dominant elites, particularly those in the federal government. But this tension between professionalization and utility is key to understanding power in (post)modernist societies, certainly as such exists in the United States. The processes of professionalization are essentially practices for gaining market control. As Larson puts it, there are several conditions necessary for the professional control of a market.[95] First, the more universal the nature of a service that is marketed, the more favorable the situation for a profession. The professions that have a clear monopoly of competence— and not only a monopoly of practice (such as teachers)—have authority over the kind of knowledge that is important for everyone's life.[96] Thus, according to this logic, what can be more universal than education? What can be more important than education? Second, the less competitive the market, the more favorable the situation for a profession; but also, the more competitive the market, the more the profession is compelled to organize along monopolistic lines. For no matter what their contributions to societies, first and foremost the professions seek to erect "no trespassing" signs between themselves and other professional groups.[97] Educational inquiry is highly competitive—anyone can do it—and indeed this is the problem the NRC seeks to address, that is, the fact that almost anything can count as education research. It thus seeks to create a monopoly for those who can engage in legitimately valuable research, of the kind that will really improve educational practice.

Third, according to Larson, the more universal the clientele the profession seeks to serve, the more favorable the situation is for the profession. Obviously, little qualifies as more universal than schools and children. Fourth, with regard to the cognitive dimension discussed previously, the more standardized and better-defined the cognitive basis, the more it permits the attainment of "what (actually) works"; and the more esoteric the body of knowledge (and the more it approaches a new paradigm), the more favorable

---

95. Larson, *The Rise of Professionalism*, 47–48.
96. Ibid., 231.
97. Kenneth S. Lynn, *The Professions in America*, ed. Kenneth S. Lynn (Boston: Houghton Mifflin, 1965), ix–xiv, xiii.

a situation is for the profession. In other words, the more education research qualifies as "scientific," the more legitimacy its cognitive basis will have. Fifth, the more institutionalized (especially in universities) the forms are for producing the professionals, the more standardized the practice of producing those professionals, and the more such production is under the profession's control, the more favorable the situation is for a profession. The NRC (and others) seek to establish a professional scientific culture for education research and propose ways of "fixing" doctoral training to ensure scientific education researchers, a topic we discuss in great detail in chapter 3.

Larson's sixth and seventh conditions for professional legitimacy seem the most important to us, as they relate most directly to the nature of power associated with establishing a science for education, and of which we will say much more in the rest of this book. The more independent a profession's market is from other markets (in our case, the more one can carve out a particular kind of expertise for education researchers that even ordinary education practitioners do not have), the more the state is compelled to protect the public by eliminating (or neutralizing) the incompetent or less competent professionals. The NRC report actually sanctions the state to intervene to control who conducts legitimate research and how. The so-called scientific community has no power to control how education researchers are produced, but the NRC's report offers federal and state governments a logic for controlling the funding of research and the training of researchers along particular (scientific/professional) lines. Thus, and finally, the final condition for professional legitimacy involves an affinity with the dominant ideologies, so that to the extent a profession's ideology coincides with dominant ideological structures, the more favorable the situation it is for a profession. As we will argue throughout this book, social science is inextricably linked to dominant political regimes, which use its knowledge to further particular oppressive practices.

For learning professions, as the sciences are, ideology is the primary tool available for gaining the political and economic resources necessary to establish and maintain their status.[98] Elliot Freidson argues that the ideal-typical ideology of professionalism is concerned with justifying the privileged position of the institutions of an occupation in a political economy as well as the authority and status of its members. To do so it must neutralize (or effectively counter) the opposing ideologies which provide a rationale for the control of work by the market (or what he calls "consumerism") and by bureaucratic entities, such as governments (or what he calls "managerialism").[99] So, with regard to our problematic, the NRC report would seek to counter consumerism by its adherence to a notion of objective knowledge (a

---

98. Eliot Freidson, *Professionalism: The Third Logic* (Chicago: The University of Chicago Press, 2001), 105.
99. Ibid., 106.

notion represented in its first five principles), and it would seek to counter managerialism both by its adherence to a notion that only the scientific community can legitimate scientific claims (a notion represented by its sixth principle) and by distancing itself from the gutter utilitarianism of the federal government's what works logic. The NRC report, when read as part of the politics of professionalism, supports Friedson's point that in the broadest sense the ideology of professionalism is premised on the belief that the work of the expert is superior to that of the amateur.[100]

These political practices of the NRC, therefore, are masked by an ideology of intellectual and moral legitimacy in the expertise of the scientist. But such legitimacy is the historic product of a struggle that divides those who try to control the processes of production underlying the system by putting forward particular definitions of those activities, and those who at any one time control the system have a tendency to exclude or subordinate those who could redefine those productions.[101] Thus, the demarcations associated with the NRC, and not only those between what counts as scientific education research and what does not, but also what counts as a legitimate researcher versus what counts as a practitioner, are premised on the notion of a "pure research function," and this is expressed in the fact that prestige is distributed throughout the learning professions according to the twin qualities of the esoteric value of what is taught and the consequent difficulties involved in attaining it *and* the audience to whom it is communicated. In other words, if the audience is the scientific community, as it would be for researchers, then that is more prestigious than if the audience was simply children, as it would be for teachers. Less prestige "is thus reserved for teachers in the primary schools to which *everyone goes* to learn *what everyone knows*."[102] Changes to this system, however, do not take place by assuming a self-regulating system, as the NRC implies in its idea of a debate within the scientific community about the justifiableness of claims, but by sudden jolts, when the principles of the dominant legitimacy are questioned.[103] So we must question the legitimacy of any attempt to create a science for education, for at stake is the ability to define and control education itself (we return to this point in chapter 3).

The notion of science as professionalism is not as natural a concept as we are led to believe by those who presumptively exalt its methods as "gold standards." This is a phenomenon that should be understood sociologically

---

100. Ibid., 111.
101. H. Jamous and B. Peloille, "Changes in the French University-Hospital System," in *Professions and Professionalization*, ed. John A. Jackson (Cambridge: Cambridge University Press, 1970), 111–52, 138.
102. John A. Jackson, "Professions and Professionalization—Editorial Introduction," in *Professions and Professionalization*, ed. John A. Jackson (Cambridge: Cambridge University Press, 1970), 3–15, 11. Emphasis in original.
103. Ibid., 142.

and historically. The professionalization of American science, according to Daniel Kevles, occurred in four more or less overlapping stages: preemption, institutionalization, legitimation, and professional autonomy.[104] The preemption stage involved the increasing esoteric quality of natural knowledge, or the "march of men of learning beyond mere fact gathering to complex relationships, to systematics, to theory," and in all disciplines this has had the same effect: the exclusion of the lay amateur from scientific discourse.[105] The institutionalization stage involved the creation of the scientific societies and the rise of the predominance of the research university, which institutionalized science and gave its practitioners the authority to pursue knowledge—and particularly "objective" knowledge. The legitimation stage centered on three notions: (1) the idea that the study of science fostered disinterested, even moral, habits of thinking, because of which (2) the scientist, now deemed an expert and morally objective, could be counted upon to supply the state with indispensable disinterested advice and guidance as it plunged into the technological age, which in turn meant that (3) the pursuit of pure science would be seen as improving the nation's wealth, health, and defense. All these factors permitted the scientist a professional autonomy, the last stage, which was premised on the belief in science's utility.[106]

Despite all the rhetoric associated with science as providing objective knowledge and benefitting society, it must be granted that the social forces discussed above converged to ensure such beliefs. The discourse on education research, then, and to repeat, is as much a practice of professional legitimation as it is an elaboration of what science is. Indeed, knowledge systems play a crucial role in any definition of a profession, and so it works as much as cultural capital as it does for solving the problems for which it is put to use.[107] Randall Collins argues persuasively that knowledge that brings professional privilege is inevitably knowledge embellished by its status image.[108] Whether the facts of science are truer than others' matters less than its success in winning over converts.[109]

Andrew Abbott similarly points out that in a given profession, the highest status professionals are those who deal with issues predigested and

104. Daniel J. Kevles, "American Science," in *The Professions in American History*, ed. Nathan O. Hatch (Notre Dame: University of Notre Dame Press, 1988), 107–25, 109.

105. Ibid.

106. Ibid., 109–11.

107. Rolf Torstendahl, "Introduction: Promotion and Strategies of Knowledge-Based Groups," in *The Formation of Professions: Knowledge, State, and Strategy*, ed. Rolf Torstendahl and Michael Burrage (Newbury Park: SAGE, 1990), 1–10, 2.

108. Randall Collins, "Changing Conceptions in the Sociology of the Professions," in *The Formation of Professions: Knowledge, State, and Strategy*, ed. Rolf Torstendahl and Michael Burrage (Newbury Park: SAGE, 1990), 11–23, 19.

109. Charles Derber, William A. Schwartz, and Yale Magrass, *Power in the Highest Degree: Professionals and the Rise of a New Mandarin Order* (Oxford: Oxford University Press, 1990), 16.

predefined by a number of individuals within a profession. These individuals have removed all complexity and difficulty in order to leave a problem at least professionally defined, although still very difficult to solve. Conversely, the lowest status professionals are those who deal with problems from which the human complexities are not or cannot be removed.[110] The professionally defined or definable is more pure than the undefined or undefinable. The "clear is more pure than the amorphous, the definite more pure than the ambiguous. Like income, purity of practice is easily ascertained in a short conversation as well as easily inferred from such characteristics as specialty. It is a ready currency for status."[111]

Thus, the training of education researchers is about status, not "skills," a point we elaborate further in chapter 3. For now, we can say that the knowledge the NRC posits as scientific, and the definitions of questions to which such knowledge legitimately can be applied, represent the power play of scientists vis-à-vis other learned professionals (such as historians and philosophers—or the "extreme postmodernists") and the practitioners that are supposed to use this knowledge. For the learned professions, the knowledge, and the issues to which it is an answer, are intrinsically connected; neither would exist without the community that defines the issues and socially validates what is accepted as an answer to them.[112]

Thus, as Aant Elzinga points out, discourses aimed at answering questions such as "Is this really science?" and "What is it good for?" (questions that underlie the NRC report's logic) may be teased out and recast as manifestations of cognitive and social legitimation strategies. The cognitive strategy involves locating a new research specialty on the map of science, thus employing arguments and definitions that distinguish this new area from "practical knowledge" (a particularly sticky problem for the professionalization of education researchers, since practical knowledge has incredible lasting power) and from other disciplines (educational inquiry, given its subject, must be distinguished from other types of inquiry by constituting it as an applied science). The social legitimation strategies run parallel to the cognitive ones, according to Elzinga, and must point to the utility of the new discipline, and thus there will be repeated references to the beneficiaries for whom it will be relevant and important (in the case of education, the entire nation is deemed a beneficiary, since our destiny is intricately tied to it).[113]

110. Andrew Abbott, "Status and Strain in the Professions," The American Journal of Sociology 86, no. 4 (1981): 819–35, 823–24.

111. Ibid., 824.

112. Collins, "Changing Conceptions," 20.

113. See, generally, Aant Elzinga, "The Knowledge Aspect of Professionalization: The Case of Science-Based Nursing Education in Sweden," in The Formation of Professions: Knowledge, State, and Strategy, ed. Rolf Torstendahl and Michael Burrage (Newbury Park: SAGE, 1990), 151–73, 160.

But, and to repeat, while scientific knowledge does indeed have social benefits, one cannot ignore the politics associated with constituting knowledge as scientific, particularly the boundaries created around who and what can be said to constitute such knowledge and the differentiating status such boundaries ensure. For monopolizing knowledge, any knowledge but particularly scientific knowledge, restricts opportunities for others to think, in effect ensuring a large class of "unskilled" workers (which is all that teachers and other mere practitioners will become), and this is the dark side of professionalism.[114] Pamela Moss is not far off, then, when she argues that the principles espoused in the NRC report, coming from an *authoritative* source such as the National Academy of Sciences, and that imply a priori judgments (such as that of experimentation as ideal for answering questions of "what works," or that replication is the hallmark of good science) disempower research communities that have concluded, based on their own good reasons, otherwise.[115]

Indeed, the movement toward professionalization, in recent times at least, sheds doubt even on moral dimensions of professionalism. As Steven Brint points out, those who claim knowledge-based authority increasingly eschew any claims to representing vital social or public interests, so that now expertise is a resource sold to the highest bidder in the market for skilled labor.[116] In the case of the emerging social scientists, the need for massive resources opened them to cooptation by those who control the resources, and the latter will almost always support experts who deliver something of value to them.[117] Such expertise only enhances the technical skills of elites or of the social-control structures.[118] We can certainly see this logic in the arguments put forth by those who argue that making education research scientific in the ways the federal government now deems legitimate is important because it holds the purse strings.[119]

What passes as objective knowledge is, really and only, a search for what elites want knowledge about. Research does not solve social problems, Daniel Rossides argues, but is an honored way to postpone tackling them. Having said this, we think it is incorrect to argue, as some have done, that

---

114. Derber, Schwartz, and Magrass, *Power in the Highest Degree*, 14.
115. Pamela A. Moss, "Understanding the Other/Understanding Ourselves: Toward a Constructive Dialogue About 'Principles' in Educational Research, *Educational Theory* 55, no. 3 (2005): 263–83, 280.
116. Steven G. Brint, *In an Age of Experts: The Changing Role of Professionals in Politics and in Public Life* (Princeton: Princeton University Press, 1994), 15.
117. Edward T. Silva and Sheila Slaughter, "Prometheus Bound: The Limits of Social Science Professionalization in the Progressive Period," *Theory and Society* 9, no. 6 (1980): 781–819, 805.
118. Daniel W. Rossides, *Professions and Disciplines: Functional and Conflict Perspectives* (Upper Saddle River: Prentice-Hall, 1998), 71.
119. See, for example, Eisenhart, "Science Plus."

scientists are bad or evil or tyrants.[120] What is important is to understand the forces that makes scientists powerful arbiters of our fate, and to offer avenues for contestation. To the extent that critics of the NRC report insist upon some other basis for legitimating educational inquiry, and fail to understand the report in the context of the political struggles over professionalism, they fail to critique, at its core, the real political problems associated with the movements seeking to make education research scientific. Kenneth Howe, for example, in opposing the scientism of SRE advocates for what he calls "experimentalism," which encompasses a "clinical" aspect in which generalizations serve as guidance for practice, encompasses a "democratic" aspect that heeds the perspectives of practitioners, and encompasses a political aspect that accounts for political values.[121] This is preferable, but misses the point that the NRC is not simply putting forth definitions of what counts as valuable knowledge; it is part of the struggle over professionalism, a struggle that must be countered, not by offering different philosophies of science, but by questioning the ideological presumptions and political practices that make it possible, particularly those granting legitimacy to scientific knowledge. Abbott argues that a profession seeks to attain what he calls a "jurisdiction" over a problem, that is, legitimate control of a problem, but this control does not necessarily entail a total dominance. In fact, many professions exercise less than dominant control in many of their jurisdictions.[122] It is only by challenging the authority of scientific discourse to dictate our lives so completely that we can open up these political practices to question, and thus to the possibility that educational inquiry will remain democratic.

We think, therefore, that a reading of the NRC report, and indeed, the entire discourse on the science of education, is a fruitful way of highlighting power in the United States. In this book, however, we would like to avoid offering a general theory of the professionalism of education researchers, and, following Larson, find it more productive to address the larger theme of the construction and social consequences of scientific knowledge and the expertise it confers on particular political actors.[123] Again, few can question that scientific knowledge has great social benefits, but there are consequences that go beyond the unethical behavior of scientists that we are used to reading in critiques of science. As Dorothy Nelkin argues, the authority of scientific expertise rests on assumptions about the rationality of

120. See, for example, Morris E. Chafetz, The Tyranny of Experts: Blowing the Whistle on the Cult of Expertise (Lanham: Madison Books, 1996), xiii.
121. Kenneth R. Howe, "The Question of Education Science: Experimentism Versus Experimentalism," Educational Theory 55, no. 3 (2005): 307–21, 317–18.
122. Andrew Abbott, "Jurisdictional Conflicts: A New Approach to the Development of the Legal Professions," American Bar Foundation Research Journal 11, no. 2 (1986): 187–224, 191.
123. See Magali Sarfatti Larson, "In the Matter of Experts and Professionals, or How Impossible It Is to Leave Nothing Unsaid," in The Formation of Professions: Knowledge, State, and Strategy, ed. Rolf Torstendahl and Michael Burrage (Newbury Park: SAGE, 1990), 24–50, 25.

their discourse, a discourse deemed rational because it is based on "objective" data gathered through rational procedures and evaluated by the scientific community through a rigorous (and rational) control process. Science is therefore regarded as a means by which to depoliticize public issues. Indeed, policy makers find that it is efficient and comfortable to define decisions as technical rather than political.[124] This is a fallacy, for legitimate political action is impossible in modernist societies without scientific knowledge, and so, we can rephrase Nelkin's point and state that science is actually the most important means of politicizing issues. In education this is particularly problematic because education often involves ideals about the nature of our world, and those ideals often reflect the political and economic interests of elites. What we must do is to highlight the political nature of science, a task we seek to accomplish, even if in small form, in this book.

THE POLITICS OF EDUCATIONAL INQUIRY

Given all we have said, we will argue in the following chapters that the discourse on the science of education research should be understood as a *politics*, that is, this discourse is made possible by other political forces, which it in turn perpetuates. This claim is not particularly novel or interesting per se, but we think that at least five major arguments flow from this claim, each forming the basis for the chapters in this book. The first argument we just discussed, that is, SRE is part of the struggle for the professional legitimation of education researchers. The second argument is that the scientism, positivism, and behaviorism underlying SRE's notion of science restrict inquiry. This will be our concern in chapter 2. There our reading sticks very close to the report, which we reinterpret primarily via the work of John Dewey. The third argument is that doctoral training will be normalized accordingly. This is our concern in chapter 3, in which, as in the latter parts of this chapter, we again move to a level of interpretation of SRE that accounts for the political conditions that make it possible. The fourth argument is that science, as part of imperatives of an informational society, will provide the necessary and very particular technology for the government of our souls. This is the focus of chapter 4, where we will take on directly the question of what science is and the power it has to govern society. The final argument with which we are concerned in this book is that money associated with scientific practices restricts practice and academic inquiry in favor of transnational capitalism, our topic in chapter 5. There we provide a critique of the "grant culture" that currently characterizes much of what happens in the name of research in universities.

---

124. Dorothy Nelkin, "The Political Impact of Technical Expertise," *Social Studies of Science* 5, no. 1 (1975): 35–54, 36.

SRE is symptomatic of these concerns and thus provides for us the point of departure for what appear to be such disparate arguments. Before we move on to a more exacting critique of SRE in the next chapter, we would like to say one thing in its defense. We agree with Eisenhart and Towne that in the debate over scientific research in education, there has been a tendency to lump together the SRE with the statements on scientifically based research in laws such as NCLB, ESRA, and in the policies and practices of the IES and WWC. The SRE, they stress, argues that scientific research in education can best be defined around principles rather than methods.[125] We believe that Eisenhart and the other authors of SRE are correct in this respect, and we will add that SRE is a reasonably written document that accurately captures what science is currently thought to be. But as Lather argues, although SRE seeks to be inclusive regarding a range of approaches to education research, in providing guidelines for rigor it is complicit with the federal government's move to evidence-based knowledge as much more about creating a policy for science than science for policy.[126]

Moreover, the NRC committee failed to recognize that in taking on its charge in the first place it was to become part of a particular, and very powerful, discourse on education that seeks to define what, how, and who gets to speak it. This reflects struggles over professionalism within and among occupations, as we discussed before, but not entirely as the rest of the book explains. As much as the authors of the report seek to distance it from those federal policies that impose a narrow view of science on education research, they cannot do so. The point that the report may indeed be different from, and more nuanced than, those federal policies is irrelevant to the larger point that it too seeks to dictate what education research, and thus education itself, is or can be, and as such it is taking a side in the struggle over the power to do just that.

---

125. Eisenhart and Towne, "Contestation and Change in National Policy on 'Scientifically Based' Education Research," 31–38.
126. Lather, "This IS Your Father's Paradigm," 19.

TWO

ON SCIENTISM AND POSITIVISM

John Dewey and Education Research

with Philip Kovacs

Is there a science of education? And still more fundamentally, Can there be a science of education? Are the procedures and aims of education such that it is possible to reduce them to anything properly called a science?

—John Dewey, *The Sources of a Science of Education*

In this chapter, our mode of interpretation stays close to the text and critiques the internal logic of *Scientific Research in Education* (SRE), arguing that the report promotes scientism and positivism and, as result, imperils democratic inquiry.[1] Via a reading that juxtaposes the NRC report with John Dewey's work, which, ironically, the report cites as justifying its stance, we explain how the report's scientism and positivism work against its intentions of promoting inquiry. We do not wish our arguments to be mistaken with many others about the scientism and positivism of the report. Such claims, as we suggested in the previous chapter, have fallen into the trap of not arguing against the internal logic of a "scientific research in education," focusing instead on what appears to be the NRC committee's rejection or

Philip Kovacs is an assistant professor in the Department of Education at the University of Alabama-Huntsville.
1. National Research Council, *Scientific Research in Education*, ed. Richard J. Shavelson and Lisa Towne (Washington, DC: National Academy Press, 2002). Available at http://www.nap.edu/ (Retrieved February 5, 2005).

deemphasizing of qualitative and interpretive approaches. We think *SRE* is clear enough in its arguments that it is strictly limiting itself to questions that can be answered empirically, and that qualitative and *other* interpretive approaches are also valid for understanding educational phenomena. The report does appear to suggest that qualitative research is supplementary to quantitative approaches, but perhaps it does not do this after all, and it is only those critics with something to lose in the overall attempt to create a "science of education," and we must count ourselves among them, who have given the report such a reading.

We will argue, however, that even if the committee did have an inclusive understanding of educational inquiry in mind when it sought to define what a science of education might look like, its attempt to define such a science is to privilege *method* over thought. We use the term "method" not in the limited sense of, say, experimental design, but in a broad sense to mean the scientific method of operating that the committee's principles imply. To say what science *is* is to privilege a method of operation, a particular kind of logic and practice premised on scientism (but not necessarily "experimentism"),[2] as science, traditionally understood, is unthinkable without it. Given this brief introduction, we now provide a more exacting reading of the report.

THE "SCIENTIFIC PRINCIPLE"

The NRC committee's explanation of scientific inquiry actually prescribes how one should speak of science in education. Scientific research, the *SRE* explains, is "a continual process of rigorous reasoning supported by a dynamic interplay between methods, theories, and findings. It builds understanding in the form of models or theories that can be tested."[3] It proposes six "guiding principles" that will qualify education research as scientific: (1) it poses significant questions that can be investigated empirically; (2) it links research to relevant theory; (3) it uses methods that permit direct investigation of the question; (4) it provides a coherent and explicit chain of reasoning; (5) it replicates and generalizes across studies; and (6) it discloses research to encourage professional scrutiny and critique.[4] Other forms of inquiry may be well and good, the report suggests, but they *should not* be called scientific.

While the NRC committee argues that what makes research scientific is not the use of a particular method, but adherence to guiding principles,

---

2. Kenneth Howe puts forward a distinction between "experimentism" and "experimentalism," the latter focusing less on scientism and more on democratic inquiry; see Kenneth R. Howe, "The Question of Education Science: Experimentism Versus Experimentalism," *Educational Theory* 55, no. 3 (2005): 307–21.

3. *SRE*, 2.

4. Ibid., 3–5.

its "scientific principles include research design . . . as but one aspect of a larger process of rigorous inquiry."[5] It states further, "In discussing design, we have to be true to our admonition that the research question drives the design, not vice versa."[6] Education research, it argues, answers three types of questions: (1) "What is happening?"—which "invites description of various kinds, so as to properly characterize a population of students, understand the scope and severity of a problem, develop a theory or conjecture, or identify changes over time among different educational indicators;" (2) "Is there a systematic effect?"—which establishes causal effects; and (3) "Why or how is it happening?"—which "confronts the need to understand the mechanisms or process by which x causes y."[7] Questions 2 and 3 apparently lend themselves to experimental designs, but question 1 lends itself to multiple forms of inquiry. Indeed,

> qualitative methods can examine possible explanations for observed effects that arise *outside of the purview of the study.* . . . In education, research that explores students' and teachers' in-depth experiences, observes their actions, and documents the constraints that affect their day-to-day activities provides a key source of generating plausible causal hypotheses.[8]

It is this kind of statement that lends credence to Patti Lather and Pamela Moss's argument that the report positions qualitative research as supplementary to quantitative research,[9] if not "outside" the research process altogether. While it is not clear to us what the committee meant by such statements, our concern is not with this point, but with the scientism and positivism of the report, a point we elaborate upon in the next section of this chapter. Here we critique each of its principles as such.

The first guiding principle states that to be scientific, education research must "pose significant questions that can be investigated empirically." This principle has two parts:

> The first part concerns the nature of the questions posed: science proceeds by posing *significant* questions about the world with potentially multiple answers that lead to hypotheses or conjectures that can be tested and refuted. The second part concerns how these questions are posed: they must be posed in such a way that

---

5. Ibid., 97.
6. Ibid., 99.
7. Ibid., 99–100.
8. Ibid., 109. Emphasis added.
9. Patti Lather and Pamela Moss, "Introduction: Implications of the Scientific Research in Education Report for Qualitative Inquiry," *Teachers College Record* 107, no. 1 (2005), 1–3, 2.

it is possible to test the adequacy of alternative answers through carefully designed and implemented observations.[10]

Later in the report, we are instructed that (scientific) questions "are posed in an effort to fill a gap in existing knowledge or to seek new knowledge, to pursue the identification of the cause or causes of some phenomena, to describe phenomena, to solve a practical problem, or to formally test a hypothesis."[11]

There are at least two observations that can be made about this principle.[12] First, despite words to the contrary, the committee does indeed establish *the* method of science as inquiring about particular kinds of questions in particular kinds of ways. As the committee states,

> Put simply, the term "empirical" means based on experience through the senses, which in turn is covered by the generic term observation. Since science is concerned with making sense of the world, its work is necessarily grounded in observations that can be made about it. Thus, research questions must be posed in ways that potentially allow for empirical investigation. . . . In contrast, questions such as: "Should all students be required to say the pledge of allegiance [sic]?" cannot be submitted to empirical investigation and thus cannot be examined scientifically. Answers to these questions lie in realms other than science.[13]

The argument that science is concerned solely with investigating "observable" phenomena is what makes this report scientistic and positivistic, as we explain later. But, also, to demarcate the kinds of questions that scientists can ask does two apparently contradictory things: (1) it limits scientific inquiry, and (2) it institutionalizes scientific inquiry. According to such an argument, science cannot deal with philosophical, moral, or political kinds of questions; its realm is the a-metaphysical, the a-moral, the a-political realm of objective empirical investigation. Yet, in defining for itself the questions over which it has authority, science has institutionalized itself in our world as the arbiter of the questions that can be asked of the world—it

---

10. *SRE*, 54–55. Emphasis added.
11. Ibid., 55.
12. Of course, it is unlikely that the NRC committee would consider our "observations" properly scientific, since they cannot be subjected to the kind of scientism it requires. This is, in some way, one of the ironies of this report. In setting forth a theory of what counts as science in what can only be called, according to its rules, a nonempirical way, since it cannot itself be subject to the kind of testing it demands, it puts forth metaphysical and epistemological claims about the testing that is required for the objects of its claim, but those very claims are themselves not tested. It is akin to the IES's privileging of randomized field trials for interventions, but the IES's own intervention in the field of education is itself not subject to such trials.
13. *SRE*, 58–59.

will decide whether a question is within its realm or not, and this gives it considerable (professional) authority in our society. In education, scientists will decide which questions are theirs, and, in such cases, everyone else must step out of the way.

The second observation that can be made about SRE's first principle is that it requires that questions "must reflect a solid understanding of the *relevant* theoretical, methodological, and empirical work that has come before."[14] This implies at first glance a progression in scientific knowledge, but it may be read just as well as ensuring that scientific knowledge always remains tied to the past. It seems to us that a truly progressive science would not tie itself so strictly to the past, and would, following Thomas Popkewitz, create "new classifications of research that make possible new ways of imagining and seeing the world."[15] Here the restrictive nature of what the report requires of scientific inquiry becomes clear, as any so-called innovation in research need *not* necessarily be tied to theoretical, methodological, or empirical work performed before it. The notions of *innovation* and *progress* might imply otherwise.

Indeed, the report's premise that scientific knowledge accumulates, paradoxically, by tying itself to the past may be one of scientists' greatest follies, since it rejects the very past it ties itself to. Some histories of the human sciences, such as Michel Foucault's, have shown that scientific inquiry has been one of *discontinuities* rather than the continuity of knowledge this report suggests.[16] Furthermore, if one, as Popkewitz points out, uses Thomas Kuhn's notion of normal versus revolutionary science as an exemplar,[17] one must recognize that the idea of science as the accumulation and growth of knowledge is partially accurate but also misleading. "Normal" science is one that dominates in any given time; "revolutionary" science is one that searches for the answers to the questions the anomalies of normal science cannot solve. The NRC, explains Popkewitz, takes the side of normal science, but it misconstrues the relations in which science is formed and changed because of challenges to the epistemological and ontological boundaries of normal science.[18] To suggest that science is the accumulation of empirically based knowledge is to rewrite history to justify what appears now to be authoritative.[19]

---

14. Ibid., 3. Emphasis added.
15. Thomas S. Popkewitz, "Is the National Research Council Committee's Report on Scientific Research in Education Scientific? On Trusting the Manifesto," *Qualitative Inquiry* 10, no. 1 (2004): 62–78, 67.
16. See Michel Foucault, *The Order of Things: An Archeology of the Human Sciences*, trans. unlisted (New York: Vintage Books, 1970); Michel Foucault, *The Archeology of Knowledge and The Discourse on Language*, trans. A. M. Sheridan Smith (New York: Pantheon Books, 1972).
17. Thomas S. Kuhn, *The Structure of Scientific Revolutions*, 2nd ed. (Chicago: University of Chicago Press, 1970).
18. Popkewitz, "On Trusting the Manifesto," 68–69.
19. Ibid., 70.

Even if a clever wordsmith could link innovative questions and ways of questioning to the past, the report's addition of the words *significant*, to the questions science answers, and *relevant*, to the prior knowledge to which these question must link themselves, ultimately renders any claims to innovation and progress meaningless, since it is unlikely that those who are the arbiters of what counts as science at any given time would consider as "significant" and "relevant" any thinking that does not conform to their authoritative discourse.[20] Elizabeth Adams St. Pierre argues that "it is often the case that those who work within one theoretical framework find others unintelligible."[21] Indeed, any attempt at questioning "regimes of truth" may be incomprehensible to those committed to those regimes.[22] We think St. Pierre is largely correct, but we will add only that in addition to, or perhaps in some cases instead of the word *unintelligible*, we might add the word *uncomfortable*. There were some members of the NRC committee who we have little doubt find many of the critical, postmodern, and poststructural critiques sufficiently intelligible, but might nevertheless see those critiques as threatening to established scientific norms, or perhaps even more accurately, to the professional community that establishes them. Marianne Bloch's question, therefore, is indeed a *significant* and *relevant* challenge to the NRC's committee's assumptions; after all, she asked, "are we reframing who is a normal researcher or scientist and who is not to be listened to?"[23]

The *SRE's* second guiding principle of what counts as scientific education research is that it must "link research to relevant theory." The report further states that "[s]cientific theories are, in essence, conceptual models that explain some phenomenon. . . . Indeed, much of science is fundamentally concerned with developing and testing theories, hypotheses, models, conjectures, or conceptual frameworks that can explain aspects of the physical and social world."[24] We have already discussed one possible concern with

---

20. The NRC committee plays its hand too early when it states that "some extreme 'postmodernists' have questioned whether there is any value in scientific evidence in education whatsoever;" *SRE*, 20. We alluded already to the dismissing of "postmodern" critiques, but it is telling that it was the word *postmodernists* that was placed within quotes, but not the word *extreme* or the word *science*. What can one say about this, then, if not that while the committee wants to be careful about how it couched its dismissiveness of what it deems postmodern, its ability to demarcate extremity, relevance, significance, reasonableness, and so forth was simply to be taken as given.

21. Elizabeth Adams St. Pierre, " 'Science' Rejects Postmodernism," *Educational Researcher* 31, no. 8 (2002): 25–27, 25.

22. Elizabeth A. St. Pierre and Wanda S. Pillow, eds., "Introduction," *Working the Ruins: Feminist Poststructural Theory and Methods in Education* (New York: Routledge, 2000), 1–23, 11.

23. Marianne Bloch, "A Discourse That Disciplines, Governs, and Regulates: The National Research Council's Report on Scientific Research in Education," *Qualitative Inquiry* 10, no. 1 (2004): 96–100, 105.

24. *SRE*, 59.

the notion of relevance put forth by this principle, but let us provide here another, somewhat similar to the first. Margaret LeCompte links notions of *relevance* to those of *agenda*. An agenda, she argues, involves "vested interests," or "a political process, informed by multiple subjectivities, possessed of multiple entrenched interests, and framed by multiple agendas."[25] Given this understanding, we ask, rhetorically, what agenda will be at work in determining that this or that research will be relevant, worthy of the title "scientific," and thus properly and legitimately funded? Will it be the conservative agenda of politicians at the federal and state levels, or the neoliberal and economically motivated agenda of governmental and private external funding agencies, or the instrumentalist, utilitarian, and political agenda of the scientific community, which, in the name of the public good and professional integrity, has claimed for itself the authority to inform policy decisions, mine knowledge for intellectual property, and define itself as the arbiter of truth in our society?

The third guiding principle, according to *SRE*, is that scientific research must "use methods that permit direct investigation of the question." According to this principle, "Research methods—the design for collecting data and the measurement and analysis of variables in the design—should be selected in light of a research question, and should address it directly."[26] Methods "can only be judged in terms of their appropriateness and effectiveness in addressing a particular research question."[27] And, regardless of the field of study, "scientific measurements should be accompanied by estimates of uncertainty whenever possible."[28] We have alluded already to the professional policing that all these principles require. But also, as we point out later in this chapter, this concern with method and certainty, even if understood broadly, is what places this report squarely within a scientism and positivism that rely upon each other for coherence and support.

Here we can also ask, what exactly does "direct investigation of the question" mean? Although we think we know the answer, how would the scientific community judge, say, Michael Erben's work? Erben uses the biographical method as one means of exploring not only the researched but also the researcher. The "life" or "self," wrote Erben, "is regarded as a text."[29] We

---

25. Margaret D. LeCompte, "Some Notes on Power, Agenda, and Voice: A Researcher's Personal Evolution Toward Critical Research," in *Critical Theory and Educational Research*, ed. Peter L. McLaren and James M. Giarelli (Albany: State University of New York Press, 1995): 91–112, 102.

26. *SRE*, 62.

27. Ibid., 3.

28. Ibid., 66.

29. Michael Erben, "The Purposes and Processes of Biographical Method," in *Understanding Educational Research*, ed. David Scott and Robin Usher (New York: Routledge, 1996): 159–74, 160.

do not seek here to substitute Erben's notion of method with those of the NRC committee's and call the former better;[30] any privileging of a method is to conjure up a professional community that polices it and excludes what is other. We reference Erben simply to ask whether his method would qualify as a "direct investigation of the question," as the committee proposes scientific studies must do. One's interpretation of a life, and especially one's own, does not lend itself to the theory of certainty that ultimately grounds this third principle in SRE. How does one, say, "estimate" the "uncertainty" associated with the answers to the questions a method like Erben's can propose? Given the provisional nature of interpretations of texts, it is clear that SRE would not consider Erben's work scientific, and so we legitimately can wonder what violence this principle does to much of scholarship. Of course, since scientific studies must also be "read," and thus "interpreted," and such readings are vulnerable to multiple interpretations, and thus structurally carry with them the element of uncertainty, we wonder too whether this principle does violence to the very form of inquiry it exalts.

SRE's fourth guiding principle requires of research that it "provide a coherent and explicit chain of reasoning." Stated differently,

> The extent to which the inferences that are made in the course of scientific work are warranted depends on rigorous reasoning that systematically and logically links empirical observations with the underlying theory and the degree to which both the theory and the observations are linked to the question or problem that lies at the root of the investigation. There is no recipe for determining how these ingredients should be combined; instead, what is required is the development of a logical "chain of reasoning" . . . that moves from evidence to theory and back again. *This chain of reasoning must be coherent, explicit (one that another researcher could replicate), and persuasive to a skeptical reader (so that, for example, counterhypotheses are addressed.)*[31]

As with the third principle, for this one it is "critical to gauge the magnitude of . . . uncertainty."[32] Popkewitz questions the committee's claim that inferential reasoning is at the core of science. Drawing on the work of Jürgen Habermas, Popkewitz posits that "the social sciences embody different cognitive interests or modes in which reality is disclosed, constituted, and acted on," and, thus, the committee reduces all thought to one type of science and "[omits] any rigorous examination of the relation of competing modes of

---

30. Though we do not make this claim about Erben's work, some forms of biographical and autobiographical work can lend themselves to a solipsism that raises its own set of restrictions for inquiry and thought.
31. SRE, 67. Emphasis added.
32. Ibid., 68.

cognition in scientific investigations."[33] As Foucault notes, "There are times in life when the question of knowing if one can think differently than one thinks, and perceive differently than one sees, is absolutely necessary if one is to go on looking and reflecting at all."[34]

We agree with this critique, but we would augment it by accounting more thoroughly for the "principle of reason" this guiding principle presupposes. Jacques Derrida is instructive here. He points out that first and foremost to respond to the call of the principle of reason is to "render reason," to explain effects through their causes, rationally.[35] SRE's claim, then, that the "chain of reasoning must be coherent, explicit (one that another researcher could replicate), and persuasive to a skeptical reader (so that, for example, counter-hypotheses are addressed),"[36] is at its roots the rendering of reason in *that* particular way. This is not a mere rendering, however, but a rendering as required by an era of purportedly "modern" reason, metaphysics, and technoscience.[37] Given the violence associated with such an era, are we sacrilegious, with Derrida, when we question what grounds and anchors this principle of reason, which itself is a principle grounding science? Indeed,

> [w]ho is more faithful to reason's call, who hears it with a keener ear, who better sees the difference, the one who offers questions in return and tries to think through the possibility of that summons, or the one who does not want to hear any question about the reason of reason?[38]

The modern dominance of the principle of reason goes hand in hand with the interpretation of the essence of beings as objects, "an object present as representation, an object placed and positioned *before* a subject."[39] The principle of reason, Derrida argues, installs empire only to the extent that it ensures that the being hiding within it remains hidden, and with it the question of the grounding of the ground itself. Derrida posits that it is growing more obvious that research may "pay off"—or for those of us in education, research must be useful in the "what works" sense—and what is opposed to this utility is "knowledge," "truth," and a "disinterested exercise of reason, under the sole authority of the principle of reason."[40] Yet, it is

---

33. Popkewitz, "On Trusting the Manifesto," 72.

34. Michel Foucault, *The History of Sexuality: The Use of Pleasure, Volume 2*, trans. R. Hurley (New York: Pantheon, 1978), 8.

35. Jacques Derrida, "The Principle of Reason: The University in the Eyes of its Pupils," *Graduate Faculty Philosophy Journal* 10, no. 1 (1984): 5–29, 9.

36. *SRE*, 67

37. Derrida, "The Principle of Reason," 10.

38. Ibid.

39. Ibid., 11. Emphasis in original.

40. Ibid., 14.

difficult to maintain the distinction between technology on the one hand and theory, science, and rationality on the other. The term *technoscience* has to be accepted, and it confirms the fact that we "can no longer dissociate the principle of reason from the very idea of technology in the realm of their modernity."[41]

Note how easy it is to read the NRC as arguing nothing other than "technoscience" in education:

> We also believe the distinction between basic and applied science has outlived its usefulness. This distinction often served to denigrate applied work (into which category education research was usually placed). But . . . great scientific work has often been inspired by the desire to solve a pressing practical problem. . . . What makes research scientific is not the motive for carrying it out, but the manner in which it is carried out.[42]

The ease with which the committee ties scientific reason with technical utility lends credence to Derrida's point. Thus, while technoscience may now characterize all academic fields, as Derrida suggests, it particularly does so for the field of education, since, by most accounts, that field is one of application. The principle of reason in *SRE*'s fourth guiding principle, therefore, only makes explicit that technoscience governs in the field of education, and it seeks to instantiate itself in areas of the field where there might be some doubt about it. For there can be no chain of reasoning that is not also a technology for creating and controlling the field, even as it purports to explain it.

We agree with Derrida that we must strive for a "community of thought in the broad sense, rather than a community of research, or science, or philosophy, since these values are most often subjected to the unquestioned authority of a principle of reason." Such community, he continues, would "interrogate the essence of reason and of the principle of reason. It must unmask—an infinite task—all the ruses of end-oriented reason, the paths by which apparently disinterested research can find itself indirectly re-appropriated, re-invested by programs of all sorts."[43]

The fifth guiding principle posits that scientific research must "replicate and generalize across studies," as replication and generalization strengthen and clarify the limits of scientific conjectures and theories. This means that observations qualify as scientific to the extent that others are able to make similar observations, and that those observations may be generalizable to other

---

41. Ibid., 15.
42. *SRE*, 20.
43. Derrida, "The Principle of Reason," 20. We will keep coming back to the notion of a "community of thought" throughout the book.

contexts. The implication of this principle is obvious, as much of qualitative and interpretive analyses, as well as participatory or action research, cannot, and seeks not to, meet this standard. We may ask, as we have been doing, who gets to decide that this is a valid standard? Moreover, if LeCompte is correct that "reality" in a social setting involves the intermingling of voices,[44] then what does that mean for this principle? This notion of voice, we argue in extending LeCompte's point, is both singular and plural, as each individual has his or her own voice, which might indeed resemble many others but is unique and not subject to be replicated. Further, the intermingling of each voice creates a social context made up of all the voices, which conform to particular conventions but also constitute "battling" voices in their nonreplicable instances, and these "battles" will change the conventions repeatedly, making it impossible to generalize beyond a fleeting moment. We may impose a convention on everyone for all time, as the practices that emanate from this principle will inevitably do, but we should not pretend even for one moment that this is not an imposition.

The final guiding principle of science, according to *SRE*, is one that requires that we "disclose research to encourage professional scrutiny and critique." The report states that the "goal of communicating new knowledge is self-evident; research results must be brought into the professional and public domain if they are to be understood, debated, and eventually become known to those who could fruitfully use them."[45] We will have occasion to revisit this principle later in this chapter in light of our Deweyan reading of the report, which requires us to attend to the democratic process of inquiry. For now, let us say that the committee's claim that "the objectivity of science derives from publicly enforced norms of the professional community of scientists,"[46] can be called nothing but professional authoritarianism, as we suggested in chapter 1. This authoritarianism "reinscribes a governing discourse that disqualifies [many] educational researchers and their (our) work, suggesting that they/we must be policed, surveyed, regulated, and taught how to be rigorous and scientific."[47] In short, this principle is about power and control. With Lather, we argue that "accountability and control are requirements for an ideology that seeks to maintain power,"[48] and thus the sixth principle must be read as imposing norms rather than encouraging sharing; that is, it taketh (control) rather than giveth (shares knowledge).

So, from these principles, what are we to take as *the* "scientific principle"? James Paul Gee seems correct to us when he argues that *SRE*'s

44. LeCompte, "Some Notes on Power, Agenda and Voice," 100.
45. *SRE*, 73.
46. Ibid., 5.
47. Bloch, "A Discourse That Disciplines, Governs, and Regulates," 107.
48. Patti Lather, "This IS Your Father's Paradigm: Government Intrusion and the Case of Qualitative Research in Education," in *Qualitative Inquiry* 10, no. 1 (2004): 15–34, 20.

principles are relatively vacuous generalities because one cannot determine anything about any of them outside of specific theories of specific domains. Who determines in these principles what are *significant* questions, *relevant* theories, *appropriate* and *effective* methods, *coherency* and *explicitness*? How can studies be *replicated* and *generalized* across domains, who gets to decide that, and who counts as the *professional community* whose scrutiny is to be sought and whose critique is to be valued? It makes little sense, Gee argues, to speak, then, of "scientific" or "scientifically driven" since these terms are relative to specific domains. The only thing we can do, he proposes, is to state some goal with which we are interested and invested, and then ask of the theories in the relevant domains if they have a good track record of meeting those goals.[49]

We can ask, more fundamentally, with Pamela Moss, how is it that the vision of social science as portrayed in *SRE* came to be privileged in the first place? To what extent is its particular image of social science likely to become more accurate, as researchers discipline themselves to conform to what is sanctioned as scientifically rigorous?[50] Indeed, the portrayal of science here implicitly admonishes the field of education for refusing its call to rigor, certainty, and control. Consider that the committee asserts that what ensures that education research is less "probabilistic" and "tentative" than scientific inquiry in the physical sciences is that it must contend with "human behavior, ideas, cultures." The corollary to this is that in education, "the 'error limits' associated with scientific inferences (not unlike confidence intervals typically cited in public opinion polls) tend to be larger in social and behavioral research, often due to the 'noise' caused by difficulties precisely measuring key constructs and major contextual factors."[51] And yet it is that very "noise" representing the humanistic, idealistic, and cultural aspects of education that we would value instead of the cold, inhumane rigor, certainty, and control the committee puts forth as more valuable.

This "noise" here, too, is not simply referring to the difficulties in attaining certainty but also to those of us who value "noise," who develop a line of inquiry that studies and celebrates it. While we might appear like "noise" in the vision of science *SRE* narrates, we say, "and that is a good thing too," since controlling for that "noise" instantiates a scientism and positivism in our work that eviscerates inquiry and thought, context and temporality, play and emotion. That evisceration is *the* scientific principle, one we argue in the rest of this chapter must be rejected if education is to promote inquiry, thought, and something akin to democracy.

---

49. James Paul Gee, "It's Theories All the Way Down: A Response to Scientific Research in Education," *Teachers College Record* 107, no. 1 (2005): 10–18, 16.
50. Pamela A. Moss, "Toward 'Epistemic Reflexivity' in Educational Research: A Response to Scientific Research in Education," *Teachers College Record* 107, no. 1 (2005): 19–29, 26.
51. *SRE*, 83.

SCIENTISM AND POSITIVISM IN EDUCATION

When one attends to the makeup of the NRC committee that authored *SRE*, it will come as little surprise that we argue that the report is slanted in favor of scientism and positivism.[52] Three members of the committee, Robert L. DeHaan,[53] Jack McFarlin Fletcher, and Robert Hauser, have nothing to do with a college of education; they represent cell biology, pediatrics, and health and aging demography, respectively. Five members—Donald I. Barfield, Rudolph Crew, Norman Hackerman, Eric Hanushek, and Ellen Condliffe Lagemann—represent private foundations.[54] Most of these foundations—WestEd (Barfield), the Stupski Family Foundation (Crew), the Robert A. Welch Foundation (Hackerman), and the Hoover Institution (Hanushek)—further positivism, scientism, and behaviorism via a business/accountability agenda that extends the tenets of the NCLB and the economic rationality that undergirds it.[55] The Spencer Foundation (Lagemann) arguably is distinct from the others, but even it was founded by Lyle M. Spencer, who headed Science Research Associates, a publishing firm later sold to IBM. One member of the committee (Paul W. Holland) is from the Educational Testing Service, and another (Robert F. Boruch) is cross-listed as being with the Graduate School of Education and the Wharton School Department of Statistics at the University of Pennsylvania. The remaining six members—Richard J. Shavelson, Jere Confrey, Margaret Eisenhart, Eugene E. Garcia, Denis C. Phillips, and Carol H. Weiss—are listed as coming from

---

52. Our point here about the committee is based on what the report indicated were their affiliations, which, of course, may have changed since then. For example, at the time of this writing, Ellen Lagemann was no longer at the Spencer Foundation.

53. Robert DeHann is listed as affiliated with the Department of Cell Biology at Emory University. We mention this because we discuss in a subsequent chapter an article that he co-authored with Margaret Eisenhart, another member of the committee, which argues for a rethinking of educational doctoral preparation to create "scientifically based education researchers." See Margaret Eisenhart and Robert L. DeHaan, "Doctoral Preparation of Scientifically Based Education Researchers," *Educational Researcher* 34, no. 4 (2005): 3–13. We could say that as a professor of cell biology he should mind his own shop and leave ours alone, but we would be wrong, because it is the replacement of our shop with his that the discourse on the science of education seeks and is effecting at great speed.

54. Ellen Lagemann is a highly regarded historian of education and served for a time as the dean of the Harvard Graduate School of Education.

55. See, for example, Joel Spring, *Political Agendas for Education: From the Christian Coalition to the Green Party* (Mahwah, NJ: Lawrence Erlbaum, 1997); Jeffrey W. Wimer and Debra S. Vredenburg, "When Ideology Sabotages the Truth: The Politics of Privately-Funded Educational Vouchers in One Urban School District," paper presented at the American Educational Studies Association, Mexico City, Mexico, November 1, 2003; and Lynn Wilson, "Controlling the Power Over Knowledge: Selling the Crisis for Self-Serving Gains," in *Schools or Markets? Commercialism, Privatization, and School-Business Partnerships*, ed. Deron R. Boyles (Mahwah, NJ: Lawrence Erlbaum, 2005): 195–215.

schools or departments of education. It is interesting and very telling of the state of affairs that of sixteen members of the committee, only six were fully affiliated with a college or school of education.[56]

This point, however, is not intended to signal that the six "education" members do not support scientism. Denis Phillips, for example, is a leading analytic philosopher whose intellectual home is in philosophy of science and science education. Jere Confrey directs the Systemic Research Collaborative for Mathematics, Science, and Technology (SYRCE) at the University of Texas-Austin. Margaret Eisenhart founded and directs the Center for Youth Science, Culture, and New Media at the University of Colorado at Boulder. Richard Shavelson is a Fellow of the American Association for the Advancement of Science. Again, our point here is that it should come as no surprise that we argue that the NRC report is premised on scientism and positivism, but this is a tricky argument for us. Let us say for now that we believe the report operates from a never-challenged position that science *is*, that is, given, a point we question further in chapter 4.

Our critique here does not seek to replicate those already made of the report (some of which we discussed here and in the previous chapter). Rather, we seek to contextualize it within the quickening pace of positivist and scientistic practices that are increasingly subsuming our lives. In the College of Education at Georgia State University, for example, in the beginning meeting of the college's faculty in August 2004, the dean and his chairs circulated a change in policy relating to course load for the 2005–2006 academic year.[57] According to the document (and among other things), faculty members engaged in "scholarship" would teach five courses per year; faculty members engaged in "research" would teach four courses per year. There was no definition, no clarification, no illustration to convey or communicate the difference between scholarship and research within the document, although the dean indicated that a driving force for the policy was Washington, D.C.'s, increasing emphasis on accountability-driven, empirical, evidence-based research.[58] When pressed to explain the distinction between "research" and "scholarship," the dean and at least some of his chairs indicated that "research" was

56. We can also count Robert Boruch, who is partly affiliated with a school of education, and Ellen Lagemann, who subsequently headed one, within these numbers without losing much of the point we make here.

57. At the time of these events, we both worked at Georgia State University. One of us has since left and is working at Florida International University, which in his opinion is even more committed to positivism and scientism than Georgia State is.

58. A slew of "helping" organizations have sought to guide people like this dean in the "art of research" as defined by the federal government. One example is the Clearinghouse on Educational Policy and Management, whose Web site provides an overview of the work furthering positivism via the U.S. government. See Ron Beghetto, *Scientifically Based Research* (Eugene: Clearinghouse on Educational Policy Management, 2003). Available at http://eric.uoregon.edu/publications/roundup/spring2003.html (Retrieved January 6, 2005).

being defined as that which answered a "question," and when pressed further, that the question had to be "empirical," which in their uninformed parlance could only mean that which used scientistic, positivistic, and behavioristic techniques. While the policy was challenged by members of the college's Faculty Affairs Committee (a debate that continues), the point was already made: scientism and positivism are alive and well. They are no longer simply ideals, or even points of debate in education; they are a way of life for some, and an imposed experience for many others.

So far, we have used the terms *positivism* and *scientism* conjointly, without much of a hint that they might be distinct. We want to distinguish now between positivism and scientism. Positivism is used here as a general reference. The term itself was first used by Claude Henri de Rouvroy, Compte de Saint-Simon to extend philosophy into the realm of scientific method. Auguste Comte adopted the term, and it came to designate a vast, worldwide movement. There are variations within positivism (e.g., social [Auguste Comte, Jeremy Bentham], evolutionary [Herbert Spencer], critical or empirocriticism [Ernst Mach], the logical positivism of the Vienna School scientists, etc.).[59] The main features of positivism include an insistence that science has the only basis for obtaining valid knowledge and observable facts are the only valid objects of knowledge.[60] In other words, only positive facts can be true, and claims can be made only about observable phenomena.[61] Positivism requires scientific techniques in the social sciences because assertions about the world must be "verifiable through experience and observation."[62] Since it recognizes knowledge as deriving only from positive facts, positivism must reduce complex social phenomena to manageable, observable units that are tested through experimentation. Positivism, therefore, denies the existence of forces or substances that go beyond the facts and laws ascertained by and through scientific methods. It opposes metaphysics and, generally speaking, any procedure that is not reducible to the scientific method, where that method presumes objectivity and value neutrality.

SRE claims *not* to emphasize objectivity,[63] but its other claims tell a different story. In summarizing its first principle, that one must pose significant questions that can be investigated empirically, it states:

---

59. See, for example, D. G. Charlton, *Positivist Thought in France During the Second Empire, 1852–1870* (Oxford: Oxford University Press, 1959); and W. M. Simon, *European Positivism in the Nineteenth Century* (Ithaca: Cornell University Press, 1963).
60. See Nicola Abbagnano, trans., Nino Langiulli, "Positivism," *The Encyclopedia of Philosophy*, Vol. 6 (New York: Macmillan, and The Free Press): 414–19.
61. George A. Lundberg, "Contemporary Positivism in Sociology," *American Sociological Review* 4, no. 1 (1939): 42–55.
62. Robert Audi, ed., *The Cambridge Dictionary of Philosophy* (Cambridge: Cambridge University Press, 1995), 445. See also, Raphael Demos, "Aspects of Positivism," *Philosophy and Phenomenological Research* 13, no. 3 (1953): 377–93.
63. SRE, 73.

Ultimately, the final court of appeals for the viability of a scientific hypothesis is its empirical adequacy. Scientists and philosophers commonly hold that the testability and refutability of scientific claims or hypotheses is an important feature of scientific investigations that is not typical in other forms of inquiry.[64]

"Testability" and "refutability" are exactly what allows scientists to claim objectivity and neutrality. Indeed, that objectivity is what is required of education research so as to gain the respectability that the committee sought for it. Scientific investigations will give the field of education, according to the report, "trustworthy, scientific evidence" on which to base decisions about education. It is the unobjective, untrustworthy hodgepodge of educational scholarship that must be replaced by the scientism and positivism presumed in the report.

More nuanced readings on the topic of scientism appear in the fields of sociology and the philosophy of science. D. C. Phillips, for example, defined scientism as "a term used in a mildly abusive way to indicate slavish adherence to the methods of science in a context where they are inappropriate (e.g., studying human affairs)."[65] Robert Bannister pointed to Freidrich von Hayek's origination of the term *scientism* in the 1940s and describes it as a "term of abuse" that means "a naive faith in the neutrality of scientific method, and a confidence bordering on arrogance that the 'modern' American millennium was just around the corner."[66] Frederick Olafson traced the roots of scientism to Enlightenment philosophers who applied "methods of inquiry that had been designed to deal with inanimate nature—with *things*"—to human beings and various human conditions.[67] In this way, scientism is a form of reductionism that de-humanizes and decontextualizes sociality. Indeed, one can say that scientism actually eviscerates sociality.

Scientism, while distinct from positivism, is nevertheless inextricably linked to it; both are mutually supportive and both restrict inquiry in

---

64. Ibid., 3.

65. D. C. Phillips, *Philosophy, Science, and Social Inquiry: Contemporary Methodological Controversies in Social Science and Related Applied Fields of Research* (Oxford: Pergamon Press, 1987), 206. See also D. C. Phillips, *The Expanded Social Scientist's Bestiary: A Guide to Fabled Threats to, and Defenses of, Naturalistic Social Science* (Lanham, MD: Rowman and Littlefield, 2000).

66. Robert C. Bannister, *Sociology and Scientism: The American Quest for Objectivity, 1880–1940* (Chapel Hill: University of North Carolina Press, 1987), 8.

67. Frederick A. Olafson, *Naturalism and the Human Condition: Against Scientism* (London: Routledge, 2001), 3–4. Emphasis in original. For a more narrow treatment of four philosophers and the implications of scientism to pragmatism, see Joseph Margolis, *The Unraveling of Scientism: American Philosophy at the End of the Twentieth Century* (Ithaca: Cornell University Press, 2003).

education.[68] Positivism, in a nutshell, eschews diverse perspectives in favor of observable facts and validates scientism for its methods of investigation; scientism attends to the observable facts by positing methods for controlling extraneous matters via positivist notions of inquiry. And this is what *SRE* requires of education research. *SRE* states, "At its core, scientific inquiry is the same in all fields."[69] Furthermore, the "accumulation of knowledge is the ultimate goal of [all] research."[70] As Kenneth Howe notes, "although the committee did some hand waiving about how scientific progress is disjointed and is characterized by uncertainty and by fits and starts, they [sic] eventually identified the general aims of scientific educational research [for everyone]."[71] Popkewitz explains that this is a project that the logical positivists promoted, that is, the elimination of metaphysical arguments in favor of a position that all knowledge fits into a single conceptual framework that explains science. This unity searches for consensus and certainty, which in turn are produced through norms of professional communities.[72] The material consequences of scientism and positivism is that they modify *seeing* the world, and thus, *being* in the world. In education, we may tie these to the gutter utilitarianism of the federal attempts to dictate a science for education, which will promote positivistic and scientistic methods and hypotheses to arrive at a simplistic notion of "what works."

Margaret Eisenhart argues that what *SRE* advocates is a notion of science in terms of postpositivism, since it accommodates both patterned behavior and human intentionality.[73] This may be correct but is beside the point.[74] Postpositivism, to be sure, seems to have supplanted positivism in education research, since the former, as Egon Guba and Yvonna Lincoln explain, acknowledges that reality only partially can be apprehended because

---

68. Moreover, as we suggest in chapter 5, scientism and positivism operate in contemporary times on an additional, mutually supportive base: economics. Scientism and positivism promote utilitarian goals by determining what counts as valid knowledge, what qualifies as the way to that knowledge, and what value one is to obtain from that knowledge. These goals are not ends-in-view or fallibilist findings of various methods; they are reductionist, procedural, economistic, prescribed functions of a military-techno-industrial complex.

69. *SRE*, 2.

70. Ibid., 24.

71. Kenneth Howe, "A Critique of Experimentalism," *Qualitative Inquiry* 10, no. 1 (2004): 42–61, 49–50.

72. Thomas S. Popkewitz, "Is the National Research Council Committee's Report on Scientific Research in Education Scientific? On Trusting the Manifesto," *Qualitative Inquiry* 10, no. 1 (2004): 62–78, 64.

73. Margaret Eisenhart, "Science Plus: A Response to the Responses to Scientific Research in Education," *Teachers College Record* 107, no. 1 (2005): 52–58, 53.

74. Eisenhart also claimed that the report does not presume that science is value-free (Ibid., 54), but, as we argued above, its claims reifying particular forms of objectivity and neutrality belie its real claims.

of flawed intellectual mechanisms and the intractable nature of social phenomena.[75] What is important, however, is that postpositivism still assumes
that there is a reality "out there," external to us, only it cannot be apprehended because of *our* inability to apprehend it. Thus, it still privileges the
scientific method; it merely exercises a bit less sanguinity in the claims it
makes. Positivism ("post" or otherwise) cannot escape the scientism that
makes its claims thinkable in the first place.[76]

The practical consequences of scientism in education are that it will
institute a notion of the curriculum as "cookbook," teaching and learning
as "proven method" or "best practices," research as "funded enterprise," and
educational inquiry as only "what works." The economic implications of
scientism are often overlooked by its critics, but scientism's significant value
in our political economy is that it can "sell" the idea of neutrality and the
institutional/scientific apparatus that defines and polices it. We spend more
time discussing these points in subsequent chapters. For now, we contribute
to the critiques of the NRC's report by pointing out something that is largely
missing in the discourse surrounding it: Its curious use of Dewey.

THE "SCIENCE" OF DEWEY

The NRC report, as we have been arguing, is symptomatic of a narrow,
positivist interpretation of what counts as knowledge in the field of education. What is curious, if not duplicitous, is the committee's claims to both
inclusiveness and Deweyan foundations. Dewey is cited in the report repeatedly but his fallibilist epistemology is subsumed by a classically-realist,
utilitarian scientism. At least one consequence follows from this curious use
of Dewey's view of science to justify what is essentially a positivist view of
knowledge and its production: it represents a major threat to opportunities
for inquiry, thought, and democracy that the corpus of Dewey's work advocates. Dewey himself addressed explicitly the question of whether there is
a "science of education," but his conclusions cannot be read as justifying
what *SRE* portrays it as being.[77]

Specifically, the committee seizes Dewey's elevation of the concept of
"science" without situating him in context. The NRC report cites Dewey

---

75. Egon G. Guba and Yvonna S. Lincoln, "Competing Paradigms in Qualitative Research,"
in *Handbook of Qualitative Research*, ed. Norman K. Denzin and Yvonna S. Lincoln (Thousand
Oaks, CA: SAGE Publications, 1994), 105–17, 110.
76. We wish to clarify that "postpositivism" is sometimes understood to include thinkers such
as W. V. O. Quine, Thomas Kuhn, and Richard Rorty. See, for example, W. V. O. Quine,
Ontological Relativity (New York: Columbia University Press, 1977); Thomas S. Kuhn, *The
Essential Tension: Selected Studies in Scientific Traditions and Change* (Chicago: University of
Chicago Press, 1979); and Richard Rorty, *Philosophy and the Mirror of Nature* (Princeton:
Princeton University Press, 1981). See, also, Susan Haack, *Defending Science—Within Reason:
Between Scientism and Cynicism* (Amherst, NY: Prometheus Books, 2003).
77. See Dewey, *The Sources of a Science of Education*.

regarding *warrants*,[78] suggesting fallibilism, but then goes on to advance foundationalism, which is antithetical to Dewey's regard for and advocacy of science qua transactional naturalistic empiricism, that is, the active manipulation of the environment as integral to learning and knowing. Here we reread Dewey's work to tease out his epistemology and conclude that such epistemology would not only *not* support *SRE*, it requires that we reject it as restricting inquiry, thought, and even democracy itself.

The relatively recent history of epistemology has been dominated by Bertrand Russell, Gottlob Frege, G. E. Moore, and others committed to an analytic view of professional philosophy. At the beginning of the twentieth century, language, correspondence theories, independent reality, and foundationalism were major foci of this analytic view. The aim of the analytic approach was to identify and reveal philosophical problems by examining and clarifying the language used to express them. This analysis led to modern logic and the recognition of the primary importance of sense and reference in the construction of meaning. Charles Sanders Peirce, William James, Dewey, and other pragmatists, however, launched an attack on the analytic approach in the early 1900s, and Dewey and Russell engaged in well-known debates about the nature of knowledge and the various requirements one must meet to be deemed to know anything at all.[79] Just prior to Russell, however, there were the new realists and the critical realists. New realists, such as William Montague and Ralph Barton Perry, who were students of the idealist Josiah Royce, mounted an effort to promote a non-Roycean pluralism that nonetheless held out hope for a doctrine of immediate perception and the independence of objects in epistemological inquiry. J. B Pratt and other critical realists rejected the new realists' doctrine of immediate perception because they did not believe that perception was unmediated. They held, instead, that the mind *is* a mediating factor between physical objects, perception, and meaning.[80]

Dewey faced criticism from virtually all of these foregoing philosophers but continually rejected the attacks on his naturalistic empiricism.[81] He set

---

78. *SRE*, 18.

79. Tom Burke, *Dewey's New Logic: A Reply to Russell* (Chicago: The University of Chicago Press, 1994), 214–44.

80. For an explanation of these movements, see Bruce Kuklick, *Rise of American Philosophy: Cambridge, Massachusetts, 1860–1930* (New Haven: Yale University Press, 1977).

81. Empiricism, generally, is the theory that knowledge stems from sense experiences and mental experiences (such as self-reflection). Dewey's naturalistic empiricism situates experience at the center of an interrelated process wherein action, enjoyment, and "undergoing" are each intertwined and central. See John P. Azelvandre, "Constructing Sympathy's Forge: Empiricism, Ethics, and Environmental Education in the Thought of Liberty Hyde Bailey and John Dewey," *Philosophy of Education* (2001): 170–78, 173–76; Peter Godfrey-Smith, "Dewey on Naturalism, Realism, and Science," *Philosophy of Science* 69 (September 2002): 1–11; James Garrison, "An Introduction to Dewey's Theory of Functional 'Trans-Action': An Alternative Paradigm for Activity Theory," *Mind, Culture, and Activity* 8 (2001): 275–96; and Deron R. Boyles, "Dewey's Epistemology: An Argument for Warranted Assertions, Knowing, and Meaningful Classroom Practice," *Educational Theory* 56, no. 1 (2006): 57–68.

out to clarify what he meant by truth, reality, and knowledge. While he accepted some of the new realist claims (e.g., reality is not dependent on human consciousness), Dewey did not accept its central premise, such at that there is an absolute independence of things from thoughts.[82] Instead, Dewey offered a theory that opposed both idealism and the variants of realism: he argued that knowledge and experience are not coextensive. Dewey also rejected defining perception (rank or base empiricism) as knowledge because of the problem of immediacy; that is, knowledge cannot be had in an instant. Knowledge takes time and is an achievement. It eventually comes, but "it is the result of situated processes that were initiated to respond to specific problems."[83] Perception is not immediate either. It too takes time and involves past habits. Perceiving, as Dewey understood it, means that data are screened, chosen, and refined.[84] Indeed, as David Hildebrand points out, such activities as perceiving and knowing "always occur within the context of larger 'situations,' a nexus of ongoing processes and purposes."[85]

In chapter 3 of the NRC report, the committee purports to define what scientific inquiry is, and thus what it should be in education. It acknowledges that differences in the interpretation of science exist but posits a view of science that disallows the very differences it notes. The report states, for example, that "well-known scientific theories include evolution, quantum theory, and the theory of relativity. In the social sciences and education," the report continues, "such 'grand' theories are rare." Yet, "generalized theoretical understanding is still a goal."[86] Indeed, the report indicates that the committee does "not make a judgment about the worth" of competing forms of research, but it does "believe strongly in the merits of scientific inquiry in education research."[87]

What makes scientific inquiry so meritorious? The answer is its "empirical method." And a reading of Dewey's specific attempt at answering the question of whether there is a science of education seems to support this, for "science signifies, I take it, the existence of systematic methods of inquiry, which, when they are brought to bear on a range of facts, enable us to understand them better and to control them more intelligently, less haphazardly and with less routine."[88] The committee appears to follow such logic, positing that the empirical method in science features "codified

82. See David L. Hildebrand, *Beyond Realism and Anti-Realism: John Dewey and the Neopragmatists* (Nashville: Vanderbilt University Press, 2003), 8–40.
83. Ibid., 24.
84. John Dewey, "The Reflect Arc Concept in Psychology," *Psychological Review* 3 (1896): 357–370.
85. Hildebrand, *Beyond Realism and Anti-Realism*, 24–25.
86. SRE, 59.
87. Ibid., 74. Emphasis in original.
88. Dewey, *The Sources of a Science of Education*, 9.

procedures for making observations and recognizing sources of bias, and the data derived from these observations are used specifically as tools to support or refute knowledge claims."[89] And, finally, empiricism in science involves "collective judgments based on logic, experience, and consensus."[90]

The report includes a footnote on page 74 where it qualifies the version of empiricism it just furthered; there the committee offers that it is not claiming that any one investigator or observational method is "objective"; rather, the guiding principles are meant to guard against bias through "rigorous methods and a critical community." If the report's prior explanation of the guiding principles did not belie the scientism and positivism of the report, this seemingly innocuous footnote clearly does. After making much of the "we do not claim objectivity" and "science is not about methods" rhetoric, the committee immediately turns around and posits that its "guiding principles are established to guard against bias through rigorous methods and a critical community" of, we might add, "objective" scientists. This is the problem of education research: "The education research community has not been nearly as critical of itself as is the case in other fields of scientific study."[91]

Let us rewrite, then, what the committee found wrong with education research: Its methods are not rigorous; it does not guard against bias; it has not been critical of itself; in short, it is not "objective." Our introductory discussion on education research in chapter 1, however, was intended to suggest that the field of education research has been more than critical of itself; indeed, it seems such criticality is all it speaks. The "education" members of the committee must surely have known this; Lagemann particularly, since she has written extensively about education research. So let us rewrite even more explicitly what the committee *really* found wrong with education research: its community of education researchers are not deemed *by* (positivist) scientists to be as critical of itself as *these* scientists think they are of themselves. Whether or not the education research community has been critical of itself is beside the point. The point is that it has yet to be fully adopted, or, dare we say, co-opted by these scientists.

To enjoin Dewey to make this and other points, the committee ends SRE's chapter 3 with this lengthy quote from Dewey's *Democracy and Education*:

> Our predilection for premature acceptance and assertion, our aversion to suspended judgment, are signs that we tend naturally to cut short the process of testing. We are satisfied with superficial

---

89. *SRE*, 74.
90. Ibid.
91. Ibid., 73. Emphasis added.

and immediate short-visioned applications. If these work out with moderate satisfactoriness, we are content to suppose that our assumptions have been confirmed. Even in the case of failure, we are inclined to put blame not on the inadequacy and incorrectness of our data and thoughts, but upon our hard luck and the hostility of circumstances. . . . Science represents the safeguard of the [human] race against these natural propensities and the evils which flow from them. It consists of the special appliances and method . . . slowly worked out in order to conduct reflection under conditions whereby its procedures and results are tested.[92]

The problem with the committee's use of the quote is that it was taken out of context. Prior to the quote, Dewey exalted science and equated it with knowledge, much like *SRE* did. He called science, in its degree,

the perfected outcome of learning—its consummation. What is known, in a given case, is what is sure, certain, settled, disposed of; that which we think *with* rather than that which we think about. In its honorable sense, knowledge is distinguished from opinion, guesswork, speculation, and mere tradition.[93]

While the quote in the report ended where it did, Dewey went on to say, "But experience makes us aware that there is a difference between intellectual certainty of *subject matter* and *our* certainty."[94] His point was to caution us on two fronts. First, we should not take science to be such a universalized worldview—nor a reified (generalized) method—that we forget context. *SRE* did claim that context is important in education, but its advocacy of rigor, certainty, and objectivity belies such a claim.

Second, we should not throw out a naturalistic empiricist interpretation of science-in-common-life. Indeed, for Dewey, "Thinking is a process of inquiry, of looking into things, of investigating. *Acquiring is always secondary*, and instrumental to the act of inquiring. . . . But all thinking is research, and all research is native, original, with him who carries it on, even if everybody else in the world already is sure of what he is still looking for."[95] The process of acquiring and accumulating scientific knowledge in education proposed by *SRE* is simply but an abstraction; such knowledge can have little effect on the process of thinking in education and in educational research, since

---

92. John Dewey, *Democracy and Education* (New York: The Free Press, 1916), 189, quoted in *SRE*, 79. The qualifier "human" in "[human] race" was added by the NRC committee.
93. Dewey, *Democracy and Education*, 188. Emphasis in original.
94. Ibid. Emphasis in original.
95. Ibid., 148. Emphasis added.

such thinking cannot be done for someone *by someone else*.[96] And yes, this will mean that educators will make "mistakes," but such is the process of thinking. And no amount of adherence to abstract principles and methods can take away this risk, because it "also follows that all thinking involves risk. Certainty cannot be guaranteed in advance."[97]

To be sure, Dewey wanted us to get away from superstition and mere opinion, as does the NRC committee. Dewey wanted us to employ scientific method, as does the NRC committee. The difference is that Dewey made an important stipulation: "The fact that science marks the perfecting of knowing in highly specialized conditions of technique renders its results, taken by themselves, remote from ordinary experience—a quality of aloofness that is properly designated by the term abstract."[98] In other words, science "as laboratory experiment" yields "scientific" results, but the connection between science and the context of everyday life is where Dewey wanted science to go. In order to do so, and in order for one to be able to be say one knows, traditional epistemology, and the version of it offered by the NRC report, is questionable on Deweyan grounds, even though the NRC committee invokes Dewey to lend legitimacy to its view. The NRC report elevates what can count only as a spectator theory of knowledge, with a quest for certainty and scientific "truth," whereas Dewey eschewed the notion of truth as standing for a static and finalized correspondence between two separate orders.[99] Here, perhaps, we have the crux of the problem. The NRC

---

96. This point echoes one made by Ralph Waldo Emerson in 1837, when he argued that "the scholar is the delegated intellect. In the right state, he is Man Thinking. In the degenerate state, when the victim of society, he tends to become a mere thinker, or still worse, the parrot of other men's thinking." See Ralph Waldo Emerson, "The American Scholar," in *American Literary Essays*, ed. Lewis Leary (New York: Thomas Y. Crowell, 1960), 21–33, 23 (emphasis in original). The reification of a particular scientific method, one that requires strict adherence to prior knowledge and theories, as the NRC report proposes in its second principle, would qualify for Emerson as "merely thinking," since it sets out from accepted dogmas. *Man Thinking* looks forward, not backward.

97. Dewey, *Democracy and Education*, 148.

98. Ibid., 189–90.

99. We could play with the term *spectator theory of knowledge* to illuminate another distressing point. The "spectator" in the theory is the detached observer, but we can add that the NRC committee puts forth another version of the "spectator theory of knowledge," where the "spectator" would be not only the detached observer, but the educators and children, who will simply "stand by and watch"—if even that much respect is afforded them—as educational researchers, reconstituted now as scientists, will experiment and otherwise act upon them, purportedly for the former's sake. But those educators and students themselves are not to be trusted with producing their own knowledge—that would simply constitute too much "noise"—and their "expertise," based solely and entirely on the vicissitudes of their contexts, is not "critical" (read as: scientific) enough to warrant that label. Indeed, they are not even worthy of judging the usefulness of this knowledge produced *by others for them*, since the NRC report makes it clear that they will not constitute the "critical community" worthy of such a task. This "spectator" theory of knowledge (production) is antithetical to Dewey's philosophy, and we will have occasion to return to it.

report elevates science as "the Method" that should drive education research seeking to determine "what works." Dewey, however, elevated science as an extrapolation of common sense, which has no intrinsic restriction.

Thus, Dewey rejected traditional accounts of epistemology just as he would reject scientism. He did so, in part, because he saw traditional episte-mology as a hollow area of inquiry given the primacy of the truth condition in the traditional syllogism (S knows that p iff: p, S believes that p, and S justifies that p). He also saw the disconnected nature of the theories phi-losophers were putting forward. In separating out the contexts of perception and the knowing that results, Dewey was frustrated by new realist, critical realist, and idealist efforts at developing a theory of knowledge. As Sidney Ratner, Jules Altman, and James Wheeler point out,

> Dewey argued persuasively that each of the main types of epistemo-logical theory which mark the course of philosophy "represents a selective extraction of some conditions and factors out of the actual pattern of inquiry." He showed that this borrowing is what gave or gives plausibility and appeal to sensationalistic empiricism, logical atomism, materialism, positivism, direct and representative [critical] realism, and perceptual, rationalistic, and absolute idealism.[100]

The appeal may exist, but the *warrant*, or justification, for that appeal is specious, in Dewey's view. The NRC report, as we discussed, privileges gen-eralizability, certainty, "model-fitting," and, we argue, causality (the latter is the goal of two of the three questions constituting education research),[101] which belies the other claims that scientific education research must heed context. But, as if responding to the NRC report rather than to sensation-alistic empiricism, logical atomism, materialism, positivism, and so forth, Ratner, Altman, and Wheeler argue that "arbitrary isolation of the elements selected from the inquiry-context in which they function invalidates their sweeping claims."[102]

Dewey did indicate that positivism and scientism do not violate ev-ery condition of inquiry as ways of knowing. Still, the NRC's selection of

100. Sidney Ratner, Jules Altman, and James E. Wheeler, *John Dewey and Arthur F. Bentley: A Philosophical Correspondence, 1932–1951* (New Brunswick, NJ: Rutgers University Press, 1964), 39. The authors' quote of Dewey is from John Dewey, *Logic: The Theory of Inquiry* (New York: Henry Holt, 1938): 513–35.

101. To remind readers, *SRE* states that education research answers three types of questions: (1) "What is happening?"—which "invites description of various kinds, so as to properly characterize a population of students, understand the scope and severity of a problem, develop a theory or conjecture, or identify changes over time among different educational indicators; (2) "Is there a systematic effect?"—which establishes casual effects; and (3) "Why or how is it happening?"—which "confronts the need to understand the mechanisms or process by which x causes y" (*SRE*, 99–100).

102. Ratner, Altman, and Wheeler, *John Dewey and Arthur F. Bentley*, 39.

conditions is so one-sided that it appears to "ignore and thereby virtually deny any other conditions which give those that are selected their cognitive force and which also prescribe the limits under which the selected elements validly apply."[103] The problem with scientism, for Dewey, is that it extracts material from their context and makes that material "structural instead of functional, ontological instead of logical."[104] The NRC report proposes scientism by way of scientistic assumptions, but it also cites Dewey, so it reflects a confusing epistemological mix of foundationalism and fallibilism. We contend that explicit engagement with theories of epistemology *can* and *should* represent an area of inquiry (and practice) that is relevant and useful for education research, especially if such inquiry works *with*, not *for*, educators to foster classroom practices that foster inquiry. Accordingly, we focus attention on Dewey's conception of "warranted assertability" since the NRC report specifically raises the point and cites Dewey for it.[105] By highlighting in the next section the distinctions between the epistemology of the NRC report and Dewey's conception of *knowing*, we hope to expose the SRE as nothing more than a promotion of a foundationalist epistemology, a bifurcation of theory and practice, and a quest for certainty, all of which Dewey rejected.

Certainty, Warrants, and Educational Inquiry

In *The Quest for Certainty*, Dewey argues for the overthrow of traditional epistemology.[106] He specifically rejects the "spectator theory of knowledge" (STK), and, some have said, argues against all of epistemology.[107] We disagree that Dewey threw out epistemology as such, but he did argue against what then defined it. In setting STK aside, Dewey sets much of *traditional* epistemology aside, but he did not argue against knowing or the known. He argues only against the reliance on ontological and metaphysical ideals entailed by traditional accounts of "pure knowledge." In place of such a traditional account, Dewey crafted a new version of epistemology—one that had as a key element the notion of warranted assertability.[108]

SRE includes a paragraph in which it accurately, if fleetingly, depicts Dewey's concept of warranted assertability:

---

103. Dewey, *Logic*, 514, op. cit., fn. 100.

104. Ibid., 534.

105. SRE, 18, 51, 59.

106. John Dewey, *The Quest for Certainty: A Study of the Relation of Knowledge and Action*, in *John Dewey: The Later Works, 1925–1953, Volume 4, 1929*, ed. Jo Ann Boydson (Carbondale: Southern Illinois University, 1988), 1–250. See, also, John Dewey and Arthur F. Bentley, *Knowing and the Known* (New York: Beacon Press, 1949).

107. See, for example, Christopher Kulp, *The End of Epistemology: Dewey and His Current Allies on the Spectator Theory of Knowledge* (Westport, CT: Greenwood Press, 1992).

108. Dewey, *Logic*, 118–72.

Dewey wrote [in *Logic: The Theory of Inquiry*] of *warrants* for making assertions or knowledge claims. In science, measurements and experimental results, observational or interview data, and mathematical and logical analysis all can be part of the warrant—or case—that supports a theory, hypothesis, or judgment. However, warrants are always revocable depending on the findings of subsequent inquiry. Beliefs that are strongly warranted or supported at one time (e.g., the geocentric model of the solar system) may later need to be abandoned (for the heliocentric model). Evidence that is regarded as authoritative at one time (e.g., ice ages are caused by the eccentricity of the Earth's orbit) can be shown later to be faulty.[109]

At first glance the sentence, "However, warrants are always revocable depending on the findings of subsequent inquiry," is an argument against traditional epistemology, that is, foundationalism. Furthermore, the report states prior to its claims about the temporality of warrants that mistakes "are made as science moves forward. The process is not infallible[;] . . . science advances through professional criticism and self-correction."[110] Yet, despite these claims, the overall report suggests otherwise. Indeed, as we explained earlier in this chapter, the point of the principles for the committee was to guard in research, as much as one can, against the uncertainty, or the "noise," that is inherent in the field of education. And, moreover, at the end of the paragraph we just cited the committee states that scientific progress is premised not only on advancing new theories or hypotheses, but also on refuting previous ones by newly acquired evidence "judged to be definitive."[111] The judge here, of course, is not the "knower" per se, but the "scientific *community* that enables science to progress."[112] This separates the "knower" from his or her own process of inquiry and grants power and action to an external body of experts.

Dewey's notion of warranted assertions replaces justification in the traditional syllogism while at the same time it critiques the syllogism itself. Where justification serves a correspondence theory of truth in the traditional account of knowledge, warranted assertions merge truth and inquiry together in such a way that correspondence to an external world is no longer the point, for Dewey, as it appears to be for the NRC committee. The point for Dewey was the interdependency of truths and the processes of inquiry: the temporal satisfaction of solved problems in a world that is not set apart from the knower's use of the world or the knower's place in that world. In this

---

109. *SRE*, 18. We wonder if the authors of *SRE* saw their theory of science as similarly historically vulnerable.
110. Ibid., 16.
111. Ibid., 18.
112. Ibid., 19. Emphasis in original.

way, the NRC report (with its blend of positivist and realist assumptions) is misguided when it describes the epistemology of an education science as a way of determining knowledge. "Knowledge" was not the focal point of epistemology for Dewey: "knowing" was.

"Knowledge" represents the end of inquiry but, according to Dewey, it was also often deemed to have a meaning of its own—disconnected from inquiry. The result is that inquiry is subordinated to the fixed end called "knowledge."[113] By "knowing" Dewey meant inquiry in a world that is not static. He meant inquiry into things "lived" by people. He meant experimenting with solving problems such that the action entailed in the solving of problems is inquiry itself and is warranted in the assertions made about the solved problem when it is (if it is eventually) solved, where "solved" is understood as temporal and a portal to further inquiry. Accordingly, in the "living" of life, problems will be faced and solved—often in serendipitous ways—such that achieving "justified true belief" (as traditional epistemology expects) is not useful.[114] As Dewey put it:

> [Warranted assertion] is preferred to the terms *belief* and *knowledge* [because] it is free from the ambiguity of these latter terms, and it involves reference to inquiry as that which warrants assertion. When knowledge is taken as a general abstract term related to inquiry in

---

113. Dewey, *Logic*, 8.

114. Dewey's pragmatist understanding of science is evident here, but his pragmatist view seems both similar to and different from Charles Sanders Peirce's, and we are more inclined to side with Dewey in this regard. Where they appeared to coincide was in the distinction they established between beliefs and truth (though Dewey eschewed the term *beliefs*, perhaps because of its connotations with dogma). But Dewey and Peirce do not seem too far apart on the distinction. Peirce, relying upon an interesting juxtapositioning of apparently contradictory notions of doubt and belief, argued that our *beliefs*, which are in the nature of habits, guide our desires and shape our actions, while our *doubts* are things from which we struggle to free ourselves so as to pass into "a state of belief." *Inquiry* is the struggle to attain a state of belief, and its sole object is the settlement of opinion, not the securing of truth; the settlement of opinion being *the* state of belief we seek, there not being a "true opinion," since all we can ever expect to achieve is a state of belief. Where Dewey and Peirce appear to part company is in Peirce's apparent privileging of the scientific method. For Peirce, there are a number of ways to fix belief, that is, to settle opinion, but the most effective is science, since it presents us with a distinction between a right and a wrong way. Granting that there are "real" things that are independent of our opinions about them, science permits us the kind of reasoning that allows us to perceive these things as they are. Science does this, Peirce argues, because of its adherence to a "method" that guards us from our feelings and intentions. See Charles S. Peirce, "The Fixation of Belief," *Popular Science Monthly* 12 (November 1877): 1–15. Available at http://www.peirce.org/writings/p107.html (Retrieved February 7, 2005).

We are not interested in comparing these pragmatist philosophies of science here, but we direct readers to such a comparison (while adding William James's), which made different, and more expansive, arguments about their similarities and differences; see Peter T. Manicas, "Pragmatic Philosophy of Science and the Charge of Scientism," *Transactions of the Charles S. Peirce Society* 24, no. 4 (1988): 179–222.

the abstract, it means "warranted assertability." The use of a term that designates a potentiality rather than an actuality involves recognition that all special conclusions of special inquiries are parts of an enterprise that is continually renewed, or is a going concern.[115]

At least two things, therefore, follow from this notion of warranted assertions. First, knowing is not sufficiently described as an abstract, semantic enterprise; it is, rather, an enterprise rooted in problems faced by people in context. Dewey argued for knowers as people who can defend their claims to knowledge—a kind of epistemic responsibility—and, thus, educational researchers (or those to whom their research is directed) cannot abdicate this responsibility to a body of experts, or, per the NRC report, the *critical* or *scientific community.* Second, one *can* know, but only fallibilistically and not foundationally. Thus, knowledge claims can exist without a commitment to universality or to linguistic correspondence to an extralinguistic "fact." This is so because, according to Dewey, there is no use or meaning that is derived *sans* living. Language is a tool to make sense of our experiences, but it derives all of its meaning and its utility from our living.

In order to better explain Dewey's notion of warrants and its application to the kind of education research we believe Dewey might have advanced, it might be helpful to distinguish between a few key concepts. "Knowing," "knowledge," and "intelligence" were distinct concepts for Dewey. "Knowing" is inquiry, that is, specific instances of applying oneself to solving problems. "Knowledge" constituted the stable outcomes of inquiry. "Intelligence" was the result of the development and accumulation of capabilities to act (i.e., inquire) in specific ways. In other words,

> Knowledge is the result of successful inquiry, whereas knowing consists in using one's intelligence in given inquiries. Intelligence is stabilized knowledge . . . which can be utilized in other inquiries, given the principle of continuity and given the fact that judgements are not merely abstract decisions but constitute a kind of conduct (assertion). . . . Knowing is to intelligence roughly what asserting is to being disposed to assert.[116]

Thus, from the standpoint of empirical naturalism,

> the denotative reference of "mind" and "intelligence" is to funding of meanings and significances, a funding which is both a product of past inquiries or knowings and the means of enriching and controlling the subject-matters of subsequent experiences. The function of enrichment and control is exercised by incorporation of what was gained in past experience in attitudes and habits which, in their interaction with the environment, create the clearer, better ordered,

---

115. Dewey, *Logic,* 9. Emphasis in original.
116. Ibid., 256.

"fuller" or richer materials of later experience—a process capable of indefinite continuance.[117]

We understand all this to mean that what counts as a Deweyan argument for educational research, despite what the NRC report says, is that only organic and natural environments for learning impel knowing and the habits of intelligence. Detachment from natural environments for learning foster only "spectators" with habits of routine. When one supports a quest for "meanings and significances" one sides with inquiry via warranted assertions. That is, given Dewey's epistemology, researchers and educators should be making knowledge claims at the very same time they are engaged in knowing (inquiry), since the means and ends are not separable for Dewey, and since the point of inquiry is not to collect detached artifacts (or pieces of the deadwood of the past). Active engagement of the sort Dewey suggested means only that researchers seek only stability rather than certainty. They are not in the business of "discovering" the basic beliefs on which traditional epistemology qua foundationalism relies. Rather, stability indicates functionality over universality.

Let us not put too much into what Dewey meant by stability either, for it too is never assured. In fact, much of the point of interacting "with the environment" is "creat[ing] the clearer, better ordered, 'fuller' or richer materials of later experience—a process capable of indefinite continuance."[118] For the kind of experience required of education research is not one of adhering to predetermined, abstract principles and methods or to the authority of a professional community, but one that is "guided by intelligent habit, rather than merely routine habit, [and it is] characterized by resourcefulness, inventiveness, ingenuity, tenacity, efficiency, and any such 'pragmatist virtue' designed to anticipate not only the regularities and constancies of experience but also the inevitable uncertainties and indeterminacies."[119] Indeed, Dewey's take on a science of education rather problematizes the notion of such a science, unlike the NRC committee's. Science, he states, "is antagonistic to education as an art because it can put a stamp of final approval upon specific procedures (upon recipes)."[120]

---

117. John Dewey, "Experience, Knowledge, and Value: A Rejoinder," in *The Philosophy of John Dewey*, ed. Paul A. Schilpp (New York: Tudor, 1939), 520–21.

118. Ibid.

119. Burke, *Dewey's New Logic*, 256–57.

120. Dewey, *Sources of a Science of Education*, 15. Indeed, the committee might have read this book prior to citing Dewey, since he appears to (but does not really) reject the very notion of an "education science." Science, he wrote, cannot exist without abstractions, which implies necessarily that, fundamentally, "certain occurrences are removed from the dimension of familiar practical experience into that of reflective or theoretical inquiry." Thus, the preoccupation with attaining some direct end or practical utility, which constitutes the field of education, will always limit scientific inquiry "for it restricts its field of attention and thought since it will attend to only those things that are immediately connected with what we want to do or get at the moment. Science signifies that we carry our observations and thinking further afield and become interested in what happens on its own account" (16–17).

In summary, epistemological fallibilism—unlike the foundationalist premises of SRE—hold that knowledge claims can be valid, even if the veracity of the knowledge claim is not universal. Dewey honed in on pragmatist notions of seeking stability with a never-ending search for meaning as a way to indicate the limits of foundationalism, and he replaced foundationalism with the warrantability of assertions and fallibilism. While not strictly arguing from the standpoint of epistemological fallibilism, St. Pierre points out the fallacy of the NRC committee's presumption of a certainty in its principles. All epistemologies and methodologies have their limits, she argues, and as we use them, we will come across these limits, which will require us to rethink these theories but also to bring others to bear on our concerns. The truly "ethical moment of inquiry [is] when we work out the failure of the known and comfortable and engage stubborn structures of intelligibility in which we must think differently, whether we like it or not."[121]

It is the struggle that comes from inquiry that the committee seeks to eliminate, and as a result it eliminates inquiry itself. Furthermore, while the NRC report gives precedence to the scientific process, rather than, and perhaps even at the expense of, the educational one, which is not to be trusted with knowing itself, it also does violence to another of Dewey's ideas: that of democracy in and of inquiry, a point that concludes this chapter.

DEMOCRATIC INQUIRY LOST

Other than to show how the NRC negates Deweyan epistemology, even as it purports to use it to justify its stance, we also propose that the report does violence to another central feature of Dewey's work, namely, democracy. John Willinsky, focusing almost entirely on the NRC report's sixth principle ("disclose research to encourage professional scrutiny"), makes what we think is a valid argument about the undemocratic nature of SRE. He argues that the sixth principle stops simply with "professional scrutiny" and does not consider the place of education research in a democracy and how it might be granted wider access to the public.[122] (Willinsky could have also situated

---

121. Elizabeth Adams St. Pierre, "Refusing Alternatives: A Science of Contestation," *Qualitative Inquiry* 10, no. 1 (2004): 130–39, 136.

122. Willinsky made a similar argument with regard to the NRC's Strategic Education Research Program (SERP) published in its 1999 report, *Improving Student Learning: A Strategic Plan for Educational Research and its Utilization* (Washington, DC: National Academy Press, 1999). The SERP proposed standards for coordination, integration, and application of education research, much of it ensuring student learning (translated often into improving test scores). Willinsky points out that while the SERP may improve the impact of research on educational practice, it could have proposed a more useful and relevant source of public knowledge, a knowledge that would advance professional development and political deliberation, "both of which are no less critical to the future of our schools . . . than improved test scores." See John Willinsky, "The Strategic Education Research Program and the Public Value of Research," *Educational Researcher* 30, no. 1 (2001): 5–14, 6.

this logic within an understanding of the struggles over professionalism, as we did in chapter 1, and made his critique accordingly.) What would make education research more important in our society, Willinsky argues, is not to require that it be conducted *like* medical research, but to constitute it as vital to the democratic process *as is* medical research. There is nothing inherently democratic about asking policy makers and school officials to use research evidence in arriving at the most effective strategies for implementing particular policies. To be called democratic, it must be part of the democratic process; it must call for situating the study of learning and teaching in classrooms, communities, and states, one that recognizes research's contribution to the educational and democratic qualities of this society.[123]

We think Willinsky is correct, but here we make a somewhat different argument. To begin, we point out the necessary interconnections Dewey established between knowing and context and between knower and inquiry. Dewey challenged the idea of dualism or any bifurcation between theory and practice. To make warranted assertions is not to have a special sect of scientists or theoreticians make those assertions for the common person. The point is to have integration of warranted assertions in all aspects of social (including scientific) life. Unfortunately, at the very point at which the NRC report suggests capitalizing on Dewey's ideas, just prior to its full discussion of the guiding principles, it diverges dramatically. The report states here, initially consistent with Dewey, that science "is an important source of knowledge for addressing social problems, but does not stand in isolation."[124]

Unfortunately, the report goes on to bifurcate scientific inquiry from the context in which its results are supposed to take effect; it bifurcates the "knower" from the supposed "user." It states, "The scientist discovers the basis for what is possible. The practitioner, parent, or policymaker, in turn, has to consider what is practical, affordable, desirable, and credible."[125] Forgetting for the moment the epistemic responsibility that goes along with claiming warrant for an assertion, in three sentences the report contradicts itself and discounts the very Deweyan epistemology it had touted in the first place. By separating "the scientist" from the "practitioner," and knowledge from its context, a haughty reality materializes: knowledge becomes an abstraction, since it is not *in* context; the scientist assumes the role of thinker and knowledge producer, and everyone else merely waits and reacts to what this "expert" says. This "expert," mind you, is an expert because he or she is not like "everyone else"; the expert is the "discoverer of the possible"—the others are unqualified and cannot be trusted to be that.

---

123. John Willinsky, "Scientific Research in a Democratic Culture: Or What's a Social Science For?" *Teachers College Record* 107, no. 1 (2005): 35–51, 43.
124. *SRE*, 49.
125. Ibid.

Dewey wrote in *Reconstruction in Philosophy* that

> educated men, cultivated men in particular, are still so dominated
> by the older conception of an aloof and self-sufficing reason and
> knowledge that they refuse to perceive the import of this doctrine.
> They think they are sustaining the cause of impartial, thorough-go-
> ing and disinterested reflection when they maintain the traditional
> philosophy of intellectualism—that is, of knowing as something
> self-sufficing and self-enclosed.[126]

Dewey might as well have been speaking of the NRC committee rather than
the rational foundationalists he actually describes in the quote. The NRC
committee is not putting forth a democratic notion of scientific inquiry, for
it is only concerned with creating a community of education scientists. Its
principles, after all, were intended to "operate like norms in a community,
in this case a community of scientists; they are expectations of how scientific
research will be conducted. Ideally, individual scientists internalize these
norms, and the community monitors them."[127]

Making scientists separate from practitioners is no different than making
traditional (analytic) philosophers separate from practitioners. The problem
is the separation itself, and the NRC report is replete with references to
such a separation. Yet, people

> do not tend to think when their action . . . is dictated to them
> by authority. . . . [when] Thinking is done for them, higher up. . . .
> Difficulties occasion thinking only when thinking is the impera-
> tive or urgent way out, only when it is the indicated road to a
> solution. Wherever external authority reigns, thinking is suspected
> and obnoxious.[128]

SRE demonstrates a repeating cadence of inclusion and flexibility at its
beginning, but then transforms itself into a prescription for what counts as
valid science and, by extension, valid education research. The point is to
have philosophies of scientism and positivism be the arbiters of education
research—even though education, schooling, teaching, and learning are
conceptually tricky and perpetually serendipitous.[129] Trickiness and serendipity

---

126. John Dewey, *Reconstruction in Philosophy* (Boston: Beacon Press, 1920), 116–17.
127. *SRE*, 52.
128. Dewey, *Reconstruction in Philosophy*, 139.
129. Or they are also what Patti Lather and Pamela Moss called the "messiness of practice-
in-context," which will always call into question the adequacy of conventional methods, or,
we might add, the gutter utilitarianism of the "what works" mentality; see Patti Lather and
Pamela Moss, "Implications of Scientific Research in Education Report for Qualitative Inquiry,"
Teachers College Record 107, no. 1 (2005): 1–3.

are cast as "problems" or "challenges," or, in a word, "noise," to be corrected and controlled, but only by the scientists themselves.

Science for Dewey was, like almost everything else, a problem *of* and *for* democracy. If the production of scientific knowledge is simply to be the work of "experts," the problem of putting such knowledge to work in actual life is going to be a problem for the democratic community, understood to be made up of everyone being affected by it, not just policy makers and scientists.[130] If people are to act intelligently, they must have the means of judging the knowledge supplied by others upon those concerns they have in common. This was one of the "problems of the public" for Dewey. Scientific knowledge had revolutionized the "conditions under which associated life goes on . . . [but not] understanding its 'how,' [the public] cannot use and control its manifestations."[131] This point, argues Peter Manicas, that science is part of a democratic (and public) mode of life, is what kept Dewey's vision of science from being technocratic, that is, concerned only with prediction and control.[132]

"Scientific research in education," for Dewey, would have meaning not because it can provide reliable information for educators by scientists, and certainly not because it instantiates a scientific culture in the field of education research, but because, and only because, it is to be obtained, judged, and used *by the educator*. The "practitioner who knows the system and its laws is evidently in possession of a powerful instrument for observing and interpreting what goes on before him. . . . His ability to judge being enriched, he has a wider range of alternatives to select from in dealing with individual situations."[133] In other words, scientific research cannot yield "rules of practice." Its value is indirect; it consists in the provision of "intellectual instrumentalities" to be used *by the educator*.[134] That is, and at the risk of repeating ourselves, which is a risk we take, given the importance of this point to us, scientific inquiry is *not* by and for experts, but by and for those who "live" the experience that we call schooling.

To instantiate science as the savior of education research, to make scientific research by scientists as that which best informs practice, is to strip those whose lives are most affected by educational decisions of the ability under a democratic process to speak of and for themselves. To have scientists dictate what the objectives, needs, and wants of education is to grant them the power to govern education. This is how "government" works, according to Foucault, as we elaborate in greater detail in chapter 4.

---

130. Dewey, perhaps in typical antidualist fashion, takes a middle stance between expert authority over scientific knowledge and its democratic use throughout society.

131. John Dewey, *The Public and Its Problems* (Athens: Swallow Press/Ohio University Press, 1957, c. 1927), 165.

132. Manicas, "Pragmatic Philosophy of Science," 212–13; op. cit., fn. 114.

133. Dewey, *Sources of a Science of Education*, 20–21.

134. Ibid., 28.

"Governmental" practices are not necessarily those of the state, but reflect myriad private and public actions and rationalities seeking to shape and manage the conduct of individuals.[135] Indeed, Dewey himself pre-dated Foucault in pointing to "government" as something distinct from state apparatuses, although he did not extend this thinking nearly as far as Foucault did. In a 1937 speech on school administration that he gave to the General Session of the Department of Superintendence of the National Education Association, Dewey argues that it is a "superficial view that holds government is located in Washington and Albany," as there "is government in the family, in business, in the church, in every social group. There are regulations, due to custom, if not to enactment, that settle how individuals in a group act in connection with one another."[136] He states further that the "way in which any organized social interest is controlled necessarily plays an important part in forming the dispositions and tastes, the attitudes, interests, purposes and desires, of those engaged in carrying on the activities of the group."[137] The point here is that the vision of science put forth by the NRC committee, and most certainly by the practices and policies of the federal government, are techniques for controlling the behavior of schools and of individuals in schools. The NRC, the federal policies and practices, and indeed this whole discourse on creating a science of education, are about nothing but "government," that is, the shaping of the conduct of children, teachers, administrators, researchers—everyone, and this "voracious desire to center and control marks the end of the democratic politics that inspire our educational system."[138]

What must be striven for, however, is the "self-government" that is part of governmental practices of control. Individuals provide for themselves the techniques that allow them to effect their own bodies, desires, wants, needs, and so forth. And with regard to scientific research, one can read Dewey as arguing for such self-government (or perhaps even a professionalization of sorts). For Dewey saw education as "autonomous," and as such it,

> should be free to determine its own ends, its own objectives. . . . Until educators get the independence and courage to insist that educational aims are to be formed as well as executed within the educative process, they will not come to consciousness of their own function.

135. See Michel Foucault, "Governmentality," in The Foucault Effect: Studies in Governmentality, ed. Graham Burchell, Colin Gordon, and Peter Miller (Chicago: The University of Chicago Press, 1991), 87–104.
136. John Dewey, "Democracy and Educational Administration," School and Society 45 (April 3, 1937): 457–62, 459.
137. Ibid., 460.
138. St. Pierre, "Refusing Alternatives," 137.

Others will then have no great respect for educators because educators do not respect their own social place and work.[139]

To suggest that science can bring respect to the field of education research is a fallacy, since it has already been deemed not to warrant the respect to police itself and thus why science is positioned as being needed by it the first place. Dewey, we should note, was not exalting one set of actors for another; that is, he should not be read as arguing that the conduct of education should be directed by educators rather than by scientists. For Dewey believed it was the "educative process, not educators themselves, that must determine educational objectives."[140] This process does have a place for scientific inquiry, to be sure, according to Dewey. The educative process "*includes* science within itself. In its very process it sets more problems to be further studied, which then react into the educative process to change it still further, and thus demand more thought, more science, and so on, in everlasting sequence."[141] The point here, however, is that science must be *a part of* that process, not outside looking in, telling it how it is to conduct itself, what it needs, what it wants, and who is capable and worthy enough of arguing otherwise.

139. Dewey, *The Sources of a Science of Education*, 73–74.
140. Ibid., 74.
141. Ibid., 77. Emphasis in original.

THREE

DEGREES OF DISTINCTION

Education Doctoral Study and the "Culture of Science"

Degree
1. any of the successive steps or stages in a process or series 2. a step in the direct line of descent [a cousin in the second *degree*] 3. social or official rank, position, or class [a man of low *degree*] 4. relative condition; manner, respect, or relation [each contributing to victory in his *degree*] 5. extent, amount, or relative intensity [hungry to a slight *degree*, burns of the third *degree*] . . . 6. *Educ.* a rank given by a college or university to a student who has completed a required course of study, or to a distinguished person as an honor . . .

—*Webster's New World Dictionary of the American Language*

Distinction
1. the act of making or keeping distinct; differentiation between or among things 2. the condition of being different; difference 3. that which makes or keeps distinct; quality, mark, or feature that differentiates 4. the state of getting special recognition or honor; fame; eminence [a singer of *distinction*] 5. the quality that makes one seem superior or worthy of special recognition [to serve with *distinction*] 6. a mark or sign of special recognition or honor.

—*Webster's New World Dictionary of the American Language*

Those of us who study higher education tend to treat academic creations as the products of rational processes rather than as the results of political struggles over the power to create, itself. The discourse on educational doctoral study, especially that calling for a "culture of science" in such study, has tended to view such doctoral work independently of this struggle, as having a unique history that illustrates progression in thought and action. We will read this discourse, however, within the long-standing debate over what kind of degree should be offered by schools of education, that is, either a practitioner- or research-oriented degree, bureaucratically manifesting itself more particularly in the Doctor of Education (EdD) or the Doctor of Philosophy (PhD). To the extent that the discourse of science is a discourse of professionalism, as we have argued, one must attend to the role of the university in this endeavor, for a necessary validation of a profession's status involves the introduction of study for the profession into the universities.[1] Given that in this movement toward an education science what is partly at stake is the professionalization of education researchers, what needs to be accomplished is the transformation of the "culture" in doctoral study. And because schools of education, like all university units, are essentially bureaucratic entities, any change in culture will manifest itself in bureaucratic terms, such as the kinds of degrees conferred.

The EdD or PhD is deemed to have particular definitions, uses, values, and, in short, a content in itself. While it is common to study the degree as a thing in itself, it seems more fruitful to study it in relation to the other, as each is the other's constitutive opposite, giving itself meaning by establishing the other as its difference. To say that our study will focus on the two doctoral degrees in relation to each other does not mean that it will be comparative, as comparisons reinforce the difference and deflect attention from the mechanisms of power that create that difference. We will treat the two doctoral degrees as products of classifying practices that guarantee, but obscure, the power of academic institutions to create and legitimate classifications of the social world in order to dominate it. Given this understanding of power, we will argue that one must be leery of the distinctions academics create. In particular, those distinctions that support the EdD/PhD debates, such as practitioner/researcher, practice/theory, professional education/liberal education, scientific inquiry/*other*, should be studied in order to uncover their underlying dialectics of power and difference.

The interpretive scheme shaping this chapter will differ from that of the previous chapter on scientism and positivism. In chapter 2, we focused our reading at the level of a text, specifically the NRC report, *Scientific Research in Education* (*SRE*).[2] We attempted to problematize this text via a reading of it juxtaposed with Dewey's work. Here we begin our transition

---

1. Everett C. Hughes, "Professions," in *The Professions in America*, ed. Kenneth S. Lynn (Boston: Houghton Mifflin, 1965), 1–14, 7; see also Bernard Barber, "Some Problems in the Sociology of the Professions," in *The Professions in America*, ed. Kenneth S. Lynn (Boston: Houghton Mifflin, 1965), 15–34, 20.
2. National Research Council, *Scientific Research in Education*, ed. Richard J. Shavelson and Lisa Towne (Washington: National Academy Press, 2002). Available at http://www.nap.edu/ (Retrieved February 5, 2005).

to a second level of interpretation, that is, a reading of a text in light of the political forces that make it possible. Prior to extending our analysis of a text by situating it beyond itself, we will remain with a close reading of a text, a follow-up report by the NRC, *Advancing Scientific Research in Education (ASRE)*.[3] Furthermore, while Dewey's work allows us to think through the distinctions (e.g., science versus nonscience, theory versus practice, and researcher versus practitioner) associated with the discourse on science in education, we will rely heavily in this chapter on the work of Pierre Bourdieu, as he offers insights into how these academic distinctions may be situated within larger political and economic struggles: those in which individuals and institutions attempt to gain control over cultural fields (such as education). This study, therefore, does not treat the distinctions associated with the discourse on a science of education as reflections of a reality independent of politics and power, but as reflections of a particular state in the struggle to control the classifications of the social world.

We provide in the following sections an overview of the discourse on the culture of science in education and the distinctions it creates, particularly between theory/practice and researcher/practitioner. We then move beyond the discourse and situate it within much older and longer-standing academic struggles, particularly those over the purposes of higher education and what its degrees will mean. Then we move beyond these academic struggles and in turn situate them within larger political struggles over cultural fields and the power that will govern how individuals will perceive the world. We read Bourdieu's work as pushing us to inquire into the extent to which these academic struggles (over what educational doctoral study will entail and what its certification will represent) are actually part of political struggles over the control of meaning-making processes that will influence not only how individuals perceive their worlds but also how they can be organized in line with those perceptions.

A "CULTURE OF SCIENCE" IN EDUCATION

We discussed in chapter 1 how the federal government has sought to establish its narrow vision of "scientifically based research" in education. We also explained how the NRC report, *SRE*, sought to provide an understanding of what scientific research in education might look like, with a view toward the professionalization of education researchers. We critiqued its scientistic, positivistic, and undemocratic vision of science in our second chapter. Here we focus on what the report requires for doctoral study in education, namely, that such study enable a "culture of science." *SRE* did not refer specifically to such a culture in doctoral study, but in its chapter on fostering science in

---

3. National Research Council, *Advancing Scientific Research in Education*, ed. Lisa Towne, Lauress L. Wise, and Tina M. Winters (Washington, DC: The National Academies Press, 2005). Available at http://www.nap.edu/ (Retrieved February 5, 2005).

a "federal education research agency," the report states that such an agency must play a role in nurturing the "community of education researchers," and that its "focus, consistent with the theme of developing a scientific culture in the agency, is on nurturing scientific norms in the field as a whole."[4] Michael Feuer, Lisa Towne, and Richard Shavelson's defense of the report explains that the report's primary emphasis was on nurturing and reinforcing a "scientific culture of education research" and on building a strong research community.[5] A "scientific culture," they argue, entails a set of "norms and practices and an ethos of *honesty*, *openness*, and continuous reflection, including how research quality is judged."[6] These norms and practices are what the guiding principles in SRE supposedly ensure. Of course, these authors might have acknowledged that rather than adhering blindly to these norms and practices of science, education researchers might be more than a little leery of the spate of ethical misconduct by scientists as reported in the media.[7] Such ethical misconduct sheds doubt on the "honesty" to which Feuer et al. and others refer, and the intellectual-property regimes that govern the production of knowledge in the sciences further shed doubt on the "openness" to which they also refer in implying that scientific knowledge should be the knowledge par excellence in education.[8]

The idea of a "culture of science" in educational study is premised on the idea that there is indeed a "scientific culture" that is distinct from one that is not. We might heed Dewey's instruction that separating science from the rest of our experiences is problematic, as we indicated in chapter 2, but for now let us assume this distinction. The distinction between a scientific culture and, for lack of a better term, a "nonscientific" culture harks back to C. P. Snow's scheme of the "two cultures."[9] Snow distinguishes the "literary intellectuals" (or what we now call the "humanities") from the "scientists" (or, more accurately, those in the so-called physical sciences) and argues that intellectual life in the "whole of Western society is increasingly being split into [these] two polar groups."[10] Each group constitutes an entirely different

---

4. SRE, 149.
5. Michael J. Feuer, Lisa Towne, and Richard J. Shavelson, "Scientific Culture and Educational Research," *Educational Researcher* 31, no. 8 (2002): 4–14.
6. Ibid., 4. Emphasis added.
7. For a study of misbehavior by scientists, where one in three scientists compromise the integrity of their research by either overlooking flawed data, failing to present contradictory evidence, and circumventing human-subjects requirements, see Brian C. Martinson, Melissa S. Anderson, and Raymond de Vries, "Scientists Behaving Badly," *Nature* 435, no. 7043 (June 9, 2005): 737–38.
8. For studies of how the privatization of knowledge has restructured the supposed norms of science, see Rebecca S. Eisenberg, "Academic Freedom and Academic Values in Sponsored Research," *Texas Law Review* 66 (1988): 1363–1404; Rebecca S. Eisenberg, "Proprietary Rights and the Norms of Science in Biotechnology Research," *Yale Law Journal* 97 (1987): 177–231.
9. C. P. Snow, *The Two Cultures* (Cambridge: Cambridge University Press, 1993, c. 1959).
10. Ibid., 3.

culture and is unable to communicate with the other. Snow does not give equal weight to each culture, however, as he saw the literary intellectuals as managing the world and guarding it from the optimism and technological progress of the scientists. Scientists have, claims Snow, the "future in their bones," while the literary intellectuals act as if "wishing the future did not exist."[11] He argues that the literary intellectuals are not only unwilling to appreciate scientific advances, but are openly hostile to them, and he believes this so strongly that he feels legitimated in calling these intellectuals "natural Luddites."[12]

This "natural Luddite" rhetoric, and the conflation it establishes between those who question science and those who are entirely opposed to technological progress, appears to us to covertly pervade the discourse on the science of education, and it supports the claims that education research is of low quality and does not address the important problems in education. Educational study that is not deemed scientific (read as: experimental) is further deemed useless, wasteful, and even harmful to children since it cannot tell us "what works," and those who oppose how science is narrowly defined in this discourse are, essentially, "Luddites." Snow, to be fair, was not entirely as naive about science as have been those supporting random field trials in education. He acknowledges the losses to our society as a result of the rise of science, particularly the fact that in "organising a society for industry [science] has made it easy to organise it for all-out war," *but*, nevertheless, the gains remain and these are the "base for our social hope."[13]

In addition to conflating inappropriately those who saw problems with the advances of science with those who opposed all technological progress, Snow also collapsed complex fields of knowledge into "two cultures," and such positivism is similarly evident in the NRC's collapsing of the various and distinct fields of knowledge into a supposed "culture of science."[14] The

---

11. Ibid., 10, 11.

12. The Luddites were a workers' movement in England in the 1800s that opposed the changes resulting from industrialism, going so far as destroying the machinery of their employers to protect their jobs. The original Luddites were squelched by the British Army and many were executed. The term now refers to, and apparently is intended by Snow to indicate, anyone opposed to scientific and technological progress.

13. Snow, *The Two Cultures*, 27.

14. Yet, having said this, even Snow, at least later in his life, may not have been as positivistic as the NRC has been with regard to establishing a unity of scientific knowledge. Snow recognizes that there are distinctions within the physical sciences, especially as some in those sciences were more likely to focus on "applied" knowledge, which is often looked down upon by those focusing on "pure" knowledge. He later also acknowledges that there are vast differences between the physical and social sciences, indicating that there may well exist a "third culture," made up of the social sciences—"intellectual persons in a variety of fields—social, history, sociology, demography, political science, economics, government (in the American academic sense), psychology, medicine, and social arts such as architecture." See C. P. Snow, "The Two Cultures: A Second Look," in *The Two Cultures* (Cambridge: Cambridge University Press, 1993, c.1964), 53–100, 70.

NRC and Snow also converge on the modernist belief in scientific progress, without attending adequately to its abuses or the political losses entailed in reorganizing society (and education) *for* science. And, more importantly for us, Snow and the NRC see the problem of establishing a culture of science as an educational one. Snow believes that education is essential for ensuring that scientific culture pervades all of society.[15] He states,

> The chief means open to us is education—education mainly in primary and secondary schools, but also in colleges and universities. There is no excuse for letting another generation be as vastly ignorant, or as devoid of understanding and sympathy, as we are ourselves.[16]

Snow's supporters can now rest easy, since science has already won its place in the precollegiate and undergraduate curricula, and consistently, especially since Sputnik, vast amounts of research and funding go into further entrenching science in those curricula. Now, at stake for science, at least in education, given the discourse on the "culture of science," is the doctoral curriculum.

In some ways, the focus in this discourse on doctoral study in education is not all that surprising. Graduate study in general seems a prize in a field of political struggles involving, among other things, financial aid and taxation policies, the proliferation of degrees, the increasing use of cheap labor for teaching and research, the unionization of academics, the external funding of research, and other things. Thus, as Patricia Gumport suggests, graduate education must be understood within larger political and economic forces, and the intersection between graduate education and research is a key site for the convergence of all these forces.[17] In particular, Gumport explains, as universities were transformed into modern research complexes, the organizational character and rhythm of academic work changed to accommodate the increased centrality of sponsored research. The training of graduate students, therefore, has become reoriented to the needs of external sponsors and obtaining further funding.[18] Indeed, the expansion of graduate education developed hand in hand with the expanding national system of sponsored research.[19]

---

15. Snow, *The Two Cultures*, 33–40.
16. Ibid., 61.
17. Patricia J. Gumport, "Graduate Education and Research: Interdependence and Strain," in *American Higher Education in the Twenty-First Century: Social, Political, and Economic Challenges*, 2nd ed., ed. Philip G. Altbach, Robert O. Berdahl, and Patricia J. Gumport (Baltimore: The Johns Hopkins University Press, 2005), 425–61, 426.
18. Ibid., 426.
19. Ibid., 433. See also Herman Feshbach, "Graduate Education and Federal Support of Research," *Daedalus: Journal of the American Academy of Arts and Sciences* 104, no. 1 (1975): 248–50; Jules B. LaPidus, "Graduate Education and Research," in *In Defense of American Higher Education*, ed. Philip G. Altbach, Patricia J. Gumport, and D. Bruce Johnstone (Baltimore: The Johns Hopkins University Press, 2001), 249–76.

We will have occasion to discuss in great detail the phenomenon of sponsored research in chapter 5. Here it is sufficient to focus on how sponsored research has altered the relationship between students and faculty, and how the movement to establish an education science relates to it. Graduate students at research universities are now more directly supervised by faculty who are little more than project managers, rather than mentor-professors, and they are treated more like employees and technicians than apprentices.[20] Gumport points out that graduate student research assistants, in particular, face the exigencies of an increasingly competitive arena for research support, so that

> time schedules of short-term project grants means less leeway for mistakes; less available grant money means more competition and pressure to produce better results; sharing capital-intensive instrumentation means long hours of work, often in other cities; increased size of research teams entails perfecting a technique on one part of the project rather than completing an entire project from beginning to end; and time spent in research is valued over time spent in the "burden" of teaching younger graduate students or undergraduates. The arrangements emphasize efficiency and productivity, which promote an organizational climate of a factory floor—or a "quasi-firm"—rather than a center of learning.[21]

Is this what we have to look forward to in education when we are told of the necessity of inculcating a "culture of science" in doctoral study? Is this the effect of, nay, is this what is the "culture of science" that is spoken of so reverently by the NRC and others? It seems to us, as we explain below, that the calls for a culture of science seek, unabashedly at times, to restructure education doctoral study in the model of the applied sciences such as biotechnology, engineering, and the health fields (particularly medicine). Gumport, supporting the "two cultures" logic, argues that in the sciences research, basic and applied, is laboratory-intensive, and a graduate student may work under faculty supervision, with the dissertation arising from a faculty member's research project. In the humanities, however, research is library-intensive, and a student may work independently with little faculty or peer contact.[22] Gumport argues that these distinctions have tended to sharpen given external demands for academic science.[23] Perhaps. We think that the calls for a culture of science in education may actually blur the lines between the supposed two cultures, or, more accurately, erase those

---

20. Gumport, "Graduate Education and Research," 452.
21. Ibid., 454.
22. Ibid., 428.
23. Ibid.

lines in favor of an all-encompassing, all-inclusive, and thus positivist, "scientific culture."

But to accomplish this "colonization," if we may say so, of educational inquiry by the sciences, the discourse on the culture of science in education correctly recognizes the need to focus on doctoral study. James Pellegrino and Susan Goldman, for example, point out that the formation of the type of community and culture envisioned by *SRE* needs to begin with graduate training programs. Graduate training in education, they argue, frequently lacks a common substantive or methods core in contrast to other disciplines and professions. If methods exist, there is little balance between quantitative and qualitative approaches, and, "Worse yet, such methods courses are sometimes pitted against each other rather than seen as complementary."[24] Again, this notion of complement reflects a positivist desideratum, that is, a wish for a unity of knowledge, which can be made instrumental in the form of particular methods. But these complex, institutionalized forms of knowledge cannot be made complementary without altering a whole set of rules and practices that dictate what can be said, who can say it, and when, since they have unique histories and discursive formations.[25] Ignoring all this, Pelligrino and Goldman advocate a restructuring of doctoral study in education in the model of the applied sciences. They posit the predominant model in education as being one of the single scholar in the social sciences, which supposedly avoids complex, practical educational problems, when those problems are best served by the multidisciplinary, methodologically rigorous, researcher-practitioner team approach prevalent in the biomedical and health sciences fields.[26] Of course, as with these applied sciences, they argue that the federal government needs to support such endeavors in education, and, they should have added, make education professors accomplices in the federal attempts to control the sciences.

More interesting to us, and reflecting the kinds of distinctions we want to tease out in subsequent sections of this chapter, Pellegrino and Goldman argue that the "community of education researchers must include practitioners if it is to understand and draw its problems from practice and study them in practical as well as theoretically relevant ways."[27] This sounds anti-dualist, and thus Deweyan at first glance, but it is not, since what it implicitly asserts is a separation of the "inquirer," that is, the researcher, from the "doer," that is, the practitioner, and, so it establishes a "community of researchers"

24. James W. Pellegrino and Susan R. Goldman, "Be Careful What You Wish For—You May Get It: Educational Research in the Spotlight," *Educational Researcher* 31, no. 8 (2002): 15–17, 16.

25. See generally, Michel Foucault, *The Archeology of Knowledge and The Discourse on Language*, trans. A. M. Sheridan Smith (New York: Pantheon Books, 1972).

26. Pelligrino and Goldman, "Be Careful What You Wish For," 16.

27. Ibid., 16.

(read as: "professionals") that derives its work, but is ultimately distinct from, the community whose problems it is now authorized to resolve. So what Pellegrino and Goldman propose of doctoral study, despite the rhetoric of including practitioners in their ideal of a "community of researchers," is not serious reconsideration of the distinction between the researcher and practitioner and what underlies it, but a maintenance of it.

This distinction between the researcher and the practitioner is pervasive throughout the discourse on education doctoral study, even when scholars attempt to reconcile this distinction. For example, in pointing out the difficulties of training education doctoral students for research, David Labaree explains that one striking characteristic of education doctoral students is that they are grown-ups, usually older than students in the arts and sciences, and they enter doctoral study only after having spent time in the schools. What makes it difficult for such students to transition into researchers, Labaree argues with a "two-cultures" kind of logic, is the differences in world views arising from the nature of teaching as a practice and the nature of education research as a practice. The shift from K-12 teaching (or, we would add, school or college administration) to education research often requires students to transform their cultural orientation from the normative to the analytical, from the personal to the intellectual, from the particular to the universal, and from the experiential to the theoretical (and, we would add, from the amateur to the professional).[28] These worldviews are not easily reconciled, but Labaree suggests that to narrow the cultural divide one must "sell" to teachers the value of the researcher view as an addition to, but not a substitute for, the teacher view, and researchers should be made to recognize how often their work involves the moral, the particular, the personal, and the experiential. This entails, for Larabee, a hybrid program that "marries theory and practice."[29]

We will have occasion to think through most of the distinctions Labaree puts forth, but for now we point out that we could translate Labaree's concept of conflicting worldviews in education doctoral work into a more basic understanding of the conflicting modes of "linguistic" existence that shape academic study: Students live in entirely different linguistic worlds than do their professors.[30] Most students are unable to cope with the technical and scholastic demand made on their use of language.[31] It is assumed

28. David F. Labaree, "The Peculiar Problems of Preparing Educational Researchers," *Educational Researcher* 32, no. 4 (2003): 13–22, 16.

29. Ibid., 21.

30. See Pierre Bourdieu, Jean-Claude Passeron, and Monique De Saint Martin, *Academic Discourse: Linguistic Misunderstanding and Professorial Power*, trans. Richard Teese (Stanford: Stanford University Press, 1994, c. 1964).

31. Pierre Bourdieu and Jean-Claude Passeron, "Introduction: Language and Relationship to Language in the Teaching Situation," in *Academic Discourse: Linguistic Misunderstanding and Professorial Power*, trans. Richard Teese (Stanford: Stanford University Press, 1994), 1–34, 4.

that in universities the ability to reconcile the language of ideas elaborated by the academic and scientific traditions and the second-order language of allusions and cultural complexities lived by students distinguishes intelligent students from all the rest. But this assumption is made possible by another assumption: that "language" is reducible to mere words. If Bourdieu and his associates are correct, however, teachers (or researchers) cannot simply step out of their linguistic and cultural "ethnocentrism"; the language they (and their students) spontaneously employ is that of a particular social group or class,[32] and these groups and classes have remarkably stable dispositions and worldviews.

Labaree's notion that one can simply "sell" the researcher view to education doctoral students, or, indeed, any call for the inculcation of a "culture of science" in education research, assumes *too much* and *too little* about language. It assumes too much about language by suggesting that one can simply learn another language, that is, the scientific and academic language, and that learning the mere *words* of these languages will go a long way toward changing the dispositions of doctoral students, and thus of education researchers; it assumes too little about language by not recognizing its role in making and unmaking social groups. Effectively introducing scientific language in education will effectively alter the lived reality of education, for it will go a very long way in restructuring groups and classes. For professorial language to work as these calls for education science suggest, it must change, as Bourdieu and his associates indicate, both in meaning and function—it must concern itself at every moment with definition and with verifying the real comprehension needs of a real public.[33] Yet, by insisting upon a simple and easily overcome distinction between the "scientist" and the "practitioner" it will always defeat itself.

We are persuaded by Bourdieu and his associates about the incompatibility of academic and practical languages, and, as a result, we think attempts to create a culture of science in education research will always be defeated by this structural incompatibility. Yet we do not find this at all problematic. Indeed, this is what gives educational study its uniqueness and vivacity. Of course, this is also what makes our classes frustrating, since many students cannot understand our language and may even go as far as to reject it. This is frustrating, however, only because we have bought into the idea that students need *to be like us*. Even granting that institutions vary, the general reality we face in education is that students are unable *to be like us* and many times refuse to be like us. We should celebrate this inability and refusal as a kind of independence, and, more important, as a kind of attempt to keep what education can mean always *open to the future*, never closed off from it. To argue otherwise—to argue that we need a common set of

---

32. Ibid., 22.
33. Ibid.

standards, or a "culture of science," as the discourse of the NRC and others tell us—is to fall into the trap, and, paradoxically, a nonempiricist trap, of seeing students as *ideals*, not as they are in their irreducible, unpredictable materialities. Students are engaged in the ever-present struggle to define themselves in the face of repeated attempts to be defined by others. In fact, attempts to establish a culture of science in educational study will require, following Bourdieu and his associates, that academics display complementary and contradictory attitudes. They will have to address themselves to fictive subjects in order to avoid the risk of putting their teaching practice on trial; they will have to address the student as she *ought to be* and discourage her from asserting her right to be only what she is, at least as she thinks it or wishes it at the moment. Moreover, professors will be unable to disguise their disdain for the "real" student, since only the fictive student deserves their respect, and really only a handful of "gifted students" need be found to prove that the fiction exists.[34]

Yet, after having said all this, we think that Bourdieu and his associates gave too little attention to the power of the idea of this "fictive student" in graduate study, since such study can take the form of an apprenticeship; that is the ideal that shapes our sense of ourselves as professors in relation to our doctoral students. Bourdieu and his associates did not account for how powerful the socializing aspects of the ideal of the apprenticeship in doctoral study are in creating normative communities of professionals. Interestingly, while never explicitly recognizing this power, the NRC appears to have known it quite well. It is this socializing power that forms the logic that governs the recommendations made by the NRC in a follow-up report to SRE suggesting, among other things, changes in education doctoral study. We think this report is illustrative of the arguments we make throughout this book, especially in this chapter, and so we turn to that report now.

"ADVANCING" SCIENCE IN DOCTORAL STUDY

In *Advancing Scientific Research in Education* (ASRE), the NRC's Committee on Research in Education (the "committee"), which includes some of the members of the committee that drafted SRE, offers "recommendations for improving scientific research in education, organized around three strategic objectives: promoting quality, building the knowledge base, and enhancing the professional development of researchers."[35] ASRE, we are told, is based on a "five-part workshop series to engage a wide range of scholars, policy makers, and educators in an action-oriented dialogue to clarify issues and to discuss ways in which current practice could be improved."[36] This is the

---

34. Ibid., 16–17.
35. ASRE, 2.
36. Ibid., 11–12.

third of three reports issued by the committee resulting from these workshops, the others focusing on implementing randomized field trials and strengthening peer review.[37] Its target audience is "education researchers and the institutions that support them—universities, federal agencies, professional associations, and foundations."[38] As we pointed out in the previous chapter, this antidemocratic understanding of research leaves out the individuals who will be most affected by the recommendations—individuals *in* schools. But our primary concern here is with its recommendations for doctoral study. We briefly summarize the report next.

The purpose of ASRE is to "spur actions that will advance scientific research in education," since the field of education lacks "a disciplinary framework like those that shape the academic study of anthropology, or economics, or psychology."[39] As with SRE, this report assumes the "deep skepticism about the quality and rigor of education scholarship," but it claims it does not find it

> necessary to denigrate or to defend the field on this point. . . . What matters is that the current landscape offers a ripe opportunity for self-reflection and improvement, and this is our point of departure: *scientific research in education could be improved, and the field should focus its energies on doing so.*[40]

Probably in response to the critiques levied at SRE, this committee is even more explicit in stating that science is defined, not by a particular method (i.e., the experiment) but by the guiding principles explained in SRE. It also reiterates that "there is more than one way to view the world and that science is not universally applicable to understanding all issues relevant to education or its improvement." This committee deemed that its

> charge was to address ways in which *scientific* education research could be improved, [and so] we do not consider the relative merits or contributions to education research that do not define themselves as scientific, approaches that include such disparate paradigms as interpretivism, postmodernism, and critical theory.[41]

---

37. National Research Council, *Implementing Randomized Field Trials in Education: Report of a Workshop* (Washington, DC: National Academies Press, 2004); National Research Council, *Strengthening Peer Review in Federal Agencies That Support Education Research* (Washington, DC: National Academies Press, 2004). These reports, as well as SRE and ASRE, are available (free of charge) at http://www.nap.edu/.

38. ASRE, 16.

39. Ibid., 9.

40. Ibid., 11. Emphasis in original.

41. Ibid., 16.

Resorting to its charge in such a legalistic and formalistic way belies the committee's real, and very political, intent to institute science in education, and thus it disparages these other forms of inquiry by implication. Further, given the politics of knowledge in universities and funding agencies, instituting science in the study of education will mean that other forms of inquiry *will* be marginalized, subordinated, or replaced.

To promote the quality of scientific research in education, at any rate, the report makes four recommendations, relating mostly to the need for federal agencies to develop criteria for peer reviewers, for researchers to use rigorous methods and high standards of evidence (read as: scientism), and for federal agencies to ensure appropriate resources for large-scale investigations and to build partnerships between researchers, practitioners, and policy makers. We do not see how this logic does not lead to an increase in experimental designs. Indeed, the committee has previously given the random-trial study the privilege of having its own workshop and its own report.[42] And these trials, as we argued in chapter 1, should be resisted, as they dehumanize individuals and risk subjecting them to unethical practices. Indeed, much of the problem here is the myopic focus on processes and the lack of ethical understanding of the effect of those processes. As Karl Hostetler writes concerning the intentions of education research:

> Good intentions do not guarantee good research. However, my argument does not hinge on the existence of bad research. Researchers may well be able to make a sound case for the ethical value of their research; but my argument is that they *do* need to be able to make that case. And that is where my doubts lie. Researchers are expected to be knowledgeable and articulate regarding the processes of research. I am not sure there are similar expectations regarding the ethical ends of research—expectations that researchers be knowledgeable and articulate regarding human well-being.[43]

Note, for example, how the committee discusses presumably valid randomization: It seeks to test "interventions" and to ensure randomness through a "*straightforward manipulation* of the number of individuals assigned to each group."[44] Yet, these individuals are, after all, *not* numbers, but human beings, and quite often children, who cannot complain that they are being *manipulated*, "straightforwardly" or otherwise. As Hostetler notes,

> The basic idea [of randomization] is to make irrelevant the influence of at least some particulars that might distinguish people from

---

42. See National Research Council, *Implementing Randomized Field Trials in Education.*
43. Karl Hostetler, "What is 'Good' Education Research?" *Educational Researcher* 34, no. 6 (2005): 16–21, 17. Emphasis in original.
44. ASRE, 30, footnote 3. Emphasis added.

one another. That can have some virtue, but it can also have the vice of suppressing just those particular factors and experiences that are essential to individuals' well-being. Imagine research that establishes a strong positive correlation between some teaching approach and students' success in reading (however that might be defined), irrespective of students' particular backgrounds. That can be valuable information; yet something is missing if the research is silent on what happens to particular students. We find a way to improve students' reading. Okay, but was it worth it? What were the costs, the tradeoffs? Did some kids enjoy the curriculum and the instruction? Were some miserable? Resistant? If the emerging theory is not somehow addressing, or at the very least acknowledging, the complexity of ethically relevant particulars that affect the well-being of particular persons, the moral task is incomplete.[45]

Moreover, educators themselves should be concerned about researchers telling them how to conduct their work, researchers who will not trust the formers' intuitions or experience. Indeed, the idea that researchers are in the best position to tell practitioners how to conduct their work constitutes a usurpation of the practitioners' field of legitimacy, as we suggested in chapter 1 and discuss later in this chapter.

A larger problem, then, seems to be that we should not raise *those* humanistic concerns, since the research process comes first and human beings are factored in, if at all, at a later time. What is touted as important by advocates of "scientific research" is not actually to advocate that research-ers connect with individuals in schools as individuals, but as subjects of research, and thus as "data." The researcher's emotional, moral, and political commitments to those individuals is subsumed by concerns with technical knowledge, stripped of its humanity. What is important is not the social, emotional, psychological, or political effects of treating people as data, but the lack of an "infrastructure or the professional norms to engage in efforts to connect and integrate theories and data across investigations."[46] Without such infrastructure, the "scientific study of educational phenomena will be fragmented," and while this cannot be avoided, one can facilitate the progression of scientific knowledge in education by "explicit efforts to promote the accumulation of research-based knowledge."[47] Other than to

---

45. Hostetler, "What is 'Good' Education Research?" 18.
46. *ASRE*, 36.
47. Ibid. The committee cites the physical sciences as the model for such accumulation, and, correspondingly, it recommends that: (1) professional associations ensure standards for data sharing; (2) education research journals require authors to make their data available to other researchers; (3) associations, journals, and funding agencies create an infrastructure for taking advantage of technology to facilitate data sharing and knowledge accumulation; and (4) educa-tion research journals develop and implement policies requiring structured abstracts.

normalize the field of education, the committee could very well recall that such accumulation may do little to reach the people most affected, since more and more knowledge in the sciences is being governed by intellectual-property regimes that enclose that knowledge and make it subject to private ownership.[48] Indeed, the "fragmentation" the committee finds so problematic in education research might be the best course for science in the era of increasing privatization of knowledge, so that private ownership of that knowledge takes place in fits and starts rather than in an all-engulfing manner. But this thinking would require self-reflection in a field that demands such self-reflection in all others but not in itself.

The last set of recommendations ASRE makes ensure the "professional development" of education research, since the "need for a diverse pool of well-trained education researchers to generate high-quality scholarship and to lend their expertise to deliberations about educational practice and policy is great."[49] The problem is *not* that there is an inadequate number of education researchers. The "real issue may not be one of quantity, but one of quality: Are current and prospective educational researchers capable of tackling the complex questions that policy makers and practitioners want answers to?"[50] This last set of recommendations, premised on the assumption that we need to develop prospective education researchers, is our primary concern in this chapter. The assumption of the need to develop education researchers led to recommendations asking schools of education to give students seeking careers in research particular competencies, that is, substantive and methodological knowledge and skills in a specialized area, as well as offering students a variety of meaningful research experiences.[51]

The problem with the field of education research, according to ASRE, is that it is too diverse, and its researchers come from virtually every discipline. Furthermore, these researchers also come to the field relatively late and thus have little prior training or experience in research.[52] The committee did purport to recognize that not all schools of education train researchers, and even in those that do the diversity of experiences and disciplinary backgrounds are assets in a field as complex as education.[53] But, and here is

48. For studies of this phenomenon in education, see Benjamin Baez, "Private Knowledge, Public Domain: The Politics of Intellectual Property in Higher Education," in *Schools or Markets? Commercialization, Privatization, and School-Business Partnerships*, ed. Deron R. Boyles (Mahwah: Lawrence Erlbaum Associates, 2005), 119–48; and Sheila Slaughter and Gary Rhoades, *Academic Capitalism and the New Economy: Markets, State, and Higher Education* (Baltimore: The Johns Hopkins University Press, 2004).
49. ASRE, 56.
50. Ibid., 57.
51. Federal agencies and publishers also have roles to play: Federal agencies should ensure review panels with a broad range of scholarly perspectives and that include traditionally underrepresented groups, and publishers should ensure that peer reviews promote the professional development of education researchers.
52. ASRE, 56–57.
53. Ibid.

the key point, "When a diverse group of students comes together in a doctoral program, however, they do not share previous experiences, a common language, or norms regarding the value and conduct of education research."[54] We read this as: Such students need to be normalized, since their diversity is really *not* an asset after all but a hindrance to the pursuit of positivist scientific knowledge. In positivistic fashion, the committee collapses very separate and diverse fields of science and professions into *one* notion of science, as "doctoral training of education researchers and the challenges associated with it are at their core very similar across social and behavioral science disciplines, as well as professional fields like social work, business, and nursing."[55] Doctoral training, therefore, "can and should be a mechanism for instilling common habits of mind—not rote standardization, but a sense of purpose around which research and teaching can be framed."[56]

This presumption about the unity of science led to three recommendations regarding doctoral study. First, "Schools of Education that train doctoral students for careers in education research should articulate the competencies those graduates should know and be able to do and design their programs to enable students to develop them." The articulation of competencies, we are told, is essential for designing course work, organizing research experiences, and developing other program elements. Such an "exercise would also define a minimum breadth of skills all would-be education researchers should have."[57] The problem for the committee is that schools of education have had little experience with scientific inquiry, since scientific research became important only in the 1960s, when the schools were linked to traditional social science disciplines that gave them rigorous methods.[58] Furthermore, and perhaps even more important, no two schools prepare researchers in exactly the same way:

> Some schools award EdD degrees; others give PhDs; others give both. (Indeed, it is not even clear what the difference between the two degrees are, as their purposes and requirements vary substantially across universities.) Some schools encourage research on teaching practice; others focus on policy research. Some schools require training in statistics; others do not. Some require experience collecting data in the field; others do not. Some require participation in supervised research and preparation of a scholarly publication prior to graduation; others do not. As currently constituted, such doctoral programs do little to ensure that the preparation

54. Ibid., 58.
55. Ibid.
56. Ibid., 59.
57. Ibid., 6.
58. Ibid., 59.

of education researchers meets at least a minimal standard of scholarly rigor.[59]

Therefore, "Specifying the competencies that every graduate of doctoral programs in schools of education—that is, the future leaders in education research—should have is critical."[60] This is not, the committee indicates, for the purposes of ensuring that all educational programs look alike, but only for ensuring minimum skills for all students. We will concede this point about the committee not recommending that all programs look alike, since, as we will argue, the point of this endeavor is not to collapse all research in the field of education into one notion of science, but to co-opt the field in its entirety.

The second recommendation is that "Schools of Education that train doctoral students for careers in education research should design their programs to enable those students to develop deep substantive and methodological knowledge and skills in a specialized area." The course work and research experiences of these students "should hone their skills and understanding in the theoretical ideas, methodological tools, and existing research in the particular area in education research they intend to pursue." For this, inter-departmental collaboration can often facilitate in-depth training by providing opportunities for students to explore areas and to work with faculty outside schools of education.[61] In addition to facilitating a breadth of knowledge in education research among doctoral candidates, schools of education should also provide opportunities for students to develop a depth of expertise in selected subfields of education research.[62] It is, according to ASRE, in the development of deep expertise in subfields of education research that collaborations with disciplinary departments and other organizational entities in a university can *pay off*, particularly for in-depth methodological training.[63]

Recognizing that faculty expertise in schools of education is not likely even to cover all specializations adequately, ASRE goes on to say that "[o]pportunities to take courses or to work with faculty outside the school of education can facilitate the honing of specialized expertise by expanding access to a wider range of subfields and specialty areas."[64] Such "collaborations" are necessary because training education researchers exclusively in schools of education shuts students off from the social and behavioral

---

59. Ibid., 59–60.
60. Ibid., 61–62.
61. Ibid., 6.
62. Ibid., 62.
63. Ibid., 62–64. Emphasis added. The suggestions for this change include the establishment of dual degrees, approval of new syllabi by university curriculum committees, flexible schedules so as to allow students to interact within and across university departments, and, of course, financial support for all of this.
64. Ibid., 64.

sciences and related departments, stunting opportunities for in-depth explorations and depriving the future leaders in the field of relevant disciplinary models and methods.[65] We read this as saying that faculty in education cannot be trusted to train their own students, and that it might be best for schools of education, if they are to claim legitimacy and prestige, for them to hand over their students to the *real* experts. Of course, given how the student-professor relationship has been altered by sponsored research, especially in the sciences so fervently revered by many,[66] this means as well that those experts in the "real" sciences will have at their disposal a steady source of cheap labor for which they are not financially responsible, since this recommendation does not suggest that the experts should have to "pay" for these students; only that there will be "payoffs," likely only *for the experts*.

The third and last recommendation explicitly dealing with doctoral work reads as follows: "Schools of education that train doctoral students for careers in education research should provide those students with a variety of meaningful research experiences." This experience, we are told, is essential to a research career, as it "facilitates the development of research skills and provides opportunities for publishing research findings in peer-reviewed journals, presenting at conferences, and participating in other activities that are the foundations of the profession." This experience will be meaningful, however, only if doctoral students "engage in research *under* the guidance of multiple faculty members who themselves are active in the field."[67] The word *under* is important here, as students will be made to serve the interests of those faculty who are active in the field, and who will subject those students only to *their* own needs, not necessarily the students', and arguably not even the schools' and colleges' needs, which are the purported objects of the research. In other words, students will provide research-active faculty with a source of cheap labor. Indeed, the independence asserted by students to which we referred previously must be stifled, as dissertation work, some of which in education may have been conducted in the fashion of the humanities, that is, as library-intensive and independent, should now be reconsidered, as such a "lone project" diminishes opportunities to learn from multiple experiences and "flies in the face of the idea of teams of researchers working together on common problems."[68] In short, education doctoral students are to be normalized to be science's doctoral students.

In line with *ASRE*, Margaret Eisenhart and Robert DeHaan, two of the *SRE* authors, advocate the inculcation of a culture of science in education doctoral study. Despite claiming to recognize Labaree's distinction between the teacher and researcher views, Eisenhart and DeHaan actually ignore it, as

65. Ibid., 65–66.
66. See generally, Gumport, "Graduate Education and Research," 450–52.
67. *ASRE*, 6. Emphasis added.
68. Ibid., 66.

a "fundamental component of training programs seeking to prepare scientifically based education researchers is to socialize students into these norms of scientific inquiry."[69] We read this as saying, unlike Labaree, not that students should be "sold" the researcher view as an addition to their views, but to replace their normative world with another. This cannot be accomplished without significantly altering academic practices, as ASRE recognized. Thus, for Eisenhart and DeHaan, education researchers need training in five broad areas: (1) varied epistemological perspectives, (2) diverse methodological strategies, (3) disparate contexts of educational practice, (4) the principles of scientific inquiry, and (5) an interdisciplinary research orientation.[70] They offer, however, only recommendations for the last two.

Eisenhart and DeHaan's recommendations for changing the current normative views in education to those of scientific inquiry requires, foremost, that the PhD program in education research should be separated from (but include parts of) the doctoral training for practice-oriented educational leadership. A separate research-intensive PhD program, we are told, opens possibilities for improving the preparation of education researchers.[71] We will take on this assumption shortly. They also propose four other recommendations. First, there should be core courses for all entering doctoral students in subjects traditional for education as well as in relevant interdisciplinary areas such as neuroscience, sociology of science, and linguistics; these courses should be scholarly, rigorous, and intense enough to familiarize students with the orienting concepts in each field, the culture of scientific inquiry, and the special demands of research in education. Second, there should be research experiences of at least two kinds under the guidance of a faculty member: One that engages students in all phases of an investigation, and another that allows them to pursue a line of research on their own and complete a report about it in the form of a technical report, a dissertation, or a series of articles. This experience should be such that students gain expertise in at least one disciplinary domain and exposure to related research perspectives and methodologies in at least one other discipline. Third, there should be a solid grounding in education practice or policy through required experiences such as teaching in a K-12 classroom, interning for a state education agency, or taking courses with teacher-practitioners. Finally, there should be interdisciplinary collaborations—not just interdisciplinary courses and seminars, but opportunities to build networks with students and researchers in other departments where studies relevant to education are conducted.[72]

---

69. Margaret Eisenhart and Robert L. DeHaan, "Doctoral Preparation of Scientifically Based Education Researchers," *Educational Researcher* 34, no. 4 (2005): 3–13, 5.
70. Ibid., 7.
71. Ibid., 9.
72. Ibid., 10.

The "culture of science" that all these reports seek to establish cannot simply be done by schools of education alone. They will need not only the expertise of the "real" scientists but the resources of the federal government. According to SRE, federal agencies must work to inculcate a scientific culture through partnerships with, among others, schools of education, as the training of education researchers is a "long-term undertaking." In schools of education, SRE points out, "students often pursue nonresearch-oriented goals (e.g., school administration) and may therefore reach the graduate level without any research training."[73] This mention of school administration is a central point, and we will stick with it a bit longer than might at first appear necessary. The mention of educational administration programs as having "nonresearch-oriented goals" is not merely indicating a state of reality;[74] it works also as a covered-over admonition, since it is the conventional wisdom that educational administration (or what tends now to be called, "educational leadership") programs, unlike many of the others, seem to those inside and outside schools of education to provide the greatest level of concern in graduate study. These programs are deemed to be the "least scientific" and least prestigious ones. Arthur Levine's recent study of educational administration programs, while not addressing the notion of an education science explicitly, apparently relied upon it for his critique of what he found wrong with such programs and what will cure their ills. The question for him was "how well current programs educate leaders for today's jobs and today's schools," but that "there is no systematic research documenting the impact of school leadership programs on the achievement of children in the schools and schools systems that graduates of these programs lead."[75] The kind of research he wants, we presume, is the kind of research the federal government and others, such as Robert Slavin,[76] deem legitimate, that is, the experiment, which they all understand, in their gutter utilitarianism, to be the best for getting at "what works."

The problem with many educational administration programs, according to Levine, is that so many practitioners are working toward a degree intended to prepare academic researchers and scholars and that has no relevance to their jobs.[77] We will leave aside the questionable presumption that a degree that is deemed for research and scholars can have no relevance for individuals

---

73. SRE, 150.

74. And it is arguable whether such a reality exists, since we know faculty and students in such programs who have nothing but "research-oriented goals," and we also know faculty and students in supposedly research-oriented programs who do not have such goals.

75. Arthur Levine, Educating School Leaders (Washington, DC: The Education Schools Project, 2005), 12. Available at http:///www.edschools.org/pdf/Final313.pdf (Retrieved July 21, 2005).

76. Robert E. Slavin, "Evidence-Based Education Policies: Transforming Educational Practice and Research," Educational Researcher 31, no. 7 (2002): 15–21.

77. Levine, Educating School Leaders, 43.

who choose not to pursue academic jobs, and question here Levine's recommendation that the EdD in educational administration should be eliminated, since it is a "watered-down doctorate that diminishes the field of educational administration and provides a back door for weak education schools to gain doctoral granting *authority*."[78] The word *authority* is important here, as we will argue later in this chapter, since it is the authority to decree degrees of distinction that is the object prize in a struggle for control of individuals and institutions. For Levine, the PhD should be reserved for preparing the small number of students seeking careers as researchers, and not only that but also the PhD should be available solely at doctoral extensive universities so that one can ensure that a small cadre of students will work with renowned faculty.[79] This repeated concern with separating doctoral study into the practitioner and researcher aspects, and the concomitant recommendations for distinct kinds of degrees, must be juxtaposed with the discourse on the "culture of science" in education research. Before we critique the distinctions established in such thinking, we digress a bit to give a short historical account of doctoral study and its bureaucratizaton in doctoral degrees. We return afterward to the distinctions, via a reading of Bourdieu.

A (VERY) BRIEF OVERVIEW OF DOCTORAL DEGREES

American research universities are presumed to be heavily influenced by German ideals of pure research and graduate study.[80] German notions were certainly influential in the development of American universities, but American institutions were also influenced by the English and Scottish notions of the undergraduate college. Thus, as James Turner and Paul Bernard argue, two "paradigms" apparently competed for dominance but were eventually reconciled in American universities. One, the "utilitarian" paradigm, stressed modern languages, mathematics, and science, and proffered "useful" knowledge for the modern commercial and technological world; it moved toward the specialization of knowledge and scientific expertise. The other, the "liberal arts" paradigm, emphasized the ancient languages, history, literature, and the fine arts; it prized breadth of knowledge rather than expertise and formation of character and intellect rather than utility.[81]

Turner and Bernard also could have explored how, even within each of these "paradigms," there developed distinctions between scholarly and

78. Ibid., 67. Emphasis added.
79. Ibid., 67–68.
80. Laurence R. Veysey, *The Emergence of the American University* (Chicago: University of Chicago Press, 1965), 125–33.
81. See James Turner and Paul Bernard, "The 'German Model' and the Graduate School: The University of Michigan and the Origin Myth of the American University," *History of Higher Education Annual* 13 (1993): 69–98, 72.

practical knowledge, and, thus, between scholars and practitioners. These distinctions played themselves out in the different types of doctoral degrees. "Doctoral" degrees apparently originated in medieval universities, which trained men for the major professions in law, medicine, and theology. The term *doctor*, deriving from the word *doceo*, referred to "teacher," and the "doctoral degree" marked the medieval qualification to teach in universities.[82] "Research," as a purpose for the doctoral degree, originated in the German university of the nineteenth century, which was redefined by Humbolt to further his belief that the various sciences constituted a "whole" unified by philosophy, and that their knowledge furthered universal enlightenment.[83] The practice of research came to the universities with the rise of the sciences, and the PhD became the qualification for such practice.[84]

The American PhD was first awarded by Yale University in 1861.[85] But it was not until the establishment of The Johns Hopkins University in 1876, modeled after German universities, that the PhD became a significant part of American universities. Yet, at Johns Hopkins, the Master of Arts (MA) and PhD originally were not considered separate degrees, or, more accurately, they were not awarded for different things. This was the case until 1909 when the university established the MA as a degree for college teachers and reserved the PhD for the small group of individuals who it judged able to make first-rate contributions to original research. From then on the holder of the PhD was deemed something of an expert on a small technical issue in a discipline.[86] By the middle of the twentieth century, however, the PhD had become, as John Brubacher and Willis Rudy explain, the "union card" necessary for college teaching, whether or not its holders actually conducted research.[87]

American universities, at any rate, oriented the PhD in the direction of potential research, even though fewer than 20 percent of PhD holders actually produced research.[88] Perhaps this fact led to the creation of different kinds of doctoral degrees. That is, there seemed a recognition that the PhD, a research degree, was not actually producing researchers, so other degrees would be necessary (reserving the PhD for researchers). Furthermore, the calls by the professions for high credentials required a rethinking of doctoral

---

82. See John Radford, "Doctor of What?" *Teaching in Higher Education*, 6, no. 4 (2001): 527–29, 528; see also, Hugh J. McDonald, "The Doctorate in America," *Journal of Higher Education* 14, no. 4 (1943): 189–94, 190.

83. Radford, "Doctor of What?" 528.

84. Veysey, *The Emergence of the American University*, 176.

85. John S. Brubacher and Willis Rudy, *Higher Education in Transition: A History of American Colleges and Universities, 1636–1956* (New York: Harper and Row, 1958), 189.

86. See Radford, "Doctor of What?" 527.

87. Brubacher and Rudy, *Higher Education in Transition*, 190.

88. Ibid.

education, and so Harvard University granted the first EdD in 1920 for practicing educators.[89] The EdD, and other doctoral degrees, however, were seen as different from, and less prestigious than, the PhD.[90]

The PhD still is seen as research-oriented and the EdD as practitioner-oriented. Because the PhD is associated with research, which is the most important function of the university, and because most of its holders spend their time solely teaching (or administration or "practice" of some kind), critiques abound. Some critics advocate different degrees for college teaching and administration.[91] Others question whether the PhD is at all necessary for college teaching,[92] although similar critiques suggest that the PhD can be redefined to account for a broader conception of faculty work.[93] Many critics, however, lament what they deem to be a watering down of the PhD degree.[94] But such a claim is possible only because the PhD is understood as being for the training and credentialing of researchers and scholars.

Despite the attributed differences between the two degrees, studies of them do not reveal significant differences. There seems generally few differences in admissions criteria, course requirements, and dissertation research (although differences may be found when comparing individual institutions).[95] For example, a 1994 study of EdD and PhD dissertations by Jack Nelson and Calleen Coorough found little differences in the kinds of studies performed, methods used, and intended audiences, although PhD dissertations were more likely than EdD ones to use high level statistics (but even this was not a large difference).[96] If there is little actual difference between PhD and EdD degrees and programs, what can account for the apparent unease with the use of the PhD for things other than research (or even college teaching)? Why have a degree for practitioners? Why do educators insist on both degrees or one over the other? What is the purpose of the doctoral degree in the first place?

---

89. Ibid.
90. McDonald, "The Doctorate in America," 190.
91. See Radford, "Doctor of What?" 529.
92. See, for example, Kenneth C. Petress, "Are Doctorates Really Needed for Non-research Positions?" *Journal of Instructional Psychology* 20, no. 4 (1993): 321–22.
93. See, for example, J. L. Lagowski, "Rethinking the Ph.D.: A New Social Contract," *Journal of Chemical Education* 73, no. 1 (1996): 1.
94. See, for example, McDonald, "The Doctorate in America," 190; Levine, *Educating School Leaders*, 67–68.
95. See Jered B. Kolbert and Johnston M. Brendel, "Current Perceptions of the Doctor of Philosophy and Doctor of Education in Counselor Preparation," *Counselor Education & Supervision* 36, no. 3 (1997): 207–15.
96. Jack K. Nelson and Calleen Coorough, "Content Analysis of the Ph.D. versus Ed.D. Dissertations," *Journal of Experimental Education* 62, no. 2 (1994): 158–68.

DOCTORAL STUDY AND THE PURPOSES
OF HIGHER EDUCATION

Those arguing that the EdD should be more "practitioner-oriented" and the PhD more "research-oriented," or that there needs to be a separation in doctoral study between the pursuit of a research career and an administrative career, seem to be making claims about higher education similar to those made by early critics. Indeed, there are in such claims traces of the disagreement between John Dewey and Robert Hutchins about the purpose of higher education; the latter arguing that general education is paramount because it "trains the mind" to deal with society's problems, and the former arguing that experiential learning better prepares students to solve those problems.[97] Indeed, in a review of Hutchins's *The Higher Learning in America*, Dewey claims that Hutchins's work establishes a hierarchy of first principles and is, therefore, authoritarian:

> There are indications that Mr. Hutchins would not take kindly to labeling the other phase of this remedial plan "authoritarian." But any scheme based on the existence of ultimate first principles, with their dependent hierarchy of subsidiary principles, does not escape authoritarianism by calling the principles "truths." I would not intimate that the author has any sympathy with fascism. But basically his idea as to the proper course to be taken is akin to the distrust of freedom and the consequent appeal to some fixed authority that is now overrunning the world. There is implicit in every assertion of fixed and eternal first truths the necessity for some human authority to decide, in this world of conflicts, just what these truths are and how they shall be taught. This problem is conveniently ignored. Doubtless much may be said for selecting Aristotle and St. Thomas as competent promulgators of first truths. But it took the authority of a powerful ecclesiastic organization to secure their wide recognition. Others may prefer Hegel, or Karl Marx, or even Mussolini as the seers of first truths; and there are those who prefer Nazism. As far as I can see, President Hutchins has completely evaded the problem of who is to determine the definite truths that constitute the hierarchy.[98]

Dewey saw the role of colleges and universities as integrating intellectualism with practicality, while Hutchins saw the role of colleges and universities as

---

97. See John Dewey, *Democracy and Education* (New York: The Free Press, 1916); Robert Maynard Hutchins, *The Higher Learning in America* (New Haven: The Yale Press, 1978 c. 1936).
98. John Dewey, "President Hutchins' Proposals to Remake Higher Education," *The Social Frontier* 3, no. 22 (January 1937), 103–104, 104.

set apart from the gritty details of real life. On Hutchins's view, thinking for the sake of thinking was enough of a purpose for higher learning. Practical and vocational pursuits would follow after a general education. Hutchins's views on pedagogy are instructive here, as they are prescient of debates surrounding the EdD and PhD (as well distinctions between education researchers and teachers). He writes that "in the university," the teacher

> should learn what to teach. He [sic] should study under all three faculties [metaphysics, social science, and natural science], and especially under that of metaphysics. If it then appears that he is destined for investigation or for vocational instruction he learn the techniques of investigation or practice in a research or technical institute. If, for example, he seems likely to be a school admin-istrator, and if a school administrator should know the number of janitors per cubic foot that school buildings require, and if a school administrator should not be trusted with a school unless he has this knowledge, then this knowledge should be gained in a technical institute.[99]

Accordingly, separating content from context means, for Hutchins, preserving academic integrity and what he understands to be rigor. The problem, for Dewey, is that Hutchins fails to value the nexus of theory and practice, content and context, and thus separates knowing from knowledge. Perhaps it is because of these sorts of epistemological conflicts that there has been constant debate over whether colleges and universities should prepare indi-viduals for the workplace, or whether they should give those individuals a liberal education so that they can participate fully in a democracy. With regard to the EdD/PhD debates in education, the privilege given to practice assumes the university should prepare individuals adequately for the world of work; the privilege given to research and theory assumes the university's purpose is to produce knowledge for, and understanding of, the world, and it is this distinction that is presumed by the calls for a culture of science in education.

For the early critics of graduate education, the distinction between the arts and sciences and the professions was clear. Thorstein Veblen, for example, asserted that the pursuit of higher learning was the *raison d'être* and province of graduate schools in the arts and sciences, and professional education (indeed, even undergraduate teaching) was antithetical to this.[100] For Veblen, the difference between the university and the "lower and pro-fessional schools is broad and simple; not so much a difference of degree as

---

99. Hutchins, *The Higher Learning in America*, 115.
100. Thorstein Veblen, *Higher Learning in America* (New Brunswick, NJ: Transaction Publish-ers, 1993, c. 1918).

of kind."[101] The lower and professional schools are "occupied with instilling such knowledge and habits as will make their pupils fit citizens of the world in whatever position in the fabric of workday life they may fall," while the university prepares "men for a life of science and scholarship; and it is accordingly concerned with such discipline only as will give efficiency in the pursuit of knowledge and fit its students for the increase and diffusion of learning."[102] While Veblen was not concerned with doctoral degrees per se, his defense of "higher learning" echoes those of critics who claim that the PhD should be concerned with research, or the pursuit of knowledge, while the EdD should be concerned with training efficient practitioners in the "workday life" they choose.

Yet, as discussed previously, most holders of the PhD do not pursue research (and never have), and now the difference between degrees seems more ideological than material. The fact of the matter is that, from many accounts, very few differences exist between the degrees produced.[103] But the distinction lives on despite the fact that it is premised on a past that never—or rarely ever—materialized in fact.[104] So the debate about doctoral education appears to be a manifestation of something other than this difference. We argue that a truer debate within academe is a struggle over the purposes of higher education, generally, and graduate education, particularly. Narratives that suggest a "watering down" of the PhD,[105] or those suggesting that the EdD/PhD differences be made clear,[106] can be read as defending the practice of research, and particularly scientific research, as the *raison d'être* of the university, while those emphasizing the value of the EdD, or those suggesting a redefinition of the PhD to account for its nonresearch uses, can be read as defending a notion of the university as also preparing individuals for the workplace, or at least for something other than research.[107]

---

101. Ibid., 14.

102. Ibid., 15.

103. See *ASRE*, 59–60; Kolbert and Brendel, "Current Perceptions of the Doctor of Philosophy and Doctor of Education in Counselor Preparation"; Nelson and Coorough, "Content Analysis"; Russell T. Osguthorpe and Mei J. Wong, "The Ph.D. versus the Ed.D.: Time for a Decision," *Innovative Higher Education* 18 (1993): 47–63.

104. Indeed, the debates about the EdD and PhD often seem to acknowledge that the world changes (or should), but they strip the PhD or the EdD of its potential for change. One is deemed "research-oriented" and the other "practice-oriented," and both are not seen as appropriately exceeding the purposes that animated them. Each is understood to represent different purposes and play different roles in a social world that is changing. Thus, our notions of the world allow for change but our notions of the degrees do not. We think that this understanding anchors the degrees in a particular time and space, but it fails to recognize that such time and space perhaps never were "real."

105. See Levine, *Educating School Leaders*.

106. Eisenhart and DeHaan, "Doctoral Preparation."

107. For an illustration of these contrasting claims at one campus, see Paul R. Smith, "A Meeting of Cultures: Part-time Students in an Ed.D. Program," *International Journal of Leadership in Education* 3, no. 4 (2000): 359–80.

There are other variations of this struggle over the purposes of higher education. Some critics suggest that the title of the degree is less important than the content of its program. For example, Ron Iannone argues that the key measure of an EdD program is whether it encourages students to become more reflexive, more critical of the status quo, and more prepared to initiate social change.[108] This assumes, of course, that universities should promote social change, rather than merely further knowledge for its own sake or simply prepare individuals to reproduce the status quo. Perhaps the status quo being challenged is the idea of what counts as knowledge. Richard Winter, Morwenna Griffiths, and Kath Green, for instance, argue that the EdD forces universities to deal with the conflict between knowledge that is reliable and unbiased and knowledge that can be used wisely toward a good purpose.[109] These argument all suggest struggle over the purposes of higher education as either to further social utility or to pursue disinterested knowledge.

Regardless of how the conflict over the purposes of higher education manifests itself—research versus practice, disinterested pursuit of knowledge versus social utility—distinctions are established and legitimated. Why are such distinctions necessary? What is at stake in the distinctions academics make? We will argue that the struggle within the academy over its purposes is part of a larger political struggle to control the classifications that will govern the world. These struggles take place not just within particular fields, such as higher education, but between fields, such as academe and the professions. The distinctions that educators live by—such as researcher/practitioner, theory/practice, liberal education/professional education, disinterested knowledge/social utility, scientist/educator, and so forth—obscure the domination that takes place when arbitrary distinctions are legitimated as obvious, natural, inevitable, and so forth. These distinctions may be arbitrary but they are not imaginary—they produce material (and psychic) effects; they produce the very reality they purport to represent. It is to the "distinctions we live by" in education that we direct the next section of this chapter.

THE DISTINCTIONS WE LIVE BY

It seems late in the chapter to mention this, but we intended the title of this chapter to be ambiguous. We wanted to set up the distinctions associated with the degrees before rereading them in the ways we do now. The terms *degree* and *distinction* in the title are used for their multiple meanings.

108. Ron Iannone, "A Critical Perspective Reform Paradigm for Ed.D. Programs," *Education* 112, no. 4 (1992): 612–17.
109. See Richard Winter, Morwenna Griffiths, and Kath Green, "The 'Academic' Qualities of Practice: What are the Criteria for a Practice-based Ph.D.?" *Studies in Higher Education* 25, no. 1 (2000): 25–37.

The word *degree*, as we indicated in the rather long epigraph of this chapter, refers to "relative condition" and "relation," as well as to the "rank given by a college or university to a student who has completed a required course of study, or to a distinguished person as an honor." *Distinction* refers to "making different," and "difference," but also to "honor" and to the "quality that makes one seem superior or worthy of special recognition." These meanings mirror the functions of power, which works by differentiation and by establishing classifications that contain hierarchies (explicit and implicit) providing value and worth. And these classifications are particularly insidious when sanctioned by institutions of higher education in the form of degrees. These classifications, with their varying *degrees* of worth, reward, and punishment, are incorporated by individuals, becoming embodied in a significant sense, and thus appearing natural and inevitable.

While many might concede to us the argument that the PhD/EdD distinction is arbitrary, few are likely to see the other distinctions that undergird this arguably superficial one as also arbitrary. Thus, the practice/theory and researcher/practitioner distinctions that support and undergird the idea of the "culture of science" in education are seen as legitimate. Indeed, the theory/practice distinction, in particular, has a long history. It has been made widely since the seventeenth century and is now not just a distinction but an opposition.[110] Raymond Williams explains, however, that theory is always in active relation to practice: "an interaction between things done, things observed and (systematic) explanation of these. This allows a necessary distinction between *theory* and *practice*, but does not require their opposition."[111] This relation, of course, can be made prejudicial when *theory* is privileged, say, in doctoral programs (especially the PhD), or when *practice* has become so conventional or habitual that theory is degraded because it challenges some customary action.[112]

This discussion about theory and practice provides a segue for discussing the struggle the academic field faces over the distinctions that matter. And in the rest of this section we extend the arguments over professionalism that we made in chapter 1. The claims made for or against the EdD belie a challenge to the authority of institutions of higher education. For example, it appears that other social institutions want to get into the degree-granting game, and not just to credential individuals but to redefine the criteria of the credentials. In almost any issue of the *Chronicle of Higher Education* one can see that multiple entities, mostly for-profit institutions but also government agencies, school districts, and corporations, want to get into the degree-granting game, and they question the emphasis on theory over practice. The author-

---

110. See Raymond Williams, *Keywords: A Vocabulary of Culture and Society*, rev. ed. (Oxford and New York: Oxford University Press, 1983), 316–18.
111. Ibid., 317. Emphasis in original.
112. Ibid.

ity to grant degrees (and to establish their criteria) has for many years been the purview of the traditional college or university. But now the academy is being challenged as the sole producer of professional credentialing, and this challenge forces it to seek to keep control of this function.[113]

The use of the EdD, or the supposed misuse of the PhD for nonresearch purposes, reflects in some ways the challenge being made to the university's social (and traditional) function. There seems a concern that traditional university education is not meeting the needs of society (and especially the professions), even as doctoral training has become increasingly necessary for credentialing individuals for high-level positions in the professions. This is certainly the case in education, and why the concerns with its research and its researchers seem so important. There seems, then, a destabilizing of the traditional role of the university as a credentialing entity. Yet the need to credential—and the doctoral degree as the credential par excellence—keeps hold even as the traditional credentialing entity is being called into question.

The challenge to the academic field (both by individuals within the field over its purposes and by those in other fields over its authority) takes place through the creation and legitimation of distinctions (or through the delegitimation of established distinctions). Distinction, therefore, is a function of power, a power that legitimates itself by legitimating the distinctions it creates. Bourdieu theorizes that social subjects distinguish themselves from, and try to gain dominance over, others by the distinctions they make.[114] And the distinctions made within the field of education, Bourdieu proposes, carry particular force: they not only classify but ensure, through the attribution of status given by degrees and certifications, the assignment of individuals into hierarchically ordered social classes.[115] Thus, the distinctions educational institutions make exercise a form of symbolic domination which reinforces material domination. As Bourdieu states,

> The official differences produced by academic classifications tend to produce (or reinforce) real differences by inducing in the classified individuals a collectively recognized and supported belief in the differences, thus producing behaviors that are intended to bring real being into line with official being.[116]

Symbolic power works by giving *recognition* to something as legitimate and worthy (or giving something else recognition as illegitimate and unworthy)

---

113. For example, universities have opposed an NIH plan to grant PhD's; see Bruce Agnew, "Scientists Block NIH Plans to Grant PhDs," *Science* (June 11, 1999): 1743.

114. Pierre Bourdieu, *Distinction: A Social Critique of the Judgment of Taste*, trans. Richard Nice (Cambridge: Harvard University Press, 1984), 6.

115. Ibid., 23.

116. Ibid., 25.

and its effects are incorporated by individuals, who then act accordingly to dominate others or to be dominated by others. The array of oppositions (such as, and in education particularly as, theory versus practice and researcher versus practitioner) find such ready acceptance because behind them lies, according to Bourdieu, the social order. The oppositions always refer back, more or less directly, to the fundamental oppositions within the social order, namely the dialectic between the dominant and dominated.[117]

Bourdieu sees the power to distinguish, that is, the power to create distinction, as instantiating a kind of cultural capital because distinctions yield a profit. He did not mean "profit" in the economic sense, but in the ability to control what is legitimate (or attractive, tasteful, distinctive, etc.) in the cultural fields (such as education, music, art, politics, etc.). Bourdieu argued that culture and economy are intricately related in a web of mutual constitution; the class distinctions of the economy inevitably generate symbolic distinctions of culture, which in turn regenerate and legitimate the economic class structures.[118] Cultural distinctions, therefore, are determined by socioeconomic structures, but they are supported by theories that deny that determination. Academic theories, in particular, attribute primary value precisely to the purity and disinterestedness of intellectual judgment, as the discourse on science in education presumes, and so they are central weapons in the exercise of symbolic power that reinforces the status quo and were developed historically to fill that role.[119] Bourdieu, accordingly, critiques all notions of universal cultural values, especially of the intelligentsia, and of the ideology of the intellectual and the cultural autonomy from economic and political determinants that the intelligentsia has constructed in defense of its material and symbolic interests, which he sees as the struggle of the "dominated fraction of the dominant class."[120]

"Academic capital," for Bourdieu, is the guaranteed product of the combined effects of cultural transmission by the family and cultural transmission by the school. That is why, he argues, we must consider what is perhaps the best-hidden effect of the educational system: the production of titles, particularly because these titles attribute status, whether positive (ennobling) or negative (stigmatizing), which every group produces by assigning individuals to hierarchically ordered classes.[121] What the discourse on science in education seeks to guarantee, it seems to us, is not just formal competence, that is, scientific competence, but the creation of a social and

---

117. Ibid., 468–69.

118. For a good discussion of this point (and others) regarding Bourdieu's theory, including its limitations, see David Gartman, "Culture as Class Symbolization or Mass Reification? A Critique of Bourdieu's *Distinction*," *American Journal of Sociology* 97, no. 2 (1991): 421–47.

119. See also Nicholas Garnham, "Extended Review: Bourdieu's *Distinction*," *Sociological Review* 34, no. 2 (1986): 423–33, 423.

120. Ibid., 424.

121. Bourdieu, *Distinction*, 23.

professional class, the education scientists, who will be creators of, indeed, a "culture." So the doctoral degree in education, which will now confer scientific competence—one of the most, if not the most powerful tools in the modern era—will be more like the patent of nobility than the title to property, which strictly technical definitions make of it.[122] To repeat what we stated in chapter 1, then, the academic training of education researchers is less about skills than about professional status. And, moreover, the worth given to this "nobility" will not simply shape the behavior of the nobles themselves, but also of others, as the creation of groups is always a demarcation and reorganization of individuals: there will be those who will be *in* the class and those *out* of it.

Scientific knowledge about education and the concepts it creates, especially the supposed causal connections between school practices and student learning proposed by the "what works" mentality, therefore, are not merely academic exercises: they will influence the way individuals, both in and out of schools, will *see* schooling or education. The capacity to see is a function of the knowledge and concepts developed to name visible (or invisible) things, and thus such knowledge and concepts constitute, as Bourdieu instructs, "programmes for perception."[123] What seems at stake in this debate over the science of education is control over those "programmes," or the establishment of scientific "programmes for perception" in an arena that is deemed to be controlled by other "programmes," such as morality, philosophy, nonce taxonomies, "practical" knowledge, intuitiveness, politics, or such *other* things. The educational classifications that will come about through the instantiation of an education science will function within and for the purposes of the struggle between social groups. Education scientists, in producing concepts, will produce groups, groups whose stake will be the power to dictate the meaning of the social world.

Schools of education create "degrees," and now they are asked to degree "scientific culture." As with the established professions, these schools will now, then, set up rituals by which a particular group of speakers are given *the* status of speakers par excellence. Like Bourdieu, Michel Foucault also helps us re-pose, though in different way, this problem of the credentialing of a new cadre of professionalized education scientists. Foucault points out that there are a number of procedures for controlling discourse, procedures whose "role is to avert its powers and its dangers, to cope with chance events, to evade its ponderous, awesome materiality."[124] Some of these procedures include rules of exclusion, taking the form of prohibitions, divisions

---

122. See, generally, Ibid., 142.
123. Ibid., 2.
124. Michel Foucault, "The Discourse on Language," in *The Archeology of Knowledge and The Discourse on Language*, trans. A. M. Sheridan Smith (New York: Pantheon Books, 1972), 215–37, 216.

(e.g., theory versus practice, reason versus folly, truth versus falsity), and the "will to truth."[125] This "will to truth," like other systems of exclusion, relies on institutional support, especially those institutions of science, such as universities, but it is "probably even more profoundly accompanied by the manner in which knowledge is employed in a society, the way in which it is exploited, divided and, in some ways, attributed."[126]

There are other rules for controlling discourse, according to Foucault, or what he calls the internal rules governing principles of classification, ordering, and distribution. The NRC's guiding principles seem to us as examples of these internal rules, which in demarcating what is scientific from what is not, will proliferate knowledge and create authors and disciplines. There are also rules taking the form of rituals qualifying speakers. The control of these rituals is what the discourse of a science of education seeks. These rituals define the qualifications required of the speaker; they lay down gestures to be made and the behavior and circumstances that must accompany the discourse; they lay down the supposed or imposed significance of the words used, their effect upon those to whom they are addressed, and their limitations.[127] What is an educational system, Foucault asks, "if not a ritualization of the word; if not a qualification of some fixing of roles for speakers; if not the constitution of a diffuse doctrinal group; if not the distribution and an appropriation of discourse, with all its learning and its powers?"[128]

Bourdieu, while coming from an entirely different perspective than Foucault, and perhaps one that can be called, if crudely, neo-Marxist, claims similar power for educational institutions and their creation of experts. The certification of experts in academic institutions, therefore, have profound consequences for the social order. The constitution of a "new" socially recognized cadre of experts in education science will, following Bourdieu, "with that deep conviction of disinterestedness which is the basis of all missionary zeal," seek to satisfy their group interests by deploying the now academically validated authority to win the "acquiescence of the classes excluded from that authority."[129] Bourdieu goes on to say about the emergence of this cadre of specialized experts, or what he calls the "new petite bourgeoisie," that it employs

> new means of manipulation to perform its role as an intermediary
> between the classes and which by its very existence brings about
> a transformation of the position and dispositions of the old petite
> bourgeoisie, [and this] can itself be understood only in terms of

125. Ibid., 216–18.
126. Ibid., 219.
127. Ibid., 225.
128. Ibid., 227.
129. Bourdieu, *Distinction*, 153.

changes in the mode of domination, which, substituting seduction for repression, public relations for policing, advertising for authority, the velvet glove for the iron fist, pursues the symbolic integration of the dominated classes by imposing needs rather than inculcating norms.[130]

The education scientists created by the "culture of science" in doctoral study, now conferred with academic credential—very likely the PhD—will, wearing the mantle of the salvation of schools while claiming disinterestedness, use their theoretical knowledge derived by rigorous scientific methods to install their "mode of domination" over schools and individuals in schools. Their theories and practices will look like help, as "what works," but in fact it will reconstruct the social order and give themselves the authority to dictate what is worthy and legitimate in education.

Bourdieu's notion of *distinction*, therefore, provides a fertile interpretive scheme for thinking through a highly symptomatic form of control in the postindustrial age—the academic creation of distinctions, their certifications in university degrees, and the cadre of experts that reshape the world even as they purport to describe it. As an interpretive framework, however, Bourdieu's notion can itself be subjected to a narrative analysis. Bourdieu's theory hinges on the notions of *habitus* and *fields*. Although we explain the habitus, and we find aspects of it heuristic, we conclude that it is inadequate to our reading of the discourse on science in education because it is too foundational and essentialist. We find more compelling, and not at all contradictory that we take part of his theory without adhering completely to another part, his theory of fields, because we think that it reposes the issues of an "education science," and its manifestations in a debate over doctoral degrees, in a different light. In the next part of this section, we discuss Bourdieu's ideas of the habitus, but we end this section emphasizing his notion of fields and the struggles by and for them.

Bourdieu's "Habitus"

Habitus explains how individuals act to reinforce class structures. Bourdieu has offered very little in the way of a concise definition of habitus but has said that

> [t]he habitus is not only a structuring structure, which organizes practices and the perception of practices, but also a structured structure: the principle of division into logical classes which organizes the perception of the social world is itself the product of

130. Ibid., 153–54.

internalization of the division into social classes. Each class condition is defined, simultaneously, by its intrinsic properties and by the relational properties which it derives from its position in the system of class conditions, which also is a system of differences, differential positions, i.e., by everything which distinguishes it from what it is not and especially from everything it is opposed to; social identity is defined and asserted through difference.[131]

The habitus, for Bourdieu, appears to be the embodied form of class dispositions, which are determined by class divisions. It apprehends differences between conditions and practices in accordance with principles and processes of differentiation that are perceived by individuals as natural. Thus, class structures are misrecognized by individuals (because of the habitus) as natural. The habitus, however, functions to dominate individuals by reinforcing class distinctions, and, therefore, class structures.

Others have explained the notion of the habitus a bit more clearly for us than has Bourdieu himself. The habitus has been defined as the internalized class norms that regulate individual practice.[132] It suggests socially constructed sets of embodied dispositions.[133] These dispositions are the embodied product of an individual's history, experience (especially in early childhood), and social location,

> becoming over time an ethos, a set of flexible but enduring mental structures and bodily schemas that organize, orient, and direct comportment in private and public space. . . . [The] habitus generates regular and immediate responses to a wide variety of situations without recourse to strategic calculation, conscious choice, or the methodical application of formal rules.[134]

In other words, the habitus is a system of schemes of perception and discrimination embodied as dispositions reflecting an entire history of the group and acquired through the formative experiences of childhood.[135]

The habitus is both constituted by social practice and constitutes social practice. First, it is constituted *by* social practices, which place limits on what is and is not thinkable, and on what are possible and sensible responses and what are not. Second, it is constitutive *of* social practices

---

131. Ibid., 170–72.
132. See Garnham, "Extended Review," 424.
133. See Robert Holton, "Bourdieu and Common Sense," *SubStance* 84 (1997): 38–52, 39.
134. Keith Topper, "Not So Trifling Nuances: Pierre Bourdieu, Symbolic Violence, and the Perversions of Democracy," *Constellations* 8, no. 1 (2001): 30–56, 38.
135. Roy Nash, "Bourdieu, 'Habitus,' and Educational Research: Is It All Worth the Candle?" *British Journal of Sociology of Education* 20, no. 2 (1999): 175–87, 177.

because it establishes the various hierarchies characteristic of social fields, the reproduction and transformation of social structures, and so forth.[136] For Bourdieu, the school, perhaps as much as the family, produces habitus by reproducing class distinctions.[137] The school functions, according to Bourdieu, as a site where competencies are constituted, and where the competencies are given positive or negative sanctions, reinforcing what is acceptable and discouraging what is not.

Given how schools have tended to reproduce social classes in Western societies, especially because, paradoxically, they do so by denying this reproduction and by exalting individualism, Bourdieu's arguments about habitus appear particularly seductive. But ultimately we find problematic the ontological status his theory of habitus confers to the idea of *class*, as if it had an empirically verifiable content of its own. It seems, in other words, to overdetermine class behavior and sets up too problematic a dichotomy between a dominant group and a dominated group. To be fair, Bourdieu argued that the habitus is not infallible,[138] and he indicates that his theory is governed by neither notions of agency nor structure. Thus, the habitus, he argues, in containing principles for the generation and structuring of practices, can be understood without presupposing a mechanical adherence to rules or an orchestration of the "action of a conductor."[139] It is hard for us to see, however, how the habitus does not entail a mechanical adherence to rules, since interpersonal relations are "never, except in appearance, *individual-to-individual* relationships and that the truth of the interaction is never entirely contained in the interaction,"[140] or since the habitus "engenders all the thoughts, all the perceptions, and all the actions consistent with the particular conditions in which it is constituted."[141]

The notion of the habitus appears to us to assume too much about class structures and too little about human agency. We think it overdetermines class structures, indicating that class distinctions are more static and stable over time and space than seems to be the case, thus, determining too completely individual action on the basis of social position. It also underestimates human agency, which clearly is constrained by class structures, but is not completely captured or defined by them. Individuals do exercise, following Judith Butler, an agency that emerges from the margins of power.[142] As Butler points out, while Bourdieu's habitus provides one important way

136. Topper, "Not So Trifling Nuances," 39.

137. Nash, "Bourdieu on Education."

138. Bourdieu, *Distinction*, 461.

139. Pierre Bourdieu, *Outline of a Theory of Practice*, trans. Richard Nice (Cambridge: Cambridge University Press, 1977), 72.

140. Ibid., 81.

141. Ibid., 96.

142. Judith Butler, *Excitable Speech: A Politics of the Performative* (London and New York: Routledge, 1997), 156.

of understanding how individuals incorporate class norms and conventions, it nevertheless fails to account for how individuals, once initiated by the habitus, resist and confound those norms and conventions that regulate them. When individuals resist those norms—by, for example, refusing to abide by traditional gender classifications—they essentially open up the habitus, Butler indicates, to an unpredictable future.[143]

Thus, while we are less sanguine than others might be about the theory of habitus, we do think that Bourdieu's notion of the struggles within and between cultural fields seems relevant to our reading of the discourse on the culture of science in education, and its corollary claims about the EdD versus the PhD. Cultural fields are shaped by habitus, but our understanding of the theory of fields need not rely upon class consciousness for our use of it as an interpretive scheme. It seems to us, at any rate, that the relevant question is not whether theory and practice, or research and practice, are important distinctions in themselves. The question should be: How does the academic field grant authority to an institution to recognize one, both, or neither as legitimate and worthy? The power to legitimate things within fields is what needs to be studied, for such power reinforces social structures but obscures this effect. It is to this concern that we now focus our attention.

Struggles Within and Between Fields

We propose that the academic distinctions associated with education doctoral degrees, such as the distinctions between researcher/practitioner and practice/theory, are created by the academic field, which faces challenges within itself and from other professional fields for the power to distinguish and to dominate by doing so. Distinctions are the effects of power relations among groups within these fields, but they appear in a misrecognized form because their logic is that of distinction.[144] In other words, these distinctions take place within particular cultural fields, which mark and reinforce group relations by establishing differences, and in academe, in particular, the worth of a position is marked by its relative distance from practical necessity. We say this even though the discourse on science and education purports to solve the problem of how research can be made useful to practitioners. In this sense, then, scientific knowledge in education will have "practical necessity." But note that the practical necessity that characterizes the knowledge produced by the scientist does not constitute a necessity for the scientist—whose legitimacy is, after all, marked by his or her distance from the "noise" constituting educational practice—but *for the practitioner.*

Scholastic culture—indeed, any "legitimate" culture—gains legitimacy, Bourdieu argues, by its ability to suspend and remove economic (or

143. Ibid., 142.
144. Garnham, "Extended Review," 425.

practical) necessity and its objective and subjective distances from practical urgencies.[145] The affirmation of power over *necessity* always implies a claim to a legitimate superiority over those who remain dominated by ordinary interests and urgencies.[146] Moreover, universities and other research institutions teach respect for the "natural" authority of scientific and pedagogic reason, and thus establish an array of hierarchies among individuals and activities, of which neither group needs to demonstrate its practical utility in order to be justified. Thus, the research institution by definition establishes a division between the practical, the partial, the tacit *know-how*, and the theoretical, the systematic, the explicit *knowledge*, a division that also creates other divisions, such as theory/practice and researcher/practitioner but also thought/methods, conception/execution, and so on.[147] Therefore, the knowledge produced by the new education scientists will be necessary *for education practitioners*, but its legitimacy, and why it is effectively dominant, is premised on its being produced by experts who are themselves *distinguished* from the former and their necessities.

This constitution of distinctions, degrees, and experts takes place within the education field. Fields are mutually supporting combinations of intellectual discourses and social institutions, which have no reference to realities beyond themselves but function to legitimate social institutions, which also have no absolute meaning beyond themselves.[148] Thus, education signifies a cultural field in which the power of individuals and institutions is largely (but not completely) determined by the cultural capital they own. Capital can take the form of academic credentials, liberal education, wealth, scholarly reputation, and, more on point, scientific legitimacy. Cultural capital is the effect of the arbitrary distinctions that maintain group coherence and legitimate social domination.

The field of education, moreover, determines the conditions by which relations within it take place. Cultural fields (and their subfields) are governed by specific laws of practice that determine both the conditions of entry into the field (e.g., economic capital, professional degrees, social connections) and the specific relations of force within it (e.g., who is authorized to speak and how). The education field may determine, for example, that the PhD will be worth more than the EdD in academe because the former credentials researchers, which are valued more than practitioners within institutions of higher education. Or, the field may legitimate scientific knowledge over and against, say, practical knowledge because the former is the province of the privileged few in the academy. Of course, in the actual field of educational

145. Bourdieu, *Distinction*, 54.
146. Ibid., 56.
147. Ibid., 387.
148. Derek Robbins, "The Practical Importance of Bourdieu's Analyses of Higher Education," *Studies in Higher Education* 18, no. 2 (1993): 151–63.

practice, that is, in schools, "practical knowledge," and thus the practitioner, may be privileged. These contradictory rules of practice indicate that fields are relatively autonomous from each other in the sense that distinctions valuable in one field or subfield (e.g., academe) are not necessarily valuable in another (e.g., in schools). Thus, the privilege given to theory over practice in higher education may not be easily translated into a similar privilege in the nonacademic workplace, which, indeed, may privilege the inverse, that is, practice over theory.

While fields are relatively autonomous from each other, they face constant struggles within themselves and with other fields. Thus, the distinctions that will matter in higher education, such as research or practice and disinterested knowledge or social utility, are constantly contested by those seeking to establish their own distinctions as more worthy than others. And the relations between education and other fields are constantly shifting as the power to legitimate distinctions is gained by one or another field. To discuss academic distinctions, such as the PhD/EdD, researcher/ practitioner, theory/practice, without accounting for the struggles within fields and between fields misses altogether the temporality of particular orderings, as power relations within and between fields do shift. In other words, the power to distinguish is, we think, what should be explored with regard to the discourses on science in education and not necessarily particular distinctions, as those change when the power to create them shifts. Distinctions are important, however, to the extent, and only to the extent, they refer one to this power.

One may say, for example, that conflicts over doctoral degrees reflect constant power struggles within the academic field over what knowledge is most worth knowing—theoretical or practical—and which practices are most worth pursuing—research, teaching, or practice. Furthermore, one can say that these conflicts, and the reforms that attempt to codify one or another kind of academic practice,[149] reflect, on deeper analysis, struggles and challenges made within fields (i.e., those between the "real" scientists and the nonscientists). Or these struggles may reflect conflicts between fields (i.e., between academic and professional fields). With regard to this latter point, the academic field exerts its power to control the other professions by granting or withholding its degrees, or seeking to make its academic degrees invaluable in these fields, but the latter fields may seek to maintain their predominance over the academic field by forcing it to abide by its (often economic) interests and urgencies. The polemics by scholars such as Veblen, Hutchins, and Dewey thus can be viewed as attempts to justify cultural distinctions that will give their versions of reality greater authority over those that challenge them. They seem to be responding to struggles over which

---

149. See, for example, ASRE, or Levine's *Educating School Leaders*, or Eisenhart and DeHaan's "Doctoral Preparation," or indeed any and all of these reports.

knowledge and practices are most worth pursing, as well as to challenges to institutions of higher education made by the professions. Such struggles are always, as Bourdieu suggests, between the "dominated fractions of the whole and the dominant fractions over the definition of the accomplished man and the education designed to produce him."[150]

Indeed, schools of education, which gain their legitimacy by privileging both academic and practical knowledge, are interstitial sites for the reworking of important relations between the academic and other professional fields. The academic field creates agents whose cultural capital, and thus, power is achieved by academic distinctions (i.e., degrees, scientific knowledge, etc.). But the "new masters of the economy," as Bourdieu has called them, have played this academic game too, and, one may say, their successes were impossible otherwise. They now rationalize their worldviews and their dominating practices through what Bourdieu calls a "management science," developed particularly within the discipline of economics, and which provides them with the sense of possessing an authority of intellectual right over the conduct of society.[151] Following Bourdieu, we think that the opposition between the "disinterested" culture of the intellectual or academic, and the "practical" and mundane culture of the other professionals and semiprofessionals has manifested itself in education in anti-intellectualism, that is, a belief in the "impractical," "unreal," "ivory-tower," and "useless" knowledge of the scholar, and an exaltation of the "what works," or "what is useful for practitioners and policy makers," knowledge of the applied scientist that the federal government, the NRC, and those scholars like Eisenhart and DeHaan seek to install in schools of education.[152]

The important point here, however, is that political struggle takes place within and between cultural fields over distinctions. As Derek Robbins points out, academic institutions do not manufacture students who possess universally valid qualifications that offer corresponding opportunities of employment (or, "research careers," as ASRE proposes).[153] Occupational opportunity provides a point of conflict in the struggle between the academic and professional fields to develop their own mechanisms for reproducing and differentiating themselves. The struggle is one in which the field of academics attempts to sustain institutional and ideological independence from other fields, while the field of the professions and other economic fields, particularly industry

---

150. Bourdieu, *Distinction*, 92.

151. Ibid., 315.

152. We do want to acknowledge, with Bourdieu, that for their part intellectuals might find a structural homology with other economically and culturally dominated groups, but they too have an interest, paradoxically, in "disinterestedness," and in all other values that are recognized as highest (*Distinction*, 317). Thus, intellectuals may find affinity with the dominated groups, but as *intellectuals* they maintain dominance over those groups by distinguishing themselves from them.

153. Robbins, "The Practical Importance of Bourdieu's Analysis."

and commerce, wish to use their own criteria for selection. The professional field seeks to appropriate the values of academe (such as the value of credentials) while the academic field seeks to accommodate the professional fields: through institutions specifically established to meet perceived needs of industry and commerce (such as professional schools), or, more on point, of practitioners and policy makers in education, and through the accommodation in the curriculum of values such as work-experience and work-based learning. This accommodation seems the point when Labaree advocates that schools of education must "sell" the researcher view to teachers,[154] and when Eisenhart and DeHaan argue that the PhD program in education research "should be separated from (but include parts of) the doctoral training for practice-oriented educational leadership."[155]

If we are correct, the discourse on the science of education, and its bureaucratic incorporation in the form of doctoral degrees, reflect struggles between the academic and other professional fields, each incorporating aspects of the other in order to dominate the other, or, at least, to thwart the threat to its legitimacy by the other. That the EdD exists as a "practice-oriented" degree is in some way a reflection that the university is losing its absolute authority to dictate what counts as valuable knowledge and cultural practice, and that it must accommodate the world of work if it is to continue to have dominance as a cultural field. Marie Brennan notes that the EdD may reflect a necessary pragmatic reaction to the pressure for increased credentials among professional groups, thereby enabling the university to live up to its "service" function for professional groups and attract students for funding faculty in times of competitive pressures.[156] Although the EdD is treated as a second-class degree in the academic field, an attitude that we think will be exacerbated by the instantiation of a "culture of science" in education research, this should not be seen as resulting from any "true" or "real" debate about research versus practical knowledge, or as having any objective meaning in itself. The EdD reflects a compromise that allows for the necessary expansion of higher degrees but which does not compete with the central function of the PhD as an induction into research and the academy generally.[157] In other words, the dual degrees in education reflect a state in the struggle within and among professional fields over the distinctions that will govern the world.

It seems to us, moreover, that the fact that the EdD and PhD programs do not necessarily adhere, in a material way, to distinctions established by the academic and other professional fields—they are often very much

---

154. Labaree, "The Peculiar Problems," 21.
155. Eisenhart and DeHaan, "Doctoral Training," 9.
156. Marie Brennan, "Education Doctorates: Reconstructing Professional Partnerships Around Research?" *Australian Universities' Review* 38, no. 2 (1995): 20–22, 20.
157. Ibid., 20

alike—illustrates that struggles within the academic field over what is worthy are quite strong. The academic field does not have the internal coherence that perhaps the other professional fields have, and thus its internal struggles may prevent it, paradoxically, from completely thwarting challenges from other fields but also from being completely dominated by them. In other words, the academic field cannot avoid the power of the distinctions the professional fields make because its struggles make it susceptible to challenge, but the struggles within it prevent those distinctions from completely taking hold because they are constantly being challenged.

These struggles, we must stress, reflect the mechanisms of power at work. To put any position in a distinction above another is to gain control over the power to do that. And one must understand power for that very fact, rather than attempt to explain a distinction as if it did not have meaning beyond itself. The power to distinguish is what is at stake in cultural fields, but this power is obscured by the embodiment of the distinctions themselves—the distinctions appear natural, obvious, and inevitable. Individual and group identities shape themselves according to these distinctions. Bourdieu explained this embodiment through his theory of the habitus. We are not sure if he was correct in this regard, but, clearly, understanding why and how individuals incorporate regulatory norms is important (an issue beyond the scope of this book). But this understanding begins, we propose, by seeing distinctions as effects of power and struggle.

Power works by establishing difference and binaries that are set up in opposition to each other, and in education some important ones are theory/practice, micro/macro, education/training, researcher/practitioner, and science/nonscience. Such binaries mislead and become more real than the processes they aim to represent.[158] Understanding them as such provides the possibility of critical agency. We are not interested, therefore, in maintaining what appears to be a structuralist view of the social order in Bourdieu's theory, particularly that of the habitus, but we find compelling the part of his theory that suggests the power of, and struggles within, cultural fields. We believe also that while those fields provide significant constraints on individuals' ability to think and act, they too are subject to unpredictable futures when individuals act unconventionally. Our overall purpose in this chapter, however, is not to provide an answer to which distinction matters in the "culture of science" and the EdD/PhD debate it perpetuates; indeed, if our premise is correct, no epistemological ground exists from which to do so. We merely seek to have academics think differently about the distinctions they make, and to spark discussion about the power of academic institutions to structure the world. In the next section we conclude the chapter

---

158. See Michael Grenfell, "Bourdieu and Initial Teacher Education: A Post Structuralist Approach," *British Educational Research Journal* 22, no. 3 (1996): 287–306.

by teasing out the implications of our argument for the doctoral training of educational researchers.

"DEGREE OF DISTINCTION"

This chapter attempted to pose in a different light the question of whether or not one needs a degree credentialing researchers over and against one credentialing practitioners. Indeed, a "need" is unrecognizable outside of the discourses about needs, which attempt to gain control over social resources by dictating how an issue will be constructed and practiced. Thus, to make a claim about any need is to engage, as Nancy Fraser argues, in a politics of needs interpretation.[159] We believe one should avoid viewing the need for either the EdD or PhD, or any manifestation that seeks to distinguish researchers from practitioners, as a reflection of a particular reality and instead engage in a study of how mechanisms of power establish, discursively and materially, the need—and distinction—in the first place.

Academic distinctions, such as theory/practice, researcher/practitioner, disinterested knowledge/social utility, scientist/nonscientist—the first term in each distinction being the privileged one in the academy—and their materialization in the certification individuals receive from doctoral programs in education, exercise a kind of domination, in that when one position is privileged over another, individuals are coerced to see themselves as more or less worthy than others depending on whether they believe themselves to be in the privileged position. More significantly, distinctions foreclose positions available for individuals to be. One must pay attention to who or what is authorizing and legitimating particular distinctions, for what purposes, and how they become embodied and thus reproduced. Such inconspicuous forms of domination, denigration, and exclusion often go unnoticed because the distinctions supporting them appear so obvious and unremarkable; they appear to be beyond the arenas of power and politics.[160]

Yet, distinctions within and between degrees, like most distinctions, are elements of power and politics. Each degree, being more or less worthy than the other, depending on the privilege given, maintains its definition and authority by its degree of distinction from the other. Indeed, it is the degree of distinction itself that is marketable. The EdD, or any degree signifying the privilege given to practical knowledge and social utility, allows one to market the claim that the theoretical knowledge provided by the PhD is unimportant, and the point of educational institutions is to train people for the world of work or for speaking to practitioners and policy makers, as we often hear in education discourse. But the holder of the PhD, or any degree

---

159. Nancy Fraser, "Talking About Needs: Interpretive Contests as Political Conflicts in Welfare State Societies," *Ethics* 99, no. 2 (1989): 291–313, 292.
160. Topper, "Not So Trifling Nuances," 42.

signifying the primacy of the research function and scientific knowledge, can market the opposite claim. Individuals, however, are regulated by either position and by the distinction. They incorporate the distinctions as being "what they are" and "what they are not." Each degree, therefore, may signify struggles over the power to create, to differentiate, to legitimate groups, and thereby to dominate the world through such creation, differentiation, and legitimation.

We do not propose, however, the end of doctoral study as such. It can be offered a new purpose, less instrumentalist and domineering for society than the discourse on the culture of science requires. But we must, first and foremost, resist the gutter utilitarianism, or the "what works" mentality, that already, in our opinion, characterized the field of education research long before the current federal government stepped in. Indeed, note how Lauren Jones, who provides an introduction to a special issue of *Educational Researcher* on doctoral preparation, *delimits* what such study can be:

> For example, how should children be taught to read or to engage with mathematical ideas? Should failing schools be reconstituted? How might the achievement gap be closed? Fundamentally, improvements in children's learning and development hinge on the richness of our understanding, which, in turn, depends considerably on the quality of our research. We faculty in education need to address these questions head on ourselves in order to strengthen the preparation (and future research) of our graduate students, who are uniquely positioned to do this work, and to do it better, in a pluralistic, global environment.[161]

This gutter utilitarianism is also what supports the discourse on science in education, since science has now been installed in our society as telling us what to do, and that discourse will only limit inquiry to the kinds of questions we just quoted. Yet, is our purpose in education solely to create such narrow visions of an educational subject? Must researchers only inquire about the ways in which such subjects can be made functional in a "pluralistic, global environment"? The gutter utilitarianism of such questions is what actually makes these questions so unassailable: Who, after all, can argue against wanting to help children read, learn math, achieve like their peers? Who can argue against wanting to graduate doctoral students who will be "uniquely positioned" to accomplish those things? What kind of person would argue against *that*?

Well, we argue against such thinking and propose that the best way to *uniquely* position our graduate students is to resist the logic of a global

---

161. Lauren Jones Young, "Border Crossings and Other Journeys: Re-envisioning the Doctoral Preparation of Educational Researchers," *Educational Researcher* 30, no. 5 (2001): 3–5, 3.

world that actually oppresses them for their *uniqueness*. The logic of this global world is to create consumerist, conformist individuals, cogs in a global market. We might educate scholars who challenge that market, who work with others to resist it and to reimagine that world. We might graduate scholars who refuse to believe that the social classifications legitimated by educational institutions are *personal*, that is, that the classifcaions indicate something essential about individuals rather than about the effects of power, which continuously seek to position individuals in particular, and more recently, economic ways.

We might seek to help students be comfortable with the elusive, slippery, contentious, serendipitous nature of schooling and educational practice. Serendipity, change, and happenstance, after all, *are* features of learning and knowing, even though they fall outside standard accounts of idealized epistemology.[162] They also are features of great frustration in doctoral study for those who are trained to believe that sequence, order, and linear reasoning are paramount. We need to overcome the "one-way" linearity of formalism that undergirds the establishment of doctoral programs of study, even those that require that students graduate promptly. Students may need to take a break, or, given the vagaries of scheduling, their courses can never be guaranteed. This, too, is a lesson about the reality we face within the nexus of "ideal" programs of study and "practical" life issues that emerge in the course of doctoral study. Life happens. We are unable to justify certitude and fixity in a world that is contentious, elusive, and slippery. Rather than argue against serendipity, we recognize and embrace it, something the scientific mentality put forth by the SRE, the federal government, and others disdain.

It might appear worthy to reframe the issues associated with the doctoral degrees as Brennan proposes. She argues that the reactions to the EdD, and the approaches to its practice, embody quite divergent views about the nature of universities, knowledge production, and the place of the intellectual.[163] In particular, they reveal the habituated dualisms between vocational and academic education, between theory and practice, and between knowledge workers in universities and in other institutions. The EdD offers, Brennan argues, a means for restructuring relations between academic and other sites of knowledge and practice by demanding a reconfiguration of university research relations with other professionals in the field. In turn, this change of relations is made possible by altering the ways in which universities have conceptualized and taught research.[164]

---

162. See Toby J. Sommer, "Suppression of Scientific Research: *Bahramdipity* and *Nulltiple* Scientific Discoveries," *Science and Engineering Ethics* 7, no. 1 (2001): 77–104; Robert K. Merton and Elinor Barber, *The Travels and Adventures of Serendipity: A Study in Sociological Semantics and the Sociology of Science* (Princeton: Princeton University Press, 2003); and William Reinsmith, *Archetypal Forms in Teaching: A Continuum* (Westport, CT: Greenwood Press, 1992).
163. Brennan, "Education Doctorates," 20.
164. Ibid., 20.

Brennan's arguments have some merit, but ultimately they too fail to account for what is at stake in the struggle over educational doctoral study. We are not sure that privileging one degree over another adequately deals with the logic of distinction and its effects in structuring the social world in ways that maintain relations of domination. If the mechanisms of power, and the social relations they engender, are to be resisted, one must understand the power to regulate through the establishment of difference. Furthermore, distinctions are not only differences, but oppositions, and as such they contain latent hierarchies. We suppose it is possible to have differences that are not also oppositions, but we are inclined to believe that distinctions always, at their roots, take the form of oppositions.

Similarly, those apparently enticing arguments about preparing education researchers which value "practitioner research,"[165] arguments that, by the way, almost always receive retorts that such research is different from university research,[166] seem to fall into the trap set up by the struggle over the power to create distinctions. And we should avoid these distinctions at all costs. It might appear that we are in agreement here with those who call for a reform of doctoral study that requires students to engage in the multidisciplinary teams or projects,[167] or with those who ask that students attain the "multiple epistemological perspectives to the point that members of different communities of educational research practice can understand one another, despite, or perhaps through, their differences."[168] But we are not, as these arguments seem to us to reflect a kind of positivism, different but related to the NRC's understanding of science, that both implies the unity of scientific knowledge and assumes that through these endeavors we can more readily approach "the real."

Reba Page made an interesting argument in her discussion of doctoral study, particularly that the point of such study might be to create a "community of dissensus," in which differences are not necessarily reconciled but permitted to exist as part of the mix that illustrates the complexity of education and schooling.[169] This argument can be deceptively seductive for us, since it refuses to take a side in the diversity of opinions and forms of

165. See Gary L. Anderson, "Reflecting on Research for Doctoral Students in Education," *Educational Researcher* 31, no. 7 (2002): 22–25.

166. See Mary Heywood Metz and Reba N. Page, "The Uses of Practitioner Research and Status Issues in Educational Research: Reply to Gary Anderson," *Educational Researcher* 31. no. 7 (2002): 26–27.

167. See Mary Haywood Metz, "Intellectual Border Crossing in Graduate Education: A Report from the Field," *Educational Researcher* 30, no. 5 (2001): 12–18; see also Eisenhart and DeHaan, "Doctoral Preparation."

168. Aaron M. Pallas, "Preparing Education Doctoral Students for Epistemological Diversity," *Educational Researcher* 30, no. 5 (2001): 6–11, 7.

169. See Reba N. Page, "Reshaping Graduate Preparation in Educational Research Methods: One School's Experience," *Educational Researcher* 30, no. 5 (2001): 19–25, 24.

inquiry in education, but we would stress that the key point is not to create a community of experts, but to consider the democratic purposes of inquiry to which all study should be directed, as John Dewey instructs. Dewey regarded "specialists" as those who were only good at one or two things, thus violating his principle of interaction.[170] Indeed, if the purpose of the EdD or PhD is merely preparation of a practitioner or researcher, then we will forgo the dynamic understanding of knowing Dewey proffers, and we will be left with the well-worn and tired practice of preparing future specialists and experts devoid of connection and interaction with others.

Rather than seeking to create a cadre of experts who know the rigors of research and can produce highly unassailable knowledge, practical or otherwise, we might seek, as Susan Talburt argues, to have students speculate about unexpected connections, relations, and complications, which will necessarily be incomplete, tentative, and unverifiable. What students produce is not meant to be "applicable" in a traditional sense, but is meant to invite readers to think differently. In this way, education researchers will offer only narratives and interpretations that readers engage with in unexpected ways, including application to or speculation about contexts that bear no objectively apparent similarities.[171] We might do better for our students, Talburt suggests, if we simply help them take responsibility for thinking through, with, and against research. And thus, rather than seeking accurate representations, theory building, or even critical change, our forms of inquiry become ethical projects that implicate "its participants in relations of here and there, now and then, reader and writer, writer and subject, and reader and subject. This implication . . . comes from complication of our texts and a refusal of interpretive closure."[172]

We might thus deflect some of the attention from the researcher and his or her communities, and refocus attention on the reader, that is, the individuals who are to make sense of the scholarship produced in schools of education. We might ask doctoral students to create, as Talburt proposes via a reading of Roland Barthes, a "writerly text," one that acknowledges the reader as an active producer of the text, the reader as meaning maker rather than information consumer, one that enters not only our, that is, the academic and policy circle of conversations, but also extends it to other unpredictable ones.[173] The so-called "community of dissensus," we would argue, then, cannot be simply, or perhaps primarily, for us as scholars, but for those communities or array of readers, who, following Talburt, can be

170. John Dewey, Experience and Education (New York: Macmillan, 1938), 33–45.
171. Susan Talburt, "Ethnographic Responsibility Without the 'Real,' " Journal of Higher Education 75, no. 1 (2004): 80–103, 92.
172. Ibid., 95.
173. Ibid., 97.

offered avenues for creating conversations into which we cannot necessarily expect to enter.

Yet, we do want to maintain in education study some attention on the researcher and scholar, but we want to offer them a different role than that called for by the NRC and others. Following Jacques Derrida, we should strive in educational study to "awaken or to resituate a responsibility, in the university or in the face of the university, whether one belongs to it or not," a responsibility of a "community of thought" for which the boundaries between theory and practice, researcher and practitioner, disinterestedness and utility, can no longer be secured. This "thought" is *not* reducible to a technique, to a science, or even to a philosophy. And this community *cannot* be restricted to academic or scientific researchers. It must be democratic in its forms and speakers, and it must at all times be vigilant to the instrumentality to which such thought will always be put to use or reappropriated, since it necessarily takes place within certain historical, techno-economic, politico-institutional, and linguistic conditions.[174] But if we can offer this "community of thought" one common practice it is that it must always seek to ward off such uses and appropriations.

We conclude this chapter, however, by saying that no "writerly text" or "community of thought" is possible until we look *at* and *beyond* the distinctions we create. If distinctions are created within the field of education, and if they reflect power at work, then it is the distinctions themselves that individuals must avoid. To act unconventionally toward a distinction, such as a degree conferring scientific or practical competence, is to resist the lure of such a distinction, which is to say, to resist the effects of its power, to refuse to give the distinction legitimacy. That may be the critical measure of the doctoral degree in education—one that challenges distinctions as reflections of the power to create distinctions and to foreclose others. A "degree of distinction" may actually be one that allows an individual to question his or her degree of distinction from others.

174. Jacques Derrida, "The Principle of Reason: The University in the Eyes of its Pupils," *Graduate Faculty Philosophy Journal* 10, no. 1 (1984): 5–29, 20–21.

FOUR

"GOVERNING" SCIENCE

═══════════════════════════════

The Scientific Imaginary and the
Creation of People in the Information Age

Life and death appeared to me ideal bounds, which I should first break
through, and pour a torrent of light into our dark world. A new species
would bless me as its creator and source; many happy and excellent natures
would owe their being to me. No father could claim the gratitude of his
child so completely as I should deserve theirs.

—Mary W. Shelley, *Frankenstein*

ON "EDUCATION SCIENCE"

In our previous chapters, we sidestepped the question of what science is,
focusing instead on the contradictions and politics within the discourse on
science represented by the federal government, the NRC, and others. In
chapter 3 we theorized, via the debates over doctoral study, how the discourse
on science may be read as part of larger power struggles over social distinctions. In this chapter, we focus more explicitly on scientific classifications,
and so we take up the question of what science is, but not to give it the
answer that the question implies, that is, not to offer a philosophy of a science of education, for if our premise is correct, no epistemological ground
exists from which to do so.[1] We are not interested in what such a science

---

1. Here we refer to a standard definition of "philosophy of science," which is an attempt to
understand the meaning, method, and logical structure of science by means of a logical and
methodological analysis of the aims, methods, criteria, concepts, laws, and theories of science.
See E. D. Klemke, Robert Hollinger, David Wÿss Rudge, and A. David Kline, "Introduction:
What is a Philosophy of Science?" in *Introductory Readings in the Philosophy of Science*, ed. E.
D. Klemke, Robert Hollinger, David Wÿss Rudge, and A. David Kline (New York: Prometheus
Books, 1998), 19–26, 20.

might look like, but why it matters that there be a science of education in the first place. What is at stake in drawing a line between science and nonscience in the field of education? It is the need to ask the question of what science is that we grapple with in this chapter.

The unifying theme of the NRC report, we are told by some of its authors, is not the displacement of alternative forms of inquiry, as its critics charge, but the necessity of establishing a "scientific culture" within the field of education.[2] This sounds deceptively simple, but it is not, as we discussed in chapter 3. Moreover, the invocation of "culture" is anything but simple. If Edward Said is correct, "culture" must be seen as much for what it is *not* and for what it *triumphs* over as for what it positively is. Culture, then, is not simply, and perhaps not mostly, a matrix of meanings that we associate with home or community or nation or whatever; it is a system of discrimination and evaluations for a particular group able to identify with it. In other words, "culture is a system of exclusions legislated from above but enacted throughout its polity, by which such things as anarchy, disorder, irrationality, inferiority, bad taste, and immorality are identified, then deposited outside the culture and kept there by the power of the State and its institutions."[3]

The invocation of "culture," then, may be as much about exclusions and displacements as it is about unity. The NRC's invocation of a "scientific culture" in education research, therefore, warrants critical attention because it will involve the exclusion and displacement of other forms of inquiry. We see this invocation as an opportunity to think about, and to make explicit, the demarcations and classifications established by science. This might imply that we will argue that science is inherently or inevitably repressive, but we will not do that, at least not with a traditional notion of repression. Though he meant it in a different sense than we would, we think that Max Horkheimer is correct in saying that science is one of humanity's "productive powers."[4] We want to attend here, therefore, to science's *productive power*, and more specifically, its power to "make up people" and to govern them in particular ways.

Given this power, the invocation of a culture of science in education is to be treated with a similar kind of foreboding to that which Mary Shelley suggests in her story of the fate of Dr. Victor Frankenstein, who took it upon himself to supersede God in dictating life and death, as our epigraph indi-

---

2. Michael J. Feuer, Lisa Towne, and Richard J. Shavelson, "Scientific Culture and Educational Research," *Educational Researcher* 31, no. 8 (2002): 4–14, 6.
3. Edward S. Said, *The World, the Text, and the Critic* (Cambridge: Harvard University Press, 1983), 11.
4. Max Horkheimer, "Notes on Science and the Crisis," in *Social Theory: The Multicultural and Classical Readings*, ed. Charles Lemert (Boulder: Westview Press, 1993), 227–30, 227. Horkheimer used "productive powers" in the Marxist sense of a means of production.

cates. When Frankenstein gives life to the creature that he has constructed from corpses, he has interfered in the Creator's plans and is punished for it. We follow Shelley in providing a tale of warning here, but not for the same reasons. We certainly do not argue that science interferes with God's scheme, nor do we argue that scientific knowledge furthers oppression and should thus be rejected. Rather, our concern is with how the production of scientific knowledge governs the world. Science, under the guises of "objectivity," "nature," "precision," and "progress," has cast all the elements of social life—all individuals; all genders, races, species; all behaviors, desires, events—into its own determinative narratives. Scientific narratives have the most profound consequences for us; they produce the world we inhabit.[5] But because science appeals to objective methods that uncover or represent facts that purportedly speak for themselves, and often put forth as being for the betterment of society, it is legitimated with the authority of being outside politics. And it is because of this authority that we argue that the idea of a "science of education" should be rejected.

Our rejection of the idea of an "education science," ironically, makes our work a part of the discourse on science, a discourse that must accept this criticism if much of what scientists say about themselves is to be believed. The skepticism that scientists believe themselves to have, which sparks them to constantly test their findings, leading them to believe themselves to be engaged in the progress of knowledge and society, cannot but admit a skepticism directed at what they do qua scientists. Thus, our critique, as critique, irrespective of its content, is part and parcel of what science has endured since its emergence, probably in the sixteenth or seventeenth century.[6] We are not naive, however, and thus we know that our critique will likely be ignored by scientists, since scientists have imagined for themselves a world in which they need only respond to other scientists. In many ways, therefore, each of us feels like an intruder in this discourse on science, or, like Susan Wells, an

> academic eavesdropper, a more or less imperfectly informed observer who is not, at least not in this role, a sanctioned member of the scientific discourse community, which takes membership very seriously. My position is both privileged and precarious. Overhearing a discourse not addressed to me, unable to speak directly with its readers and writers, unable to understand much of what is being said or all of what is being meant, I face the perennial embarrassment

---

5. Laura Dassow Walls, "Textbooks and Texts from the Brooks: Inventing Scientific Authority in America," *American Quarterly* 49, no. 1 (1997): 1–25, 20.

6. Leo Marx, "Reflections on the Neo-Romantic Critique of Science," *Daedalus: Journal of the American Academy of Arts and Sciences* 107, no. 2 (1978): 61–73, 61.

of eavesdroppers: how can I report, publicly, what I was not meant to hear?[7]

Even if we are given the benefit of the doubt and read by the very community we speak about, we are also not naive enough to think that it will not survive this recent critique, as it has done many times before. Nevertheless, critique we must, and, to be sure, the skepticism required by scientific thinking, if it is to be taken at face value, would demand nothing less. And, if the community that we speak about does not heed us, then hopefully those it seeks to govern will.

But, what kind of critique is ours? If Leo Marx is correct, the critiques of science can be classified into two kinds: those focusing on science as a mode of cognition and those focusing on science as an institution.[8] The first kind, a critique of science as a mode of cognition, is what we think most of the critiques levied against the NRC report and other elaborations on an education science have been. This kind of critique questions whether the conception of reality implicit in scientific methods is adequate to our experience. The second kind of critique directed at the institution of science questions whether the methods and products of scientific inquiry are compatible with the expressed and tacit goals of our society.[9] We find the first kind of critique rather tedious, and after Thomas Kuhn and Michel Foucault, as we explain later, not particularly novel or important.[10] Any attempt at understanding science as a mode of cognition, that is, any philosophy of science, merely reflects what we believe at a particular moment in our history, and perhaps this is an engaging academic pastime, but it is nothing more.

Our critique, then, if Marx's classification has merit, will likely fall into the second camp. We critique the institution of science, though we do not ask whether science is compatible with society's goals, at least as Marx explains it, since such a conceptualization presupposes an order of operation that we will question rather than assume: that society is *before* science, such that it has particular goals, distinct from those of science, to which the latter must be compared. We think it wise to question this order of operation and to ask whether it is possible that the more accurate order is in reverse. That is, is it possible that science creates much of what counts as "society," so that the goals of science are indeed those of society? We think science has the

7. Susan Wells, *Sweet Reason: Rhetoric and the Discourses of Modernity* (Chicago: University of Chicago Press, 1996), 60.

8. Marx, "Reflections on the Neo-Romantic Critique of Science," 62.

9. Ibid.

10. Thomas S. Kuhn, *The Structure of Scientific Revolutions*, 2nd ed. (Chicago: University of Chicago Press, 1970); Michel Foucault, *The Order of Things: An Archeology of the Human Sciences* (New York: Vintage Books, 1970); Michel Foucault, *The Archeology of Knowledge and The Discourse on Language*, trans. A. M. Sheridan Smith (New York: Pantheon Books, 1972).

power to tell us what society *is*. Thus, we find it important to disturb the actual order of operation (i.e., science before society), and to argue actually for the assumed order (i.e., society before science), so that the question of whether science's goals are compatible with those of society will become an actual question of debate, rather than a rhetorical device for obscuring a symptomatic form of power in the (post)modern age.

What we want to do in this chapter, in short, is to implicate scientists in what the world is and how the world functions—not as outside observers who intentionally or unintentionally influence social reality through the knowledge they produce, but as instrumental to the creation of that reality. This means that we will read the discourse on education science as *political*. By this, we follow Fredric Jameson in arguing for the priority of the political interpretation of texts. The political interpretation of texts does not simply assume that scientific texts have political resonance; it deems itself the "absolute horizon of all reading and all interpretation."[11] Jameson locates this absolute horizon in Marxist theory, but we do not define the political horizon so grandly or so narrowly, depending on one's view. We mean only to say that for us the political interpretation of texts seeks to understand how people are created and governed, and economic considerations, while perhaps very significant, are but parts of the strategies of governing.[12] We are not simply saying, therefore, that the discourse on scientific research in education will have political effects, but that such research is itself political. Indeed, the idea that research has political effects constructs a temporal space between the act of research and its effects on the world. We want to argue against such temporality, and to say that the world cannot reach us—it is unavailable to us—except through narratives, the most important in Western cultures being the narratives coming from science.

Wells argues that among the texts of modernity, none are more forbidding than those of the sciences, particularly the natural sciences, to which the social sciences seem to aspire, with all their equations, graphs, charts, and inaccessible language—barely language at all, actually.[13] But, despite their difficulty, these texts are read and cited, and the impact on the world these texts have is undeniable. Wells also points out that despite the difficulty of reading scientific texts by nonscientists, there is an academic practice of reading the "rhetoric of science," a mode of inquiry that seeks to understand these texts as labors of language.[14] We think this is a good practice, and we hope it is taken up rigorously in the field of education now

---

11. Fredric Jameson, *The Political Unconscious: Narrative as a Socially Symbolic Act* (Ithaca: Cornell University Press, 1981), 17.

12. We will, however, take up economic considerations of the discourse on science in our final chapter.

13. Wells, *Sweet Reason*, 53.

14. Ibid., 54–55.

that its privileged research must qualify as "scientific." But our interest here lies less in reading actual scientific texts than in reading *science as a text*, a text that represents a symptomatic form of power in the modernist era: the creation of "souls" and their "government."

In the next section, we summarize how scholars answer the question of what science is. We reread this discourse as elaborating what we call a "scientific imaginary," manifesting particular directives in the information age. We then offer a *political* reading of this imaginary, that is, we offer a reading that situates science as part of the practices of government, or the techniques for regulating the behavior of individuals. Scientific discourses are not the only techniques for governing individuals, of course, but we argue they are the most powerful. We then conclude with elaborations of why scientific discourses have such power. We propose that scientific narratives are *performative*, in the sense that they enact what they purport to describe or explain. We conclude by offering education researchers an alternative way of thinking about their work.

THE "SCIENTIFIC IMAGINARY"

The NRC argues that scientific inquiry involves "a continual process of rigorous reasoning supported by a dynamic interplay between methods, theories, and findings. It builds understanding in the form of models or theories that can be tested."[15] We think that the NRC's philosophy of science is well supported by previous philosophies of science. But we also think it is instructive to ask, not whether the NRC's view accurately represents what scientific inquiry is, but what kind of subject does it conjure up? Who, or what, is the scientist it imagines will be conducting education research?

We read into the NRC's philosophy of science the elaboration of a number of ideas about the scientist, which we call, collectively, the "scientific imaginary." We borrow from psychoanalysis the notion of the "imaginary," which we offer not as a psychology of the scientist, but as a metaphorical device that allows us to represent what the discourse on science conjures up as the scientist. The imaginary is the realm of illusions and images that we idealize as our selves and to which we direct our desires.[16] The scientific

15. National Research Council, *Scientific Research in Education*, ed. Richard J. Shavelson and Lisa Towne (Washington, DC: National Academy Press, 2002), 2. Available at http://www.nap.edu/ (Retrieved February 5, 2005).
16. Briefly, Jacques Lacan locates the "imaginary" first in the infant's "mirror stage," the stage when the child identifies himself with his image in a mirror. The significance of this stage is that the child, who previously only understood himself in fragments (e.g., a hand, a foot) and who saw only "others" (e.g., a parent, a sibling), now sees and understands a "self." But this understanding of a self is a misrecognition, since the self that is recognized is simply that of an image, which is idealized as the self. See Jacques Lacan, "The Mirror Stage as Formative of the Function of the I as Revealed in Psychoanalytic Experience," in *Écrits: A Selection*, trans. Alan Sheridan (New York: W. W. Norton, 1977), 1–7.

imaginary in the NRC report, and in other proposals for a science of education, conjures up a new "education scientist" on the basis of certain ideas of
what a scientist is imagined to be. There may be more, but we deal here with
just four: (1) the scientist is objective; (2) the scientist is concerned with
the empirical; (3) the scientist must "tame chance"; and (4) the scientist
ensures progress. We explain, and critique, these ideas in order.

The Scientist is Objective

In our reading we discovered competing philosophies of scientific practice.
It appears to us, however, that these philosophies generally propose that
the scientist engages in two kinds of practices. First, whether dealing with
natural or social phenomena, the scientist explains general regularities by
subsuming them into general laws or theories.[17] Second, and perhaps most
importantly, whatever theories are posited, the scientist must engage in a
process of falsifying, refuting, and testing his and others' theories.[18] The
NRC appears to imagine the scientist in the same manner. That is why it
proposes that scientific research in education must build understanding in the
form of models or theories that can be tested. But why are these practices
privileged as scientific? To us, they seem necessary because how else can
one trust that the scientist is speaking objectively? The positing of theories
that must be tested is what ensures that scientific knowledge is "objective."
Karl Popper says as much when he argues that what distinguishes scientific
inquiry from other forms of inquiry is its objectivity. The scientific method
is objective, he argues, because its task is not to determine truth per se,
but to eliminate theories. It relies upon the need for the espousal of many
theories and for the severe tests of those theories.[19] The scientist, then, is
not personally or politically invested in her theories.

There is something paradoxical about this premise of theory building
with testing. Following Wells, we think this premise seems to ask us to
read science in this way: the scientist claims to have found something he
posits as, at least temporally, "true," but also invites others to prove him
wrong. Thus, the scientist speaks the truth of what he utters but must appear indifferent to it; the scientist will tell us what he truly believes but
then invite others to challenge that belief.[20] So, if we look in education for
what the NRC imagines the scientist to be, then what we are going to see

17. See, for example, Carl G. Hempel, "Studies in the Logic of Explanation," in *Introductory Readings in the Philosophy of Science*, ed. E. D. Klemke, Robert Hollinger, David Wÿss Rudge, and A. David Kline (New York: Prometheus Books, 1998), 206–44, 207, 212.

18. See, for example, Karl Popper, "Science: Conjectures and Refutations," in *Introductory Readings in the Philosophy of Science*, ed. E. D. Klemke, Robert Hollinger, David Wÿss Rudge, and A. David Kline (New York: Prometheus Books, 1998), 38–47, 42.

19. Karl R. Popper, "What is Dialectic?" *Mind* 49, no. 196 (1940): 403–26, 404.

20. Wells, *Sweet Reason*, 58–59.

is the proliferation of researchers who will tell us what they think is true of education, but also ask us not to believe it.

The idea that the scientist is objective, paradoxical as it is, works because it is premised on the model of the scientist offered by the natural sciences, where, arguably, it appears possible to step back and discard all of one's "cultural baggage." But what is particularly remarkable to us about this notion of objectivity, and what allows us to call it a crucial part of the scientific imaginary, is that this idea seems accepted even by many epistemologists and many sociologists of knowledge, who propose that knowledge is socially determined or constructed, which means, in a sense, that all knowledge is "cultural baggage."[21] Robert Merton, for example, in elaborating upon what he called "insider" versus "outsider" knowledge (that is, knowledge about a group by those within the group versus knowledge about a group by those outside the group) argues that sociological understanding

> includes an empirically confirmable comprehension of the conditions and often complex processes in which people are caught up without much awareness of what is going on. To analyze and understand these requires a theoretical and technical competence which, as such, transcends one's status as Insider or Outsider. The role of the social scientist concerned with achieving knowledge about society requires enough *detachment* and trained capacity to know how to assemble and assess the evidence without regard for what the analysis seems to imply about the worth of one's group.[22]

A social scientist can have such "detachment," it appears, only when she brackets off or controls for any emotional or political commitment to her group, or even to the theories she proposes.

We can, even with cursory look, locate the idea of scientific objectivity in a larger imaginary: the Western Rationalist Tradition, or the scholarly ideal of the disinterested inquirer engaged in the quest for objective knowledge that will have universal validity, as John Searle proposes it to be.[23] We also need not look too far to see the fallacy of this idea. For example, Said

---

21. See Charles W. Mills, "Alternative Epistemologies," in *Epistemology: The Big Questions*, ed. Linda Martin Alcoff (Oxford: Blackwell, 1998), 392–410; Steve Fuller, *Social Epistemology* (Bloomington: Indiana University Press, 2002); Frederick F. Schmitt, *Socializing Epistemology: The Social Dimensions of Knowledge* (Lanham: University Press of America, 1997); Karl Mannheim, *Ideology and Utopia: An Introduction to the Sociology of Knowledge*, trans., Louis Wirth and Edward Shils (San Diego: Harcourt, 1936); and Robert K. Merton, *Social Theory and Social Structure* (New York: The Free Press, 1968).

22. Robert K. Merton, "Insiders and Outsiders: A Chapter in the Sociology of Knowledge," *American Journal of Sociology* 78, no. 1 (1972): 9–47, 41. Emphasis added.

23. John R. Searle, "Rationality and Realism, What is at Stake?" *Daedalus: Journal of the American Academy of Arts and Sciences* 122, no. 4 (1993): 55–83, 69.

describes how the West has come to understand itself as a contrast to the
"Other," a process supported by a host of vocabularies but especially those
of science.[24] What we know about ourselves in the West may have been
cultivated during the many years of its colonial rule, which was exercised
first through force, then through "culture," especially the creation of history,
geography, literature, and the like, which worked by differentiation, exclusion,
and the creation of "others."[25] Scientific knowledge, therefore, cannot be
deemed "objective," since it serves always a political imperative of exclusion
and separation, now not strictly and perhaps not even primarily through
force, but through—and this is more insidious—what counts as good, just,
beautiful, and so on, and, consequently, through abjection.

Yet, this idea of objectivity is not simply fallacious, since such an ac-
cusation presupposes that it is possible to have an objective science, even
if we do not have one now. The idea of objectivity in science is also an
impossibility. If Kuhn is correct about paradigms in the natural sciences,
then scientists cannot be "objective" in the sense presumed by Popper and
others. Paradigms are universally recognized scientific achievements that
for a time provide model problems and solutions to a community of practitioners.[26] "Normal science," which is supported by the prevalent paradigm,
does not discover new things; it only confirms what its paradigm requires it
to confirm. Anomalies, which arise, paradoxically, because of the practice
of constant testing, when they appear, do not appear as new "facts" at all.[27]
When the anomalies persist, as they will, scientists seek to reconcile them
with the existing paradigm; if they fail, it is the fault of the scientist, not the
theory.[28] When anomalies cannot be reconciled with the prevailing paradigm,
then the paradigm is replaced by another, a process that Kuhn refers to as
revolutionary, since the world in which the scientist operates changes:

> [P]aradigm changes do cause scientists to see the world of their
> research-engagement differently. In so far as their only recourse to
> that world is through what they see and do, we may want to say that
> after a revolution scientists are responding to a different world.[29]

A different world indeed: different "problems" emerge, different "facts" are
discovered, different theories become the object of experimentation, different

24. Edward Said, *Orientalism* (New York: Pantheon Books, 1978), 39–46; see also Linda Tuhiwai Smith, *Decolonizing Methodologies: Research and Indigenous Peoples* (London: Zed Books,
1999).
25. John Willinsky, *Learning to Divide the World: Education at Empire's End* (Minneapolis:
University of Minnesota Press, 1998).
26. Kuhn, *The Structure of Scientific Revolutions*, viii.
27. Ibid., 53.
28. Ibid., 80.
29. Ibid., 111.

achievements become universally accepted, different methods are created, and different texts are written, all to fit the new paradigm. One can say in reading Kuhn, therefore, that scientific objectivity, possible only within a paradigm, is actually an inability to see any other alternative, an inability to see the world differently.

Similarly, Foucault argues that it might be more instructive to refer to scientific theories as discursive events rather than as "truths," even temporary ones, which presuppose empirical verification. He instructs us to question how it is that a particular scientific statement appeared as opposed to another.[30] By statement, Foucault means a function in a system of dispersion, a system in which knowledge is grouped, separated, used, limited, challenged, appropriated, and so on. Groups of statements form discourses. Discourses systematically form the objects of which they speak; they are thus *practices*. And groups of discourse form *archives*. Somewhat like Kuhn's paradigm, we think, an archive is the general system of the formation and transformation of statements. An archive cannot be completely described, and it is not possible to describe our own archives. All we can do, it appears, is to describe its possibilities on the basis of those discourses that are no longer valid or sayable. A science, for Foucault, therefore, is not linked to that which must have lived, or is lived, that is, not to the empirical domain, but to that which must have been said—or must be said—if a discourse is to exist that complies, if necessary, with the experimental or formal criteria of "scientificity." "Knowledge," scientific and otherwise, is that of which we speak in a discursive practice, and any discursive practice may be defined by the knowledge that it forms.[31]

To take on the ideological functioning of a science in order to reveal or modify it, Foucault argues, is not to uncover the philosophical presuppositions that may lie within it, or to return to the foundations that made it possible and that legitimated it, but to question it as a discursive practice, that is, to question its formation of its objects, its types of enunciation, its concepts, its theoretical choices—it is to treat it as one practice among others.[32] In other words, the point of a history of ideas, for Foucault, involves discovering how objects constitute themselves in *discourse*, how they are entered into sorts of *laws*, and how they fall under certain *kinds* of things.[33]

Kuhn's and Foucault's histories seem to render any philosophy of science problematic, since what counts as "science" is less a particular mode of cognition that can lay claim to universal validity than professional or cultural norms of what can be said and not said. Thus, they open the door

30. Foucault, *The Archeology of Knowledge*, 27.
31. Ibid., 182–83.
32. Ibid., 186.
33. See Ian Hacking, "Michel Foucault's Immature Science," *Nous* 13, no. 1 (1979): 39–51, 51.

to the history and sociology of science.[34] Yet, their arguments are often easily misunderstood by many scholars, even by important philosophers of science. For example, Popper misunderstands the sociology of knowledge when he argues that it emphasizes science as a process in the mind of the scientist, and that it fails to account for the social aspects of the scientific method, from which scientific objectivity does not result via the attempts of the scientist to be objective but from the "friendly-hostile co-operation of many scientists."[35] This is not what the sociology of knowledge does at all. The point is not that there are no "scientific facts," but that, as Karl Mannheim points out, such facts are always asserted in an intellectual and social context.[36] This view is premised on the idea that society is constitutive of human beings, and that society's influence extends into the structures of human experience in the form of ideas, concepts, and systems of thought.[37] We think the socially determined or socially constructed view of scientific knowledge[38] would be problematic for Popper because it appears to put the privilege accorded to science into question. Yet, he need not have worried too much, for scientific knowledge does have a privileged position *in* society, even if it is not outside *of* society. We need only ask from this why it holds such a privileged position in our society.

Now that education research will ostensibly become more "scientific," we hope educational scholars seek to understand scientific "thought," not "thought as such" but the ways social and historical conditions give such thought intelligibility. We hope, that is, for history and sociology of "education science." Our task in this chapter, however, is not to account for what the scientists actually *say* but to what they *do* in saying something. So, yes, we offer an account of scientific knowledge, but only to explain how that

---

34. Kuhn's and Foucault's work are two of the most important in the history of science; for an important work in the sociology of knowledge, see Peter L. Berger and Thomas Luckmann, *The Social Construction of Reality: A Treatise in the Sociology of Knowledge* (New York: Anchor Books, 1966).

35. Karl R. Popper, *The Open Society and its Enemies, Volume II, The High Tide of Prophecy: Hegel, Marx, and the Aftermath* (Princeton: Princeton University Press, 1962), 217.

36. Mannheim, *Ideology and Utopia*, 102.

37. E. Doyle McCarthy, *Knowledge as Culture: The New Sociology of Knowledge* (London and New York: Routledge, 1996), 1.

38. McCarthy identified two propositions within the sociology of knowledge. The first is that knowledge is socially determined, a proposition that has dominated the sociology of knowledge since its inception. This was the view of Mannheim and Merton, and it assumes that all human thought and consciousness develop out of real life, the actual social conditions that particular individuals share (see Mannheim, op. cit., 22n; Merton, op. cit., 22n). The second proposition, epitomized by Berger and Luckmann, is that knowledge constitutes a social order, and it assumes that knowledges are not merely the outcome of the social order but are themselves key forces in the creation and communication of a social order (see Berger and Luckmann, op. cit., 35n). The latter proposition seems to receive the greatest attention today (McCarthy, *Knowledge as Culture*, 12).

knowledge gains the power to enact what it says, how science is *political* in that way, and what consequences for education, and thus for society, such power entails.

The idea of the objective scientist is part of the scientific imaginary that will be idealized in education research if the supporters of an education science get their way. We are to imagine science and politics as separate and distinct kinds of practices. But we might wonder instead how it became possible to conceptualize a difference between political and scientific practice in seemingly apolitical terms.[39] What happens to education when it is dressed up as "scientific," and thus apolitical? Does it lose, ironically, its political potential to create the better world we hope for by invoking an education science? We do not think it loses its political potential to create worlds, and, indeed, it will gain a powerful discourse for doing so, but we fear that in doing that it will be imagined as apolitical, distinct from politics, and removed from democratic critique as a result.

The Scientist Is Concerned with the Empirical

At the risk of being tautological, education research, if it is to be scientific, will constitute a *social* science. No one that we know of argues that the study of education phenomena can qualify as anything but that. The NRC's idea that scientific research in education must build understanding in the form of models or theories that can be tested empirically will make education research a social science, but the idea itself is premised on the philosophy of the natural sciences. Yet, there is universal agreement—indeed, even to mention it appears like the basest of truisms—that the social and natural sciences each deal with distinct kinds of phenomena. The NRC committee sees no paradox in proposing for the study of the social realm what is considered "natural" for the study of the natural realm, obviously, because in typical positivist fashion, it collapses diverse fields of scientific inquiry into a particular scientific imaginary, one premised on a unity of knowledge, which the study of natural phenomena appears to offer.

But the belief that the social sciences should be like the natural sciences is not universally shared. While there is almost universal agreement that the social and natural sciences address themselves to different phenomena, there is almost universal disagreement about whether they share a common philosophy of science. The only valid recourse for the social sciences, it appears to us, given this debate, is either to appropriate the philosophies of the natural sciences or to establish their own. The most common philosophy of social science that is not premised on that of natural science typically looks like Charles Taylor's, who proposes that while natural science proceeds from

39. See Jens Bartelson, *The Critique of the State* (Cambridge: Cambridge University Press, 2001), 26–29.

mathematical inference and empirical verification, the "sciences of man" must be based on interpretation.[40] Interestingly, Kuhn takes exception to Taylor's distinction between the natural and social sciences, arguing that knowledge in the natural sciences is also culturally dependent and thus is also interpretive.[41]

Yet, a science of education, if we are to understand the NRC committee's logic, can have no other model for understanding itself than that of the natural sciences. Indeed, how else can it call itself a science? Even arguments that the social sciences are interpretive in nature do not question the model of the natural sciences as valid; they question only whether that model suits the social sciences. This desire to be like the natural sciences, therefore, is worth exploring farther. Roger Trigg points out that the enormous success of the modern physical sciences in manipulating the world has made it appear that their methods provide the key for the extension of human knowledge in all areas. So any discipline that seeks legitimacy must appear "scientific" in precisely the manner in which, say, physics is; otherwise it may be deemed not to produce any contributions to genuine knowledge at all.[42] Thus, despite the fact that two competing philosophies guide our understanding of the social sciences—humanism, which deems humans different from physical objects and sees the function of the social sciences as interpreting and rendering the social realm intelligible rather than invoking causes; and naturalism, which takes natural science as its model and seeks to establish laws and causality—it is the latter, naturalism, which has had the most influence on the social sciences.[43] The NRC report, in distinguishing "scientific education research" from other interpretive approaches, such as history, philosophy, and even much of qualitative inquiry, appears to privilege naturalism as the philosophy that guides its vision of an education science.

Naturalism in the social sciences comes in many guises, but what seems to shape it is the positivist belief in the unity of the sciences, the irrelevance of metaphysical claims, and an empiricism that assumes that the aim of science is to measure, describe, control, and predict observable facts.[44] A major tenet of this empiricism is a separation of fact from value, and thus the privileging of a "value-free" science. Social scientists should

40. Charles Taylor, "Interpretation and the Sciences of Man," in *Complementary Methods for Research in Education*, 2 ed., ed. Richard M. Jaeger (Washington, DC: American Educational Research Association, 1997), 293–323, 297–98.

41. Thomas S. Kuhn, "The Natural and Human Sciences," in *Introductory Readings in the Philosophy of Science*, ed. E. D. Klemke, Robert Hollinger, David Wÿss Rudge, and A. David Kline (New York: Prometheus Books, 1998), 128–34, 132–33.

42. Roger Trigg, *Understanding Social Science: A Philosophical Introduction to the Social Sciences* (Oxford: Basil Blackwell, 1985), 2.

43. Ibid., 2–3.

44. Ibid., 3–4.

establish "facts" about society in the same way that we believe a physicist or a chemist uncovers "facts."[45] The irony is that this belief in a "value-free" science, as we explained, is as fallacious in the natural sciences as it is in the social ones.[46] There can be no removal of value from science, as Richard Rudner argues, since no scientific hypothesis is ever completely verified, and in accepting a hypothesis the scientist must make a decision that the evidence is *sufficiently* strong or that the probability is *sufficiently* high to warrant the acceptance of the hypothesis.[47] But that is neither here nor there, for the idea of a value-free science that comes from focusing entirely on the empirical realm is part of the scientific imaginary; thus, it is an idealized illusion of the scientist, which, in turn, also becomes the object of her desire and what she strives for more than anything else.

If the idea of objectivity is traceable to the Western rationalist tradition, from where does the idea of the empirical come? It too comes from Western rationalism, but more specifically we think it is traceable to a theory of empiricism espoused by David Hume. For Hume, all objects of inquiry may be divided into two kinds: "relations of ideas and matters of fact," and the latter is determined by the relations of cause and effect, by which, and arguably only through which, we can go beyond the mere evidence of our memory and senses.[48] Knowledge of this kind is not

> attained by reasonings *a priori*; but arises entirely from experience, when we find that any particular objects are constantly conjoined with each other. . . . [Thus the] proposition, that causes and effects are discoverable not by reason but by experience will readily be admitted.[49]

Hume's theory of empiricism evolved into positivistic theories of experience, which focus strictly on that which can be observed and separates "facts" from "interpretations." But such strict positivism is likely untenable today. And so Margaret Eisenhart is likely correct when she argues that the NRC's notion of empiricism is probably a postpositivistic one, since it can accommodate the "role of *both* patterned behavior and human intentionality in human activity."[50]

---

45. Ibid., 6.

46. See David L. Miller, "Science, Technology, and Value Judgments," *Ethics* 58, no. 1 (1947): 63–69, 63.

47. Richard Rudner, "The Scientist *Qua* Scientist Makes Value Judgments," in *Introductory Readings in the Philosophy of Science*, ed. E. D. Klemke, Robert Hollinger, David Wÿss Rudge, and A. David Kline (New York: Prometheus Books, 1998), 492–98, 493.

48. David Hume, "An Enquiry Concerning Human Understanding," in *The Empiricists: Locke, Berkeley, Hume* (New York: Anchor Books, 1974), 307–430, 322–23.

49. Ibid., 324.

50. Margaret Eisenhart, "Science Plus: A Response to the Responses to *Scientific Research in Education*," *Teachers College Record* 107, no. 1 (2005): 52–58, 53. Emphasis in original.

The NRC report is postpositivistic in another sense: its idea of empiri-cism, perhaps unintentionally, gives way to theory. The NRC argues that education scientists must develop theories or models that can be tested empirically. Thus, while the realm of the scientist is the empirical, this realm is intelligible only via theories that give it coherence. The NRC does not imagine a scientist that poses metatheories, since that would take the scientist far askew of the empirical realm, but the research must be linked to "relevant" theory. Jeffrey Alexander argues that in the social sciences, there is consistent disagreement about the precise nature of empirical knowledge, and arguments about scientific truths do not, and cannot, refer only to the empirical level. They cut across the full range of nonempirical commitments which sustain competing points of view.[51]

Positivism, in its strict sense, rejects theory in favor of pure sense expe-rience. It treats social interactions as if they were the "colliding of physical objects," and explains why behaviorism, which seems predominant in educa-tion, has led to systemic exclusion of whatever could not be scientifically tested in a laboratory-like setting.[52] Postpositivism emphasizes sense experience but also assumes that our ability to understand the social realm is limited, not just by the limits of measurement but also by the fact that competing theories hold sway. The existence of multiple theories means also that any "empirical" claim in the social sciences is also an attempt to "rationalize and systematize the intuitively grasped complexities of social analysis and social life. . . . They reflect efforts by [social scientists] to articulate criteria for evaluating the 'truth' of different non-empirical domains."[53] Thus, as Trigg argues, in the social sciences it is not a question of neutral observations forming the basis for theory; the observations we make, the way we classify them, and even what count as relevant observations, are governed by the theories we hold. The NRC report is, then, representative of theoretical shifts in the social sciences, and its claim that an education scientist deals with theories that can be tested empirically actually reflects that the social sciences have indeed moved away from the strictly empirical (i.e., sense data) to the role of theory or the conceptual schemes for making sense of the world.[54] Thus, we can say that the notion of the education scientist as concerned with empirical facts is an illusion of the scientific imaginary.

We can critique the idea of empiricism in the social sciences from another angle as well, one even more fundamental than the point that social scientists privilege the nonempirical while arguing otherwise. The human sciences, if Foucault's study of biology, philology, and economics is even remotely correct, are under a significant misimpression: that "man" is an

---

51. Jeffrey Alexander, "Postpositivist Case for the Classics," in *Social Theory: The Multicultural and Classic Readings*, ed. Charles Lemert (Boulder: Westview Press, 1993), 557–62, 558.
52. Trigg, *Understanding Social Science*, 41.
53. Alexander, "Postpositivist Case for the Classics," 561.
54. Trigg, *Understanding Social Science*, 9.

empirical reality. "Man" is a recent creation, and probably reflects no more than a transformation in how we conceptualize the order of things. Order, for Foucault, is anterior to words and perceptions, which are then taken to be more or less exact expressions of it. It is important to ask in what ways a culture has made manifest the existence of order.[55] Before the end of the eighteenth century, *man* did not exist. In the classical age, there was no specific domain proper to man, that is, there was no difference between "nature" and "human nature"—all appeared in an ordered continuity of beings.[56] Classical thought was encyclopedic, represented best by the figure of a table in which the human being might appear next to a tiger. There was only nature, a continuous order of things. For Foucault, the eclipsing of classical thought occurred when natural history became biology, when the analysis of wealth became economics, when reflections upon language became philology, and when man appeared in his ambiguous position as an object of knowledge and as a subject that knows. Modern thought begins when man became an "empirical individual," of an order that now belongs to things themselves and which has interior laws.[57]

The belief that man's experience is an empirical reality, of all time and for all time, would indeed make the question Foucault asks below seem aberrant, if not crazy:

> The true contestation of positivism and eschatology does not lie, therefore, in a return to actual experience . . . but if such a con-testation could be made, it would be from the starting-point of a question which may well seem aberrant. . . . The question would be: *Does man really exist?* To imagine, for an instant, what the world and thought and truth might be if man did not exist, is considered to be merely indulging in paradox. This is because we are so blinded by the recent manifestation of man that we can no longer remember a time, and it is not so long ago, when the world, its order, and human beings existed, but man did not. . . . Ought we not to remind ourselves—we who believe ourselves bound to a finitude which belongs only to us, and which opens up the truth of the world to us by means of our cognition—ought we not to remind ourselves that we are bound to the back of a tiger?[58]

The point we want to stress here is that one of the most significant ideas of the scientific imaginary—"man as empirical reality"—may be premised on a nonempirical conception of order. The human sciences appeared when man

---

55. See Foucault, *The Order of Things*, xxi.
56. Ibid., 309.
57. Ibid., 312–13.
58. Ibid., 322. Emphasis added.

constituted himself in Western culture as that which must be known and which can know himself. Man "became that upon the basis of which all knowledge could be constituted as immediate and non-problematized evidence; he became, *a fortiori*, that which justified the calling into question of all knowledge of man."[59] Empiricism, then, is an illusion, for the social sciences are systems of thought by which man represents himself to himself.

If, therefore, we must take a side in the debate over a philosophy of social science, those who argue in favor of its interpretive, rather than empiricist, basis seem more accurate to us. (Of course, Kuhn pointed out that the natural sciences are also, when all is said and done, interpretive too.) And yet, the scientific imaginary idealizes the notion of an empiricism that determines theory, and not the other way around. Is it because the empirical realm still offers the chance for measurement and precision, while the world of interpretations does not?

The Scientist Must "Tame Chance" (in the Informational Society)

Friedrich Nietzsche wrote that science has been our way of "putting an end to the complete confusion in which things exist, by hypotheses that 'explain' everything—so it has come from the intellect's dislike of chaos."[60] This dislike of chaos, for Nietzsche, explains why "mechanistic" interpretations of our world "stand victorious," and why "no science believes it can achieve progress and success except with the aid of mechanistic procedures."[61] We think Nietzsche alludes to an important component of the scientific imaginary: the need to "tame chance," a phrase we borrow from Ian Hacking's brilliant study of the use of statistics in Western societies.[62]

Before we provide a reading of this need to tame chance in the scientific imaginary, we would like to alert the reader that we will situate this narrative within larger political forces which make it possible and which it in turn makes possible, namely, the imperatives of what can be termed the "informational society."[63] If science is, as Horkheimer indicated, one of humanity's "productive powers,"[64] then we want to ask, what exactly does it *produce*? It produces scientific knowledge about the world, of course. But perhaps not *of course*, for if our premise is correct that the creation and manipulation of information is a key aspect of our political landscape, then we must rethink

---

59. Ibid., 345.
60. Friedrich Nietzsche, *The Will to Power*, ed. Walter Kaufman, trans. Walter Kaufman and R. J. Hollingdale (New York: Vintage Books, 1967), 324.
61. Ibid., 332.
62. Ian Hacking, *The Taming of Chance* (Cambridge: Cambridge University Press, 1990).
63. "Informational society" refers broadly to a phenomenon in which the creation and manipulation of knowledge has become the basis for cultural, economic, and political activity. See generally Manual Castells, *The Rise of the Network Society* (Oxford: Blackwell, 1996).
64. Horkheimer, "Notes on Science and the Crisis," 227.

such knowledge as having a particularly salient role to play. We will argue that science produces a world of "data," which (1) allows that world to be "tamed," and (2) converts it into "information" for easy administration. We discuss the taming of the world first, then its "informationization."

Taming Education. The need to tame chance probably comes from, again, the natural sciences, which are characterized by a "widespread instinctive conviction in the existence of an *Order of Things,* and, in particular, of an *Order of Nature.*"[65] This order is hidden, of course, and so our task is to uncover it. We must control for indeterminancy in order to uncover the secrets of nature. What is interesting about the need to tame chance, which is perhaps premised on a dislike of chaos, is that it comes concomitantly with the belief that our world is actually governed by chance. Hacking explains that the most decisive conceptual event of the modern era has been the discovery that the world is not deterministic; causality, or the idea that the past necessarily determines what happens next, was toppled, and a space was cleared for chance. Coinciding with the evolution of the belief in chance also came the practice of the enumeration of people and their habits by state bureaucracies. That is, society became statistical.

Statistics, as the word itself suggests, were originally data collected by state bureaucrats to aid them in carrying out the affairs of government. These bureaucrats derived their statistics from censuses, cadastral surveys, tax rolls, public health records, crime statistics, and other sources, and they allowed its readers not only to summarize facts but also to discover social truths.[66] These two events, the belief in indeterminancy and the enumeration of people, brought into being laws, analogous with those of nature but pertaining to people, expressed in terms of probability. These laws carry with them the connotations of normalcy and of deviations from the norm.[67] These laws, in other words, create "normal people," defined as such if they conform to the central tendency of such laws, while those at the extremes are pathological.[68]

The idea of the "normal," as Hacking explains, has always been part of a pair: its opposite is the pathological. For a short time, its domain was chiefly medical, but then it moved into the sphere of everything: people, behavior, states of affairs, diplomatic relations, molecules—all these may be normal or abnormal. The word *normal* became indispensable because it created a way to be "objective" about human beings.[69] In a sense, the concept

---

65. Alfred North Whitehead, *Science and the Modern World* (New York: The New American Library, 1925), 11. Emphasis in original.
66. Lisa Anderson, *Pursuing Truth, Exercising Power: Social Science and Public Policy in the 21ˢᵗ Century* (New York: Columbia University Press, 2003), 9.
67. Hacking, *The Taming of Chance,* 1.
68. Ibid., 2.
69. Ibid., 160.

of the normal tames the indeterminable human "beast." The magic of the word is that we can use it to say two things at once: how things are and how things ought to be. The normal stands indifferently for what is typical, the unenthusiastic objective average, but also for what has been and for what needs to be. That is why the benign and sterile-sounding word *normal* has become one of the most powerful ideological tools of our time.[70]

The taming of chance, coinciding with the creation of a "society of statistics," made up people: the normal, the pathological, the educated, the poor, and so on. Population studies, with their classifying practices, put people into categories.[71] With the pervasive classification taking place in schools, we might inquire, how are people made up? When and how, for instance, were the "gifted," "the ADHD," the "intelligent," the "at risk," the "high achiever," and for that matter, the "leader," the "teacher," the "educated citizen" made? Hacking proposes that in thinking about "making up people" two vectors of analyses might be useful: the vector of labeling, pressing from above by a community of experts who create a "reality" that people make their own; and the vector of the autonomous behavior of the person so labeled, which presses from below, creating a reality every expert must face.[72]

But all this is not simply a matter of creating people by the social sciences. From their statistics could also be developed statistical laws which did not need theory, only numbers. One need only collect more numbers and regularities (and anomalies) would appear. The more numbers one has, the more inductions one can make.[73] These laws did not matter just for their own sake; they dictated freedom and constraint. "Statistical fatalism," therefore, was born, according to which if a statistical law applied to a group of people, then the freedom of individuals in that group could be constrained.[74] In this way, institutionalized violence is made "scientific." Yet, the scientist, now powered by the magic of numbers, cannot be held responsible for such violence, since she could appear to be simply and neutrally explaining human behavior through "laws of nature." The scientist is apolitical, and thus not subject to political control, since she is simply developing laws from numbers and other kinds of data: she can say, "The truth is in the numbers, not in the scientist." (One can see how this narrative links up with the first: the scientist is objective.)

To see events and people as "data," however, whether quantitative or qualitative, required a radical break in how the world was ordered. As

---

70. Ibid., 169.
71. Ian Hacking, "Making Up People," in *Reconstructing Individualism: Autonomy, Individuality, and the Self in Western Thought*, ed. Thomas C. Heller, Morton Sosna, and David E. Wellbery (Stanford: Stanford University Press, 1986), 222–36.
72. Ibid., 234.
73. Hacking, *The Taming of Chance*, 62–63.
74. Ibid., 121.

Thomas Popkewitz explains, it required both: (1) the objectification of the individual, so that the inner characteristics of the person could be known as data and used for change—the individual, that is, became an "empirical fact" that could be observed and made an object of knowledge, irrespective of the feelings and values of the observer; and (2) the reinscription of the data into positive strategies by which groups and individuals would become agents of change.[75] The social world, and its individuals, could now be made into "things" that could be ordered systematically and taxonomically within a functional system that was administrable.[76]

The problem of modern science, natural and social, is to make observable that which was previously hidden so as to make it subject to administration. To do this, scientists must fix space in time, so that the former becomes understandable in terms of, and only in terms of, the latter—people, schools, and events develop and change *in time*—and this is important since time could be measured in a linear, sequential way. This need to tame chance is irresistible. Let someone propose an antistatistical idea to reflect individuality or to resist creating probabilities of the universe, and the next generation effortlessly co-opts it so that it becomes part of the standard statistical machinery of information and control.[77] Precise measurement controls for indeterminacy, and so the task of the social scientist is to develop precise measures in a world that resists it, and precisely because this world is understood as resisting precision, more and more sophisticated mechanisms are necessary to tame it.

We may now read *SRE* or any attempt at establishing a science of education as a very significant political act in the administration of individuals. Given the indeterminacy of the world, the enumeration of people, and the needs of administration, we can now create an education scientist who will carry a very powerful and very particular function in this world. This education scientist will come into the school precisely because schools resist statistical laws. Indeed, this resistance is not only the problem the scientist seeks to solve, but is also the very reason why she was invited into the school in the first place; its resistance is a spark for more measurement and precision. The invocation of a culture of science of education, therefore, has to be understood as part of this mechanism of taming chance and the "statistical fatalism," or scientific violence, to which it inevitably leads. The newly created education scientist will be graciously invited into a realm of absolute indeterminacy, the public school, in order to measure it, to establish its laws, to make up its people, and, in short, to "tame" it.

75. Thomas S. Popkewitz, "A Changing Terrain of Knowledge and Power: A Social Epistemology of Educational Research," *Educational Researcher* 26, no. 9 (1997): 18–29, 19.
76. Ibid.
77. Hacking, *The Taming of Chance*, 141.

Informationization of Education. There is another aspect of the taming of chance, to which we already alluded, that warrants discussion: the taming of chance permits the transformation of knowledge into information. The measurement and precision the taming chance requires allows for the transformation of all that was previously imprecise, indeterminable, and unknowable into "data." Jean-François Lyotard wrote that the nature of knowledge in the postmodern age has undergone (and is undergoing) dramatic change, largely as a result of the proliferation of information-processing machines. "Knowledge" is being transformed into "quantities of information," easily translatable into databases, easily used by anyone with a computer, and easily exchanged and sold. This "informationization" of knowledge also transforms relations between and among myriad institutions and individuals, all of which are being converted into "data" that can be stored in a database. So knowledge must now fit new channels and become operational only if learning is translated into quantities of information.[78]

We should ask ourselves how much of what "education" now means to us can be represented by the figure of the "database." Institutions, individuals, education, teaching, learning, diversity—everything and anything—can be converted into an information byte and stored in a database. Indeed, "accountability," a concept appearing often throughout contemporary education discourse, is unintelligible outside a system of databases, a system that gives us what we now call knowledge, which then is turned back on the system to spark conversions of new things into data. The figure of the database, by the way, is a metaphorical device and is not meant literally. One can see the logic of the "database" in what we see is a rise in encyclopedia, compendia, edited books, treatises, and other sources that purportedly provide all-engulfing or comprehensive information in one easily transferable place.

We may say that we have been attending to only part of the problem with the federal government's privileging of experimental research in education, especially of the type that is collected and reported in the What Works Clearinghouse (WWC). Recall that the WWC aims to promote informed education decisions through a set of easily accessible databases and user-friendly reports that provide "education consumers" with ongoing, high quality reviews of the effectiveness of replicable educational interventions that intend to improve student outcomes.[79] It also puts forth guidelines for determining the validity of studies, privileging the randomized field trial. We thought of this privileging of the randomized field trial, and the mechanistic logic of reporting them in its particular ways, as ideological, as dictating a

---

78. Jean-François Lyotard, *The Postmodern Condition: A Report on Knowledge*, trans. Geoff Bennington and Brian Massumi (Minneapolis: University of Minnesota Press, 1984, c. 1979), 4.
79. What Works Clearinghouse, *Who We Are* (Washington, DC: Institute for Education Sciences, n.d.). Available at: http:www.whatworks.ed.gov/whoweare/overview.html (Retrieved April 18, 2005).

narrow scientism for education research. It is that, to be sure, but it may not be only that. If knowledge must be transformed into information, as required by the new channels of cultural and economic exchanges, then the experiment is not merely a scientific method, it is also a technology of informationization, that is, a technology for transforming knowledge into a database. The WWC will require that experiments in education be conducted in particular ways, will collect their results in particular ways, and will report them in particular ways, not only because this privileges a narrow vision of the knowledge of education, but also because this will permit the easy reduction of educational knowledge into information bytes that anyone can use and manipulate for whatever purposes they wish, since information is "democratic"—anyone can use it and manipulate it. Indeed, we wonder whether the NRC knew this all along, and its attempt to define an education science that was not reducible to the experiment of the type the WWC requires was actually a way of legitimating the expertise of the scientists of a very specialized knowledge, one the scientific community, and only that community, can decipher and validate.

For how long will we be able to think of education outside of a system of databases? This "informationization" of knowledge, we must stress, is not simply a *practical* matter. That is, the information is not just useful for acting upon the individuals and institutions in education. The "informationization" is also an *epistemological* matter, for it will become what we can know, and an *ontological* matter, for it will become what *is* education. Moreover, as we indicated, this informationization of knowledge is also *technological* in that it makes all phenomena numerical, calculable, and reproducible.[80] This point will make even more sense if one heeds what Walter Benjamin indicated is one of the most significant forces shaping modernity: reproducibility, where the reproduction of things becomes the end.[81] In other words, reproducibility, brought about by technological progress, becomes the logic of production, so that the end of productive forces becomes solely the *reproduction* of objects. The originals are no longer valued as such; they are valued to the extent they can be reproduced. What we lose is the essence, uniqueness, and authenticity of the object itself; we lose its value for itself and for the moment.[82] We may see this, then, as the problem to which the discourse on the science of education now addresses itself: education research, and thus education itself, is not reproducible. The "what works" logic is a logic

---

80. See Nigel Thrift, "Movement-Space: The Changing Domain of Thinking Resulting from the Development of New Kinds of Spatial Awareness," *Economy and Society* 33, no. 4 (2004): 582–604, 584–85.
81. See John Lechte, "Walter Benjamin," in *Fifty Key Contemporary Thinkers: From Structuralism to Postmodernity* (London and New York: Routledge, 1994), 203–207, 204.
82. Walter Benjamin, *The Work of Art in the Age of Mechanical Reproduction* (Los Angeles: UCLA School of Theater, Film, and Television, n.d., c. 1936). Available at http://www.marxist.org/reference/subject/philosophy/works/ge/benjamin.htm (Retrieved August 26, 2005).

of reproducibility and informationization. And so now the discourse on education science, and the need to tame chance in the scientific imaginary supporting it, make a certain kind of sense: we will need an education scientist who will "tame" the irreproducibility of education, one who will restructure education, convert it into data, so that education can be fixed *in* time, reproducible, efficient, easily transferable, and for *all* time.

The Scientist Ensures Progress

Richard Rorty seems correct to us when he points out that there are two desiderata for the vocabulary of the social sciences: (1) it should contain descriptions that permit prediction and control; or (2) it should contain descriptions that help one decide what to do.[83] The first desideratum is actually a desire to be like the natural sciences, since the need to predict and control is a major tenet of their philosophies, as we have been saying. This desire also is probably at the root of why behaviorism is a predominant ideology in the social sciences. What behaviorists seem to agree upon is that the test of a good social science should be its ability to predict and explain observable behavior, whether of individuals or groups.[84] The second desideratum implies that the social sciences are inherently utilitarian, and, arguably, unlike the natural sciences, do not, and cannot, subscribe to a notion of knowledge for its own sake. The social sciences *serve* some *one* or some *thing*. We will reinterpret this second desire as the idea that the scientist ensures progress, an idea that makes the other three ideas of scientific imaginary thinkable.

The idea of progress is evident in the NRC's two reports on scientific research in education that we have discussed in this book. The NRC states in *ASRE* that "a basic premise of our work is that the pursuit of scientific understanding can be a powerful tool for the betterment of society."[85] This belief in the notion of science as progress was even more evident in the section of *SRE* that has received considerably less attention in the literature than the other sections, that is, the section of the report providing guidelines for fostering a scientific culture in a federal education research agency. After all, the NRC states, the "federal government has an important and legitimate role in supporting research as a public good, including research in education."[86] What strikes us about this statement is how presumptive it is.

---

83. Richard Rorty, "Method, Social Science, and Social Hope," in *The Postmodern Turn: New Perspectives on Social Theory*, ed. Steven Seidman (Cambridge: Cambridge University Press, 1994), 46–64, 52.
84. Alexander Rosenberg, *Philosophy of Science*, 2nd ed. (Boulder: Westview Press, 1988), 59.
85. National Research Council, *Advancing Scientific Research in Education*, ed. Lisa Towne, Lauress L. Wise, and Tina M. Winters (Washington, DC: The National Academies Press, 2005), 15. Available at http://www.nap.edu/ (Retrieved February 5, 2005).
86. *SRE*, 127.

Why are we to take as given that the federal government's role in supporting research is *important*, *legitimate*, and a *public good*? We are certain that some readers of this book will think that our even asking such a question proves that we have come from outer space, or, more accurately, that we are crazy, since to "come from outer space" actually requires scientific advancement. But here is the point: science always takes progress, and thus itself, as given. "American culture," our sense of ourselves in relation to others, our superiority over others in the world, is based on scientific prowess. Many of us look to science to tell us what we are—what we are in the natural world, and what we are in the social world—and what we are not—we are not "backward," "primitive," "underdeveloped" like *them over there*. Some of us might look at science negatively, either because we have Luddite-like tendencies or because we see science as contrary to our religious faiths. But whether or not we accept science, it defines us positively or negatively in relation to itself. What is at stake in this whole discourse on science, therefore, is the determination of who and what we are and who and what we are going to be. And these are high stakes indeed.

The idea of science as progress has been contested, of course. Paul Feyerabend argues, for example, that all ideologies, including scientific ones, should be deemed fairytales, which have interesting things to say but also wicked lies, and scientific ideologies, like most ethical prescriptions, may provide useful rules of thumb but are deadly when followed to the letter.[87] Science's ideological character, for Feyerabend, consists primarily in the belief that it produces good results. Also, the criticism of science by the often-called "postmodernists" rejects the empiricist, positivist, rational-logical model of modern science, a criticism made possible not only by skepticism toward its metanarratives, but also by, among other things, an impatience at the failure of modern science to produce the results it promised.[88]

Nevertheless, there is considerably widespread belief in the idea of science as a sign of progress, and this belief illustrates most clearly that modernist beliefs still have force in our society. The idea of science as progress reflects the modernist belief that knowledge can be used for the social good, and, if the NRC reports are any indication, it appears to be as strong today as it was almost eighty years ago when Sigmund Freud stated that "civilization . . . includes . . . all the knowledge and capacity that men have acquired in order to control the forces of nature and extract its wealth for the satisfaction of human needs."[89] What characterizes the sciences since

---

87. Paul Feyerabend, "How to Defend Society Against Science," in *Introductory Readings in the Philosophy of Science*, ed. E. D. Klemke, Robert Hollinger, David Wÿss Rudge, and A. David Kline (New York: Prometheus Books, 1998), 54–65, 55.

88. Pauline Marie Rosenau, *Post-Modernism and the Social Sciences: Insights, Inroads, and Intrusions* (Princeton: Princeton University Press, 1992), 9–10.

89. Sigmund Freud, *The Future of an Illusion*, trans. W. D. Robson-Scott, ed. James Strachey (New York: Anchor Books, 1957, c. 1927), 2–3.

the nineteenth century, Whitehead explains, is the "invention of the method of invention," from which science was conceived less for its principles than for its results: science became a storehouse of ideas for utilization.[90]

The social sciences were integral to the making of Western modernity. The "science of society" articulated ideals of the new social order, designed maps for constructing institutions and cultures, provided legitimation for a centralized bureaucratic state and its aspiration to reorder the social world, offered techniques and skills to manage large shifts of population from the countryside to the cities, and provided strategies of social control through defining identities and social norms.[91] Thus, two justificatory strategies were pivotal to the legitimation of the social sciences in Western society. First, theories of the nature of knowledge were advanced that distinguished between knowledge and religion, opinion, ideology, or myth. Second, the legitimation of the social sciences invoked grand stories of human evolution which interpreted the rise of these sciences as both a sign of progress and a contributing cause.[92] Science is progress because it has taken us out of the "dark ages."

E. Doyle McCarthy explains that at the center of what we call Western civilization is the twofold idea of science and reason, and, because of scientific knowledge and technology, people have come to believe that they possess the capacity to live better lives and to achieve the equality they doubly claim as both the foundation and the hope for their democracies. This idea, McCarthy indicates, has inevitably stemmed from industrial capitalism's requirement of change and movement and its consequent emphasis on the virtues of newness and inevitable progress. The confident embrace of science, then, as a progressive force for our future rests on the idea that scientific knowledge pursues universal laws whose discovery leads all peoples toward their natural destinies. Science, Doyle argues, as the practical embodiment of impersonal reason, has provided us with its grandest and most vital stories.[93]

We can now bring together the four ideas of the scientific imaginary in the discourse on the science of education. The impersonal scientific study of "empirical facts" constituting educational phenomena will allow us to get rid of the "noise" in education, to establish verifiable theories that can be tested with relative precision, and which are reproducible and generalizable across time and space. Only through this method can we be sure that we have improved schools, teaching, learning, and, in a word, *education*. Education provides the key to our individual and collective destinies, and, given that science is progress, an education science is our destiny.

---

90. Whitehead, *Science and the Modern World*, 91.
91. Steven Seidman, Introduction to *The Postmodern Turn: New Perspectives on Social Theory*, ed. Steven Seidman (Cambridge: Cambridge University Press, 1994), 1–23, 3.
92. Ibid.
93. McCarthy, *Knowledge as Culture*, 85–86.

An education science will shape our destiny because, of course, it will shape educational policy. After all, as Bruce Albers, president of the National Academy of Sciences, states in the forward to SRE, the NRC has been "designed to elevate the role of education research in improving policy and practice."[94] There seems, then, a link between science and political government we would like to tease out here. Lisa Anderson's study of the social sciences appears to make this point. She explains that the ideas and institutions that support social science research reflect a historically and culturally specific commitment to a sort of traditional American liberalism, one that was simultaneously skeptical of and reliant upon the state, not very self-conscious of its embrace of the rhetoric of equality and the reality of privilege, but supremely confident in the susceptibility of social problems to human intervention.[95] In the United States, science supported the cause of liberalism by breaking with tradition, questioning authority, and celebrating the individual, both as citizen and, ultimately, as a "unit of analysis." Liberalism in turn supported the pursuit of science by supporting the freedoms of belief, assembly, and association, which were important to unfettered inquiry.[96] Anderson, however, fails to question the value of this link in an otherwise convincing account of how social scientists have gained power by donning the mantle of objectivity and assuming its illusion of truth. She states rather uncritically that "public policy will be enhanced by such exposure to social science but also that closer familiarity with the challenges that face policymakers is salutary for social science itself."[97]

It is this unquestioned, and apparently unquestionable, link between science and the state that supports the federal government's investment in science. As Vannevar Bush's influential 1945 report providing justification for the massive federal support of science explains:

> Advances in science when put to practical use mean more jobs, higher wages, shorter hours, more abundant crops, more leisure for recreation, for study, for learning how to live without the deadening drudgery which has been the burden of the common man for ages past. Advances in science will also bring higher standards of living, will lead to the prevention or cure of disease, will promote conservation of our limited national resources, and will assure means of defense against aggression. But to achieve these objectives—to secure a high level of employment, to maintain a position of world

---

94. SRE, viii.
95. Anderson, *Pursuing Truth*, 6.
96. Ibid., 13.
97. Ibid., 3.

leadership—the flow of new scientific knowledge must be both continuous and substantial.[98]

The NRC's rationale for such federal investment in educational research echoes Bush's, except that national defense is no longer the logic that guides such investment but *economics*:

> [The] United States is no longer a manufacturing society in which people with little formal education can find moderate- to high-paying jobs. It is now a service- and knowledge-driven economy in which high levels of literacy and numeracy are required of almost everyone to achieve a good standard of living. . . . To meet these new demands, rigorous, sustained, scientific research in education is needed.[99]

The federal government's interest in science, we want to say again, transcends any particular political orientation, and thus the critique of the NRC report as yet another Republican attempt to control education is correct only in a specific sense. We should critique particular political uses of science, of course, but we should be careful not to imply in this critique that science can be free of such control, as any support of science serves *a* political agenda. And, besides, many of these critics would themselves argue for the use of science to further a progressive agenda.

The creation and proliferation of scientific experts in the service of democratic ideals, Popkewitz argues, was made possible by a linking of academic and scientific knowledge with populism.[100] In other words, it is the popular belief in the idea that science can be used for good that supports the proliferation of these experts, the public funding they receive, and the knowledge they produce. The scientific imaginary, then, explains the views held by people such as Popper, who, in his attack on what he calls the historicism of Plato, Hegel, and Marx, tries to justify a particular (and we would say, "governmental") role for the social scientist. This scientist must become a "social engineer." The social engineer, Popper argues, believes that a scientific basis for politics would consist of the factual information necessary for the construction and alteration of social institutions in accordance with our wishes and aims. She does not care for how or why institutions were originally formed; she cares only whether the institution is organized to serve our aims.[101]

---

98. Vannevar Bush, *Science: The Endless Frontier* (Washington, DC: United States Government Printing Office, 1945). Available at http://www.nsf.gov/od/lpa/nsf50/vbush1945.htm (Retrieved July 16, 2003).
99. *SRE*, 11–12.
100. Popkewitz, "A Changing Terrain," 22–23.
101. Karl R. Popper, *The Open Society and its Enemies, Volume I: The Spell of Plato* (Princeton: Princeton University Press, 1962), 22–23.

Note, however, the power that is authorized by such a view, for, if Pierre Bourdieu is correct, the function of the social engineers is also to

> supply recipes to the leaders of private companies and government departments. They offer a rationalization of the practical or semi-theoretical understanding that the members of the dominant class have of the social world. The governing élite today needs a science capable of (in both senses) *rationalizing* its domination, capable of reinforcing the mechanisms that sustain it and of legitimizing it. It goes without saying that the limits of this science are set by its practical functions: neither for the social engineers nor for the managers of the economy can it perform a radical questioning.[102]

Yet the views of both Popper and Bourdieu overdetermine the matter. We question neither that science can become the tool for individual and social progress, nor that science is a tool for class domination. We do question the temporal gap these views establish between the *uses* of science and its *effects* on the world. We would like to have readers consider SRE and ASRE as less representative of a political attempt to control science than as science's attempt to make itself indispensable in yet another context, education. Science, by legitimizing what counts as truth, positions itself squarely within political arenas but, paradoxically, by putting itself forward as being separate and distinct from them. So, we are to understand, science should influence the politics of education, but only in a one-way relationship, that is, science can influence educational policymaking, but it cannot be influenced by it in return.

Our interest in answering the question of what science is via the metaphorical device of the scientific imaginary was not intended simply for itself. We used it to give the discourses on science a reading, and now we subject this scientific imaginary itself to a further reading. That is, we want to interpret it in view of the role it plays in creating and governing individuals. We move next into science's role in "governing souls."

THE "GOVERNMENT OF SOULS"

H. S. Pritchett was more correct than he imagined himself to be when he said in 1900 that "it may be accepted as a fact that the government of this country is passing rapidly into the hands of the educated man."[103] He meant by the "educated man" the scientist, who should be supported by the State so that he may serve it with useful knowledge that will allow state

---

102. Pierre Bourdieu, *Sociology in Question* (Thousand Oaks: Sage Publications, 1993), 13.
103. H. S. Pritchett, "The Relation of Educated Men to the State," *Science* 12, no. 305 (1900): 657–66, 659.

officials to govern effectively. We too believe that government is passing rapidly into the hands of scientists, but unlike Pritchett we do not mean by "government" only the formal or political institutions of the state. We follow Foucault in thinking of an older sense of the term. Foucault, with his characteristic neologisms, used the term "governmentality" to refer to the "conduct of conduct," or the ways in which not only political institutions but also a host of other public and private entities seek to shape the conduct of individuals.[104] This study of "government" looks to the ways in which political and civic institutions rationalize, guide, shape, and direct the behavior of individuals, and to how individuals themselves seek to direct their own behavior. In other words, attention to "governmentality" accounts for how the juridical, fiscal, organizational, psychological, and scientific all get deployed to direct the conduct of individuals. It asks, for example, how do the "technologies of power" come together with the "technologies of self" to produce governable subjects.[105] Foucault explains that the "contact point, where individuals are driven by others is tied to the way they conduct themselves, is what we can call, I think, government."[106]

We propose here that an education science will serve governmental practices; that is, it will provide the key technologies of power for rationalizing and governing individuals. Popkewitz seems to make a similar argument when he explains that the progress of science was made possible by three events. We discussed one of these events in the previous section, that is, the linking of scientific knowledge with populism. A second event linked progress to a particular kind of humanism and anthropological motive: individuals were no longer understood as governed by mythical, religious, or transcendental theories, but came to be seen as beings that possessed agency. Thus, social administration could now be directed at producing the individual's own freedom. Closely linked to this event was another that focused the social sciences, especially psychology, on the "soul" of an actor, that is, on microprocesses, so as to produce individuals who were "self-motivated," "self-responsible," and "reasonable." The individual's innermost desires, affects, and bodily practices

---

104. See Michel Foucault, "Governmentality," in *The Foucault Effect: Studies in Governmentality*, ed. Graham Burchell, Colin Gordon, and Peter Miller (Chicago: The University of Chicago Press, 1991), 87–104.

105. For Foucault, the "technologies of the self" are those techniques or operations that individuals use to affect their bodies, souls, thoughts, conduct, and ways of being, so as to transform themselves in order to attain a certain state of happiness, purity, wisdom, perfection, immortality. These technologies are different from what Foucault has elaborated as the discursive regimes of truth, or the "technologies of power," which we elaborate upon in greater detail in this chapter. The technologies of power control individuals through the production of knowledge about them. See Michel Foucault, "Technologies of the Self," in *Technologies of the Self: A Seminar with Michel Foucault*, ed. Luther H. Martin, Huck Gutman, and Patrick H. Hutton (Amherst: The University of Massachusetts Press, 1988), 16–49, 19.

106. Michel Foucault, "About the Beginning of the Hermeneutics of the Self: Two Lectures at Darmouth," *Political Theory* 21 (1993): 198–227, 203.

were normalized, classified, and made objects of change. The modern school, Popkewitz argues, is a site invested with practices for governing the soul, for administering and disciplining the social environment and the identity of its subjects to achieve individual freedom and responsibility. It is a site where political rationalities are converted into pedagogies.[107]

The sciences are not the only practices addressing themselves to the soul. A host of state bureaucracies, philanthropic and civic organizations, churches, and schools look to the soul, to the depths of the heart and the thoughts, the will, the inclinations of individuals.[108] Foucault refers to these practices as disciplinary mechanisms or technologies of power. The "body" and its "soul" became the new sites for, and investment of, power relations, which did not seek to oppress the individual, but to *produce* him, to make him the subject of knowledges and practices intended to direct his actions and desires, to effectively administer him in relation to others, to make him more "useful." What the social sciences do is give "scientific status" to such political technologies.[109]

In other words, disciplinary mechanisms were born when the body, or more accurately, its soul, became the site of a concerted (but not necessarily organized) and calculated manipulation of its elements, its gestures, its behavior:

> The human body was entering a machinery of power that explores it, breaks it down and rearranges it. A "political anatomy", which was also a "mechanics of power", was being born; it defined how one may have a hold over others' bodies, not only so that they may do what one wishes, but so that they may operate as one wishes, with the techniques, the speed and the efficiency that one determines. Thus discipline produces subjected and practised bodies, "docile" bodies. Discipline increases the forces of the body (in economic terms of utility) and diminishes these same forces (in political terms of obedience). In short, it dissociates power from the body; on the one hand, it turns it into an "aptitude", a "capacity", which it seeks to increase; on the other hand, it reverses the course of the energy, the power that might result from it, and turns it into a relation of strict subjection.[110]

Disciplinary mechanisms are the most significant forms of power of the modern age, especially if they attain scientific status, because they "make

---

107. Popkewitz, "A Changing Terrain," 22.
108. Michel Foucault, *Discipline and Punish: The Birth of the Prison* (New York: Vintage Books, 1977), 16.
109. Ibid., 24.
110. Ibid., 138.

up individuals." But, we stress, this power is not "repressive" per se, or even triumphant, as Dr. Frankenstein seems to be in the epigraph of this chapter. This power understands itself as acting in the best interest of the individual, as liberating the individual even. It seeks to make her "normal."

Techniques of normalization, therefore, became important instruments of power. The power of normalization imposes homogeneity, but it also individualizes, Foucault argues, by making it possible to measure gaps, to determine levels, to fix specialties, and to render the differences useful by fitting them one to another.[111] Hacking, as we explained previously, indicates that normalization is made possible by statistics. We agree that statistics makes normalization easier, for they allow for the control of the entire population, but normalizing practices address themselves both to the population and to the individual. And the "examination" epitomizes this population-individual nexus. Foucault explains:

> The examination combines the techniques of an observing hierarchy and those of a normalizing judgement. It is a normalizing gaze, a surveillance that makes it possible to qualify, to classify and to punish. It establishes over individuals a visibility through which one differentiates them and judges them. That is why, in all the mechanisms of discipline, the examination is highly ritualized. In it are combined the ceremony of power and the form of the experiment, the deployment of force and the establishment of truth. At the heart of the procedures of discipline, it manifests the subjection of those who are perceived as objects and the objectification of those who are subjected. The superimposition of the power relations and knowledge relations assumes in the examination all its visible brilliance.[112]

Given that a science of education will surely direct itself primarily to teaching and learning, the examination will take on greater prominence in schools. For the examination opens up two correlative possibilities:

> firstly, the constitution of the individual as a describable, analyzable object, not in order to reduce him to "specific" features . . . but in order to maintain him in his individual features, in his particular evolution, in his own aptitudes or abilities, under the gaze of a permanent corpus of knowledge; and, secondly, the constitution of a comparative system that made possible the measurement of overall phenomena, the description of groups, the characterization

---

111. Ibid., 184.
112. Ibid., 184–85.

of collective facts, the calculation of the gaps between individuals, their distribution in a given "population."[113]

So now we can see that the privileging of quantitative methods by the NRC and the federal government makes absolute sense; they reduce educational phenomena to quantifiable, reproducible, and generalizable data that will give us statistics, which in turn permit the objectification of individuals as individuals and as parts of a host of populations (e.g., racial, national, etc.). Indeed, given the importance of the examination, and the ease with which it can be converted into statistics, an education science will be a "science of government" par excellence, since it is in education that the examination is mostly thinkable and practicable. The discourse on science, then, seeks the "scientification" of a very powerful disciplinary apparatus in the government of souls.

One can see, if we may reiterate, the role an education science will play in the governing of souls: it will entrench particular political technologies in the school and give them scientific status. But this technology requires a technologist, for not everyone will have the skills or be able to use the information effectively (thus, why doctoral study also comes into play in these discourses on education science, as we indicated in chapter 3). The discourse on education science is not merely ideological, as its critics, ourselves included, have been arguing; it is also "technical" to the extent it rationalizes, offers techniques, and legitimate practices that will govern subjects, as well as those that will instruct their "governors," that is, the education scientists.

We may reread, then, the notion that schools are failing, which has led to the intensification of "scientific research in education." The "failing school" is a fabrication with a particular purpose: to intensify disciplinary mechanisms having the status of science. They will bring with them more examinations, more experiments, more surveys, and, yes, more "naturalistic inquiries" that can reach the innermost feelings of their subjects, and the findings of all these technologies will be transferred into databases that permit increasingly sophisticated statistical analyses for more exacting individualization of students, who then can be made subject to comparisons, and of government practices at the individual, group, national, and international levels. But more. Not only is the "failing school" a fabrication, so is the "individual," the "population," and even the "society" itself that will be conjured up by the education scientists, working within mechanisms of power, and who are warmly invited into the school by the fabrication of its failure.

The social sciences as a whole are instrumental in a symptomatic form of government, one premised on individual freedom and self-reliance.

---

113. Ibid., 190.

Popkewitz explains that the social sciences cannot be separated from modern developments such as organized capitalism, the welfare state, and urbanization. With these developments also came the "democratization of the individual," or when people came to see, and to be seen, as individuals who could act on the world. The individual became a citizen of a nation, and as such, had certain obligations and freedoms. These obligations and freedoms became tied to social administration. Thus, a new relationship developed in the liberal state between the governing of the state and the governing of the individual, a relationship that required the latter to exhibit self-discipline and self-motivation. In other words, these "free" individuals became a problem of administration for the modern state, which utilized the social sciences to develop policies that would remove strife and lead to social development. The project of creating self-governing, morally directed individuals, Popkewitz argues, was largely conceptualized by the emerging social sciences, and especially psychology, which conjured up a consciousness committed to hard work and democratic principles.[114] And so our use of the term *sciences of government* in referring to the social sciences from now on will make a certain kind of sense. For these sciences provide the rationality and techniques necessary for directing the behavior of people.

We want to point out, again, that all this could happen because the individual is "respected," in a sense, by the sciences of government, which are not seeking to oppress her, but to liberate her, to help her, to make her normal.[115] Thus, this belief in emancipating the individual accounts, we think, for why even democratically minded scholars were seduced by the sciences of government. For example, Popkewitz argues that even John Dewey was complicit in this linking of individualism with social administration. Dewey, he argues, inscribed political/moral assumptions of progress into his conception of personal development within "community." The idea of "community" embodied a Protestant notion of hard work, a commitment to science as a problem-solving device in a democracy, and an Emersonian notion of citizen "voluntarism" in social affairs.[116]

We think Popkewitz is correct that Dewey was complicit in the linking of sciences with social administration, but not because he believed in a notion of science as corresponding with reality, a belief we think was absolutely crucial to why social scientists were complicit in the ways they were. Recall that they took as their model that of the natural sciences, creating for them an imaginary in which they saw themselves involved

---

114. Popkewitz, "A Changing Terrain," 19.
115. We do not deny, however, the oppressive uses of scientific knowledge as epitomized by eugenics, which at first glance appears to have been discredited, but, as Bernadette Baker explains, has simply taken on new forms in education. See Bernadette Baker, "The Hunt for Disability: The New Eugenics and the Normalization of School Children," *Teachers College Record* 104, no. 4 (2002): 663–703.
116. Popkewitz, "A Changing Terrain," 19.

in the neutral observation and analysis of the social world and the particularities of individuals, and is thus why they emphasized prediction and control. But, as we pointed out in chapter 2, Dewey's democratic vision of science did not privilege prediction and control. Indeed, as Rorty points out, Dewey rejected the idea of science as working toward a correspondence with reality. Dewey did not see science as useful in and of itself; science was useful only to the extent that it works better than another vocabulary for a given purpose.[117] Nevertheless, despite the fact that Dewey did not emphasize the *expert* but the *purpose* to which scientific knowledge would be put, he did believe that the "methods of science also point the way to the measures and policies by means of which a better social order can be brought into existence."[118] So Popkewitz seems correct that the historical relationship between the governing of the state as a force in the governing of the individual remains in the social (and educational) sciences, even in critical traditions such as Dewey's.[119]

The sciences of government gave the state the ability to become invested in "bio-power," a regime of knowledge and power whose end is life itself and which operates at both the level of the individual, through pastoral and individualizing technologies of power, and at the level of the species, through the sciences of the state, the most important being statistics related to the population.[120] The sciences of government make possible the revelation of the problems of the population, that is, its health practices, its economic behavior, its educational attainment, its psychology, everything. "Government" involves, therefore, a particular relation between state, civic practices, and the sciences of government, and it is through this relation that the individual and the population can best be governed.[121]

What we see in the discourse on science in education, therefore, is a rationalization for that particular governmental relation. The "student" is not an empirical reality, but a *political field* of practice and knowledge, where scientific apparatuses and public and private institutions will have great hold over it. Baker, for example, argues that the "child" is not a natural phenomenon with natural laws guiding its natural development, but a political space for the production of categories, distinctions, techniques,

117. Rorty, "Method, Social Science, and Social Hope," 47–48.
118. John Dewey, *Experience and Education* (New York: Touchstone, 1997, c. 1938), 81.
119. Popkewitz, "A Changing Terrain," 19. To be clear, Dewey promoted scientific inquiry, but inquiry that was applied *in* social life rather than *to* it.
120. For a discussion of bio-power, see Michel Foucault, *The History of Sexuality: An Introduction Volume I*, trans. Robert Hurley (New York: Vintage Books, 1978), 135–59. See also, Michel Foucault, *"Society Must Be Defended:" Lectures at the Collège de France*, ed. Mauro Bertani and Alessandro Fontana, trans. David Macey (New York: Picador, 1997), 239–64.
121. Michel Foucault, "The Political Technology of Individuals," in *Technologies of the Self: A Seminar with Michel Foucault*, ed. Luther Martin, Huck Gutman, and Patrick Hutton (Amherst: University of Massachusetts Press, 1988), 145–62, 150–51.

and reasonings.[122] We can say that about other objects of knowledge in education, such as the "teacher" and the "parent."[123] Thus, the "student" will become the site for government rationalities and techniques that will, following Foucault, "invest it, mark it, train it, . . . force it to carry out tasks, to perform ceremonies, to emit signs."[124] The "student" that the educational reformers and educational scientists have set their eyes upon has become a *measure*, "not of things, but of power."[125] That education research needs to be "practical" is more true than at first meets the eye—it is "practical" if it conducts conduct well, that is, if it gives efficiency to the control and direction of individual behavior.

Among disciplinary mechanisms he addresses, Foucault seems to give more space to the sciences of government in the creation of individuals and their consequent subjection. But he refused to grant more authority to any one form of power over another. We believe, however, that Foucault could have given the sciences of government the greatest authority in the bio-power regime. We think, and this is perhaps where we part company with Foucault, that the sciences of government have the greatest authority in the governing of individuals because they can enact in reality what they purport to represent in theory. Their authoritative discourse is guaranteed by particular conventional arrangements apart from their links to state apparatuses. In other words, scientific discourses have performative power, an argument we expand upon next.

"PERFORMING" SCIENTIFIC RESEARCH IN EDUCATION

In 1961, Michael Young published a brilliant fable (that seems to have come true) about the reorganization of British society through educational testing.[126] In his fable, the use of intelligence tests leads to a meritocracy that replaces an inefficient and unpopular social order that allocates rewards and status on the basis of a hereditary system with one that allocates rewards and statuses on the basis of this formula: merit = IQ + effort. Young's meritocracy, reinforced by science, has catastrophic consequences on people's lives and on a democratic form of government. Eventually, the masses revolt in a revolution that leads to the death of the narrator himself. Young's thesis

122. See Bernadette Baker, " 'Childhood' in the Emergence and Spread of U.S. Public Schools," in *Foucault's Challenge: Discourse, Knowledge, and Power in Education*, ed. Thomas S. Popkewitz and Marie Brennan (New York: Teachers College Press, 1998), 117–43, 138.

123. For how the "parent" is created and manipulated by neoliberal governmental practices, see Benjamin Baez and Susan Talburt, "Governing for Responsibility and with Love: Parents and Children Between Home and School," *Educational Theory* 58, no. 1 (2008): 25–43.

124. Foucault, *Discipline and Punish*, 25–26.

125. Ibid., 74.

126. Michael Young, *The Rise of the Meritocracy 1870–2033: An Essay on Education and Equality* (New York: Penguin Books, 1961).

is worth the read, especially for how it helps one critique the notion of merit in educational discourse.[127] But here we focus only on his point, rather prophetic, that the "scientists have inherited the earth."[128] We want to offer a theory of why the "scientists have inherited the earth." However, again, we do not want to be read as "psychologizing" scientists, as we think that a more serious accounting of the power of scientists treats the issue histori-cally, philosophically, and sociologically. Scientists are subjects of their own discursive practices; their "intentions" are to be understood within these discursive practices. Of course, other discursive practices also exercise power over individuals, but our argument here is that scientific practices have a particular kind of power that makes them more efficient than others.

To start this inquiry, we need not stray too far from where we started. The NRC report states, "Science is a communal 'form of life.' "[129] Scientific knowledge, therefore, is never a private act. Indeed, Popper's explanation of the scientific method highlights its "public" character, its "free criticism" and its avoidance of "speaking cross purposes."[130] Science, we are told by another philosopher of science, does not just acquire information or posit only noncontradictory theories; "its goal is a consensus of rational opinion over the widest possible field."[131] All this means to us is that science is, at its most fundamental level, a ritualized performance. It comes about through particular speech, uttered through particular rituals, to particular individuals, who will respond in particular ways. That is, the scientist speaks through the scientific method, does so to other scientists, who confirm or refute that speech, also through the scientific method, until a consensus is reached.

There is then a politics that is associated with this ritual culminating in consensus, for this ritual is "governmental," that is, it seeks to shape and direct the conduct of scientists. Marianne Bloch is correct, even if not on point, when she argues that what the NRC report represents is how the community of "good scientific researchers in education" monitor or police the consensually reached normative values, reproduce them, and discipline and regulate those who do not follow the norms established in the report.[132] There will be, it appears, a sanctioning of "abnormal" educational scientists. Science, then, is inherently *political*. We do not mean to say by this that

---

127. For one example of such a critique, see Benjamin Baez, "Merit and Difference," *Teachers College Record* 108, no. 6 (2006): 996–1016.
128. Young, *The Rise of the Meritocracy*, 107.
129. *SRE*, 53.
130. Popper, *The Open Society and its Enemies, Volume II*, 218.
131. John Ziman, "What is Science?" in *Introductory Readings in the Philosophy of Science*, ed. E. D. Klemke, Robert Hollinger, David Wÿss Rudge, and A. David Kline (New York: Prometheus Books, 1998), 48–53, 51.
132. Marianne Bloch, "A Discourse That Disciplines, Governs, and Regulates: The National Research Council's Report on Scientific Research in Education," *Qualitative Inquiry* 10, no. 1 (2004): 96–110, 102.

science makes political action possible; it does, of course, make political action possible but only because it is itself political action par excellence. Scientific research is an interpretive act, and, thus, it is a sense-making act, but one that through its interpretations and conventional authority reinforces or destabilizes other narratives in the world. There is, however, an understanding that science is a valid form of obtaining knowledge about the world; science is the empirical way of knowing. This understanding establishes science as separate and distinct from the experience it takes as its object of study.

We question this narrative about science. To illustrate our point, we offer as example the recent research supporting the use of affirmative action in higher education.[133] The NRC, the federal government, and other supporters of scientific research in education would likely consider William Bowen and Derek Bok's *The Shape of the River*, or similar studies that seek to justify affirmative action with "empirical" data, as epitomizing the scientific uses of education research to inform public policy.[134] This research presents the experiences of White and Black students at prestigious institutions of higher education as empirical evidence of the educational benefits of racial diversity. They measure and compare individuals along a number of variables, such as test scores, grades, graduation rates, graduate-school attendance rates, salaries, civic commitments, attitudes, and so on. This work seeks "facts" in order to transcend the moral and ideological rhetoric associated with affirmative action. But read as a narrative, this research also produces its own objects. That is, by *comparing* individuals along racial lines, this research *produces* racial difference and renders possible institutional practices to deal with it (e.g., affirmative action, multicultural curricula). These practices in turn provide the bases for further studies (to see whether they "work").

We do not question the moral or political imperative of this research on the benefits of diversity. It is intended to counter centuries-long discriminatory practices based partially, and ironically, on science. Stephen Jay Gould's classic work, *The Mismeasure of Man*, for example, points out how racism has shaped the scientific study of race.[135] His eye-opening analysis of scientific practices shaped by an ideology of biological determinism disproves the myth of science as an objective enterprise. What Bowen and Bok, and others, could have heeded, however, was Gould's point that science suffers from particular fallacies: it reifies abstractions as concrete entities (such as

---

133. For a more extensive elaboration of this point, see Benjamin Baez, "The Study of Diversity: The 'Knowledge of Difference' and the Limits of Science," *Journal of Higher Education* 75, no. 3 (2004): 285–306.

134. William G. Bowen and Derek Bok, *The Shape of the River: Long-Term Consequences of Considering Race in College and University Admissions* (Princeton: Princeton University Press, 1998).

135. Stephen Jay Gould, *The Mismeasure of Man* (New York: W. W. Norton, 1981).

intelligence, or in our illustration, diversity), assigns them a number, and then ranks people in a single series of worthiness. This is the "mismeasure of man" of which Gould speaks.[136] Furthermore, Bowen and Bok, and Gould for that matter, fail to account for how their very discourse *produces* race. While science was instrumental to the creation of race classifications premised on biological determinism, the sciences of government, specifically, have also redefined them. In particular, the work of Franz Boas was important in redefining race as a cultural construct.[137] More recently, Michael Omi and Howard Winant have elaborated a theory of race that highlights how particular political projects give meaning to racial categories.[138] All this work clearly can be termed a progression in knowledge about race, but our point is simply to highlight the power of scientific narratives to constitute their own objects, and in this case, *race*.

But from where does this power come? Kuhn, Foucault, and others, as we discussed previously, illustrate that the sciences represent systems and processes that determine what can be said and known, and they are given legitimacy by a slew of institutional and conventional arrangements. We also pointed out how professional legitimation authorizes scientists to speak authoritatively. To ask how "scientific research in education" will create what it purports to study and represent requires an inquiry into the conventional practices that will give this research the authority to study and represent. The diversity studies, for example, are given their legitimacy by the sciences of government, their links to academic institutions, as well as by the very practices produced as a result of the research performed (e.g., diversity studies require confirmation or negation). Our concern here relates not to the content of research per se (we do not argue that results of such studies are inaccurate or improper), but to the practices and discourses that guarantee, and are produced by, the act of scientific research. This understanding requires that scientists think of themselves as engaged in producing the world and not just representing it. Researchers, therefore, must reflect on the ethics of producing knowledge, itself.

An education science will be a "political" science, in a sense, because it will create and govern the world we inhabit. Bourdieu argues that political action is possible because agents have knowledge of the world and act on the world by acting on that knowledge.[139] Their actions are attempts to produce

---

136. Ibid., 24–25.
137. See Alice Littlefield, Leonard Lieberman, and Larry T. Reynolds, "Redefining Race: The Potential Demise of a Concept in Physical Anthropology," *Current Anthropology* 23, no. 6 (1982): 641–55; Roger Sanjek, "The Enduring Inequities of Race," in *Race*, ed. Stephen Gregory and Roger Sanjek (New Brunswick: Rutgers University Press, 1996), 1–17.
138. Michael Omi and Howard Winant, *Racial Formation in the United States: From the 1960s to the 1990s*, 2nd ed. (New York and London: Routledge, 1994).
139. Pierre Bourdieu, *Language and Symbolic Power*, ed. John B. Thompson, trans. Gino Raymond and Matthew Adamson (Cambridge: Harvard University Press, 1991), 127.

and impose representations of the world that transform or manipulate the representations of others. Scientific theories, for Bourdieu, have particular authority in politics because of what he calls their "theory effects."[140] This means that by expressing in coherent and empirically valid discourse that which is supposedly implicit (such as the educational benefits of diversity), science transforms the representation of the social world (for instance, to one that rejects "color-blindness" as a valid description of reality), and, consequently, transforms the social world itself, to the extent it renders possible practices that conform to this transformed representation (such as affirmative action). Science, and thus the new educational research apparatus it wants to bring into existence, will bring about what it declares.

We must look at this education science, therefore, following Bourdieu, to understand its creation of "rites of institutions." That is, this science will establish "rites" or "passages" (such as the techniques for measuring diversity's benefits) that legitimate arbitrary boundaries (such as the difference between Whites and Blacks). These "rites" draw attention to passages but obscure the lines that are drawn (such as those creating racial differences). These rites, Bourdieu argues, may constitute a simple difference (say, a phenotype) into a legitimate distinction, "an institution." An institution of identity, for example, defines someone as *some thing*, and in doing so it imposes arbitrary boundaries on what is available for that person to be.[141] These boundaries may be arbitrary but are not imaginary; they have political and psychological effects. They signify to an individual what his or her identity is in front of others, the others treat that individual accordingly, and the individual feels obligated to comply with the boundaries.

When research relates to social groups, such as racial minorities or "at risk" students, it involves but covers over, following Bourdieu, struggles over classification, "struggles over the monopoly of the power to make people see and believe, to get them to know and recognize, to impose the legitimate definition of the divisions of the social world and, thereby, to *make and unmake groups*."[142] Researchers who put forward empirical evidence about individuals and groups would be well advised to remember, Bourdieu warns, that such empirical evidence captures only a particular moment or state in the struggle to make and unmake groups. In other words, such evidence records the particular material or symbolic forces between those who have a stake in one or another kind of classification, and who often invoke scientific authority to establish in experience the *arbitrary* division they seek to impose. If any of this is possible, we might see scientific education research as both a weapon and a prize in a political struggle. As we indicated in chapter 3, what will be at stake in making education research "scientific," then, is control

---

140. Ibid., 133.
141. Ibid., 117–21.
142. Ibid., 221.

over meaning-making processes in education and in the cultural fields that use education to further various aims (for democatic goals in some cases, of course, such as the use of affirmative action in higher education). Because it uses science, however, such research is *performative*, to the extent that it imposes its theories of particular definitions of the world as true.

A performative is an utterance that enacts what it says. For example, saying "I promise" in the context of bartering for a bicycle is not merely expressing an intention or describing a particular event, it is the forming of a contract. Saying "I do" in the context of a wedding is the act of marrying. But what gives such utterances their power? J. L. Austin proposes that for a performative to be effective, that is, for an utterance to perform the action that it names, certain conditions are necessary: (1) a convention that gives an utterance effect when performed by particular individuals in certain circumstances; (2) the particular persons and circumstances must be appropriate; and (3) the actions performed must be executed correctly.[143] Leaving aside for the moment the point that because the performative relies on convention it contains a structural vulnerability (that the convention will not be executed properly),[144] to think of scientific discourse as performative would require, then, an inquiry into the conventions, persons, and circumstances that give effect to such discourse. Bourdieu indicates that when speakers speak, the entire social structure is present in each interaction. Performatives, he argues, can be understood in terms of symbolic domination; that is, the weight of individual agents' speech depends on their symbolic capital, or the recognition, institutionalized or not, they receive from a group.[145] Thus, explaining the power of a discourse involves an inquiry into the conditions by which an individual can find herself and her speech invested with the power to impose itself as authoritative, as legitimate, as truth.

We propose that what would give scientific education research the performativity to legitimate particular definitions of education and individuals are (1) the conventional legitimacy accorded to science's pursuit of knowledge and truth, (2) its institutionalization in universities, which have conventional legitimacy to pursue knowledge and truth, and (3) the conventions associated with scholarly expertise and professional autonomy. We have discussed throughout this chapter the conventional authority granted to the sciences of government, grounded in the scientific imaginary and put into the service of governmental practices.

---

143. J. L. Austin, *How to Do Things with Words* (The William James Lectures Delivered at Harvard University in 1955), ed. J. O. Urmson and Marina Sbisa (Cambridge: Harvard University Press, 1975), 14–15.
144. See Jacques Derrida, "Signature Event Context," in *Limited Inc*, ed. Gerald Graff (Evanston: Northwestern University Press, 1988), 1–23.
145. Bourdieu, *Language and Symbolic Power*, 72.

Here we address the latter two conventions giving scientific narratives performative power. With regard to the second convention, the institutionalization of science in universities, we can note that universities have become the chief sites for the production of knowledge. Indeed, with the incorporation of the sciences of government, the university became the chief site for the production of all kinds of knowledge about individuals and the social world. Thorstein Veblen could state, without blinking an eye, we are sure, that the "university is the only accepted institution of the modern culture on which the quest of knowledge unquestionably devolves."[146] Despite Veblen's argument, we can certainly question how it is that knowledge came to devolve from universities.

The university, of course, is not the sole site for the production of knowledge. Knowledge is produced in a multiplicity of places and through a multiplicity of relations. For instance, if Stanley Aronowitz is correct, "practical knowledge" is produced everywhere, but "intellectual knowledge" is produced in the university.[147] But intellectual knowledge is more authoritative than practical knowledge, and so the universities are the sites for the most powerful forms of knowledge: those emanating from the sciences. Indeed, but for universities, the sciences of government might not have been possible. Randall Collins explains that for "objective" knowledge of the social world to develop, two things had to happen: first, societies had to become rationalized; second, there had to emerge an institutional apparatus for the support of intellectual specialists.[148] This apparatus received its foundations in the Middle Ages with the rise of universities in cities such as Paris, Bologna, and Oxford.[149] These early universities were religiously affiliated, and so a further requirement for the rise of the sciences of government was the secularization of these universities. Today, social scientists are anchored primarily in universities, but they also occupy a range of other institutions (e.g., state agencies, private foundations, think tanks, private corporations, and so forth).[150] The idea of the independent scientist, a hero of the scientific imaginary, is a thing of the past.

---

146. Thorstein Veblen, *The Higher Learning in America* (New Brunswick: Transaction Publishers, 1996), 11.
147. Stanley Aronowitz, *Roll Over Beethoven: The Return of Cultural Strife* (Hanover: Wesleyan University Press, 1993), 203–204.
148. Randall Collins, *Four Sociological Traditions* (Oxford: Oxford University Press), 5.
149. Ibid., 8–9.
150. See Philip Kovacs and Deron Boyles, "Institutes, Foundations, and Think Tanks: Conservative Influences on U.S. Public Schools," *Public Resistance* 1, no. 1 (May 1, 2005): 1–18. Available at http://www.publicresistance.org (Retrieved November 12, 2005); and Deron Boyles, *American Education and Corporations: The Free Market Goes to School* (New York: Falmer, 2000), 41–60.

The university as the primary site for the pursuit of knowledge "for itself" is the product of the Enlightenment, with its belief that knowledge of all things is its ultimate goal. The birth of the university as we know it today occurred in Germany, with the establishment by Humbolt of a university in Berlin in 1809, whose mission was science and nationalism.[151] In America, the establishment of The Johns Hopkins University in 1876, premised on the German Enlightenment ideal, prompted the institutional-ization of the university as the primary site for the pursuit of knowledge. Johns Hopkins' mission, according to its first president, Daniel Coit Gilman, was the "encouragement of research . . . and the advancement of individual scholars, who by their excellence will advance the sciences they pursue, and the society where they dwell."[152]

It was in the university that the sciences of government were organized along disciplinary lines (e.g., sociology, anthropology, economics, etc.); the boundaries between these sciences and the humanities hardened; and these sciences underwent a process of mathematization and professionalization.[153] Once these sciences were institutionalized in universities, they proliferated research, as well as a host of institutional practices that ensured its continuation. Frederick Rudolph notes that without research, "there would be no departments, no departmental chairmen, no hierarchy—only teachers."[154] Research, according to Rudolph, created its own institutions and practices, such as learned journals, learned societies, university presses, and sabbatical leaves.

Indeed, because of the expanding American university system and the generous support of a distinctly American institution, the large private foundation, American social scientists constructed a special position for them-selves in society, distant from the compromising fray of both politics and the market, yet engaged in what seemed to be disinterested service on behalf of social progress through science.[155] The institutionalization of these sciences in colleges and universities, which are exported and reproduced globally, also introduces the American sciences of government in a world that had no prior need for them, and which might have questioned their presumptions. If scientific knowledge is the powerful force in disciplinary power in the modern age, then the exportation of the American sciences of government should be made central in understanding the effects of globalization.

The university's installation as the primary site for the pursuit of knowl-edge created a new kind of subjectivity: the researcher, one who saw her

---

151. See Clark Kerr, The Uses of the University (New York: Harper and Row, 1966), 11.
152. "A Brief History of Johns Hopkins University." Available at www.jhu.edu/news_info/ jhuinfo/history.html (Retrieved October 24, 2000).
153. Steven Seidman, introduction to The Postmodern Turn, 4.
154. Frederick Rudolph, The American College and University: A History (Athens: The University of Georgia Press, 1962), 404.
155. Lisa Anderson, "The Global Reach of American Social Science," The Chronicle Review (November 26, 2003): B7–B9, B8.

identity in terms of the pursuit of knowledge, and who developed an ethic around such an identity (e.g., that associated with academic freedom). And this point leads to our explanation of the third convention giving science is performative power: scholarly expertise and professional autonomy. This professional autonomy as we know it today depends on the notion of the university as the institution of the intellectual. The modern university not only provides the training and intellectual tradition, but also incorporates the legitimating structure of authority and competence.[156] We are led, again, to the nineteenth century and to the German universities' cry for *libertas philosophandi*, or the freedom of philosophizing.[157] The German professors, in speaking of such freedom, had in mind *lernfreiheit*, freedom to learn, and *lehrfreiheit*, freedom of inquiry, both of which formed the basis for the American notion of academic freedom.[158] In the United States, in part to protect their autonomy to pursue knowledge and truth, academic scholars organized the American Association of University Professors (AAUP) in 1915 and began to develop guiding principles for the pursuit of knowledge they claimed would ultimately benefit society.[159] Indeed, what is unique about the university might be, as John Brubacher noted thirty years ago, the expertise of the scholar in assaying knowledge.[160] This claim to expertise legitimates, we think, the concurrent claim to professional autonomy, which in turn legitimates the claim to expertise. For example, consider Thomas Haskell's justification for such professional autonomy:

> Academic freedom came into being as a defense of the disciplinary community (or, more exactly, the university conceived as an ensemble of such communities), and if it is to do the work we expect of it, it must continue to be at bottom a denial that anyone outside the community is fully competent to pass judgment on matters falling within the community's domain.[161]

---

156. John A. Jackson, "Professions and Professionalization Editorial Introduction," in *Professions and Professionalization*, ed. John A. Jackson (Cambridge: Cambridge University Press, 1970), 3–15, 4–5.

157. Robert B. Sutton, "The Phrase *Libertas Philosophandi*," *Journal of the History of Ideas* 14, no. 2 (1953): 310–16, 310.

158. See Walter Metzger, "Academic Freedom and Scientific Freedom," *Daedalus: Journal of the American Academy of Arts and Sciences* 107, no. 2 (1978): 93–114; Rudolph, *The American College and University*, 412. We take up the notion of academic freedom again in chapter 5.

159. See Walter P. Metzger, "The 1940 Statement of Principles on Academic Freedom and Tenure," in *Freedom and Tenure in the Academy*, ed. William W. Van Alstyne (Durham: Duke University Press, 1993), 3–77.

160. John S. Brubacher, "The Theory of Higher Education," *Journal of Higher Education* 41, no. 2 (1970): 98–115, 100.

161. Thomas L. Haskell, "Justifying the Rights of Academic Freedom in the Era of 'Power/Knowledge,'" in *Legal Rights: Historical and Philosophical Perspectives*, ed. Austin Sarat and Thomas R. Kearns (Ann Arbor: The University of Michigan Press, 1996), 113–76, 128.

It seems that for Haskell professional autonomy protects the disciplinary community, which requires professional autonomy in order to be defined as a disciplinary community. This rather circular argument essentially authenticates the academy as an institution made up of experts whose claim to expertise is constituted almost entirely by their being given the legitimacy to pursue knowledge autonomously.

Our specific point in discussing these conventions is to give an account of what gives scientific narratives their performative power, for this power is "conventional." The overall point here is that inquiry into the performativity of educational research should account for the institutional practices that legitimate the academy and researcher as producers of such knowledge. This inquiry might include analyses of disciplinary discourses, as well as of practices insulating its sciences from critique, including specialization, departmentalization, confidentiality of peer review, and reward systems. Furthermore, such inquiry should attend to how the scientists legitimate themselves by citing themselves and by circulating their narratives throughout the social milieu. Thus, the most important practice in the production of knowledge cannot be ignored: the creation of the scientist, who is constituted as expert, professionally autonomous and objective. This scientific imagination views herself as the author of knowledge rather than the effect of the mechanisms of knowledge production.

The field of education is already one where worldviews are transmitted, cultures reproduced, ways of life passed, and persons created.[162] And this field is exported all over the world. Thus, instituting a science of this field will ensure that its determinative classifications will govern the world.[163] To understand the complexity of the link between knowledge and power in this field, however, one must not view such a link as innately repressive. The knowledge created by power, and the power engendered by knowledge, are in a significant sense *productive* of identity, culture, morality, ethics, and a "people." The modern forms of knowledge, as Jürgen Habermas explains with regard to Foucault's work, is determined by a "will to truth" for which any frustration is only a spur to the renewed production of knowledge.[164] This will to truth is the key to the nexus between power and knowledge. The sciences of government make use of a perspective that analyzes the individual as a being that relates itself to classifications created by itself. These sciences, following Habermas, in the wake of this will to truth, have

---

162. E. Vance Randall, Bruce S. Cooper, and Steven J. Hite, "Understanding the Politics of Research in Education," *Educational Policy* 13, no. 1 (1999): 7–22, 8.
163. See generally, Thomas S. Popkewitz, "Is the National Research Council Committee's Report on Scientific Research in Education Scientific? On Trusting the Manifesto," *Qualitative Inquiry* 10, no. 1 (2004): 62–78, 66–67.
164. Jürgen Habermas, "The Critique of Reason as an Unmasking of the Human Sciences: Michel Foucault," in *Critique and Power: Recasting the Foucault/Habermas Debate*, ed. Michael Kelly (Cambridge: The MIT Press, 1994): 47–77, 69.

been on a journey of a boundless productive increase in knowledge about individuals.[165] The very production of scientific knowledge in education, then, *is* the mechanism of power at work, and not necessarily subject to a separate power that uses it for its own purposes.

This can be stated differently. In sketching narratives of human evolution, the sciences of government established themselves as both signs of progress and contributing causes. Once society and individuals became objects of knowledge, and human behavior the subject of study, analysis, and resolution, these sciences were linked to the mechanisms of power that present humans and society as problems to be resolved and set themselves up as providing solutions to those problems. One should understand the relationship between power and knowledge as one in which there is a constant articulation of power on knowledge and knowledge on power.[166] If so, it is inappropriate, as is often the case, to claim merely that power uses knowledge; rather, the exercise of power itself creates objects of knowledge.

The science of government in education, for example, will establish, say, the student as a *problem* to be studied and itself as providing the means for understanding and resolving it. And yet, this science seeks to appropriate for itself the scientific imaginary of the natural sciences and thus will insulate itself from politics. But because it sketches narratives about society and its individuals, it is implicated in the mechanisms of power and control and must be open to critique. This critique should not be that its knowledge cannot serve democratic goals—we do not dispute that imperative—the critique is that it produces "empirical facts," tentative as they are. The "scientific education research" being promoted by the NRC and others will implicitly create and legitimate particular views of the world, and as such, it will be taking a side in the struggle over the power to impose such views on the world. Such research, therefore, should not be seen merely as creating empirical knowledge about human experience in education; it is an attempt to recast narratives in particular contexts. Scientific research *is* political, therefore, and thus justifications for such research should be part of a democratic process of critique at each and every moment it seeks to speak about education.

We hope we are not read as saying that all scientific research should be thwarted at all cost—though we do say that about experimental designs—but we do want to offer scientific researchers a different purpose than that offered by the NRC, the federal government, and other advocates of a science of education. It is to this different purpose that we direct the conclusion of this chapter.

165. Ibid.
166. See Michel Foucault, *Power/Knowledge: Selected Interviews and Other Writings 1972–1977*, ed. and trans. Colin Gordon (New York: Pantheon Books, 1980).

ON "EDUCATION SCIENCE," REDUX

It is difficult for us to argue against any research that seeks to improve poor schools, to close the achievement gap between wealthy and poor students, to make better the conditions of social minorities, and so on. But even when scientists adopt the particular vantage points of those who suffer oppression, if they fail to describe the game in which those vantage points, and the beliefs underlying them, are produced, then they have invoked one among many contributions to the creation of beliefs whose foundations and social effects should be described.[167] It is by letting go of the dream of "royal science," as Bourdieu puts it, or the power to decree union and separation, that scientists can take up as their object the game whose stake is the power to govern the vision of the world, and in which researchers have no choice but to mystify or demystify that game.[168]

We would like to warn against the invocation of an education science for the reasons we have just given, but this does not mean that we reject scientific narratives outright. Those narratives should be ones among *many* narratives circulating in a political field such as education. We offer educational researchers, then, a purpose different from that offered by the NRC and others seeking to install scientific research as the narrative par excellence in education, and in this regard, we extend the points we made in concluding our previous chapter. Educational researchers should recognize how they produce what they purport to study, and they must be willing to discard their theories as soon as it becomes clear that those theories are becoming "evident." It may seem odd to suggest that researchers should discard their theories, but, as Bourdieu argues, researchers can free themselves from the mechanisms of domination only by bringing to light the social conditions engendered by the circulation of their fundamental concepts and creations. Education researchers should take as their object of study, following Bourdieu, the social operations of naming (and classifying) and the "rites of institutions" that result from them. Education researchers, therefore, must include in their studies a theory of their "theory effects," a theory of the performativity of their work. This means that researchers must question their power to make up people and to govern them with their narratives, rather than relying on the guise of an "objective" science.

Education researchers must also acknowledge the power of the texts they create, and this acknowledgment necessarily challenges their own discursive formations. Their texts create the reality they purport to describe. For instance, Said illustrates how much of what we know about many things reflect *textual attitudes* and not what we gleam from firsthand, personal ex-

---

167. Bourdieu, *Language and Symbolic Power*, 226.
168. Ibid., 227–28.

perience.[169] That is, we tend to know the world and others, not through actual, face-to-face interactions with them, but through the texts created by others, such as researchers, journalists, novelists, artists, and others who seek to represent the world. Indeed, such texts have a powerful influence on what we personally experience. Said explains that when later Western explorers and travelers went to the Orient, they "saw" what they had already read in the texts of previous Western colonizers. We might heed, then, how what we *see* in research might actually reflect a textual attitude, the effect of prior narratives about schools and their individuals.

This purpose we offer education research is *ethical*, and so it might seem at odds with all we have just argued regarding the performativity of scientific narratives. How can one discard an utterance that has enacted itself? But we might recall now that the power of the performative is "conventional" and thus structurally vulnerable to things "that can be and will go wrong."[170] We must be attentive to the theory-effects and textual attitudes and refuse the rituals that give them performative power. We must refuse the lure of establishing a "royal science" in favor of discourse that questions its representations and theories, and that is attentive to how those theories create the world and initiate and mediate the experiences people can have. This purpose for education researchers does not prohibit the creation of knowledge—indeed, nothing can—but it does insist upon the temporal nature of all knowledge claims, as well as a greater concern with how knowledge gets used in multiple contexts. Our concern is that we, as researchers, become ethically responsible for our production of knowledge and for how such production makes and unmakes lives.

We hope we are not read as saying that all of "scientific education research" is a pack of lies, but only that it is a crucial part of a considerable material investment in how we will come to understand and govern education, individuals, and even the world. The very fact of knowledge production implicates power—to have knowledge of something is to have authority over it. Education researchers exercise power that controls people, even if they see themselves differently from those that they know deliberately try to control people. SRE and the other proposals for establishing an education science, therefore, must be critiqued, not only for their narrow definitions of science or their exclusion of multiple forms of inquiry, as critics have tended to do, but for how they justify the sciences of government in yet another domain that, in a sense, and fortunately, has held them at bay.

---

169. Said, *Orientalism*, 92–96.
170. Austin, *How to do Things with Words*, 14.

FIVE

ENTREPRENEURSHIP AND THE
"GRANTS CULTURE"

―――――――――――――――――――――――――――――

Privatization of Research and Academic Freedom

The future arrives first at Georgia State through our research. Within Georgia State's research community, new discoveries have the potential to transform student and faculty learning into a mutually reinforcing experience. Students can be active contributors to the knowledge base rather than passive *consumers*. Faculty researchers develop intellectually and become better *teachers*.

—Georgia State University President Carl V. Patton

ON SPONSORED RESEARCH

One of the often-ignored imperatives of an education science will be the establishment in the study of education of a research enterprise focused on external funding, and our task in this chapter will be to uncover the inner workings of such an imperative. We start with our epigraph. When Carl Patton, the president of Georgia State University, claims that "new discoveries have the potential to transform student and faculty learning into a mutually reinforcing experience," that "students can be active contributors to the knowledge base rather than passive consumers," and that "researchers develop intellectually and become better teachers," he is not alone in his thinking. Indeed, his comments are typical in higher education, but, remarkably, usually go unchallenged. The rhetoric of positioning students as "active contributors" versus "passive *consumers*" of knowledge indicates that the production of knowledge and the imperatives of consumerism go hand

167

in hand. Furthermore, the claim that research makes one a better teacher is not only debatable but perhaps not even provable, since faculty at Georgia State University, as is the case at other universities, often "buy" themselves out of teaching to pursue externally funded research.

What makes the president's remarks particularly disturbing to us, how-ever, is that he ties the mission of the university specifically to externally funded research:

> The mission of our university—learning (teaching), discovery (research) and engagement (public service)—is more important to *our* community, *our* state and *our* nation than ever before. *Research is what sets us apart.* We understand the impact of *our* research on economic growth, and *we* are able to produce the educated people and new ideas that keep the economy growing. *Our* continued capacity to innovate will determine how *our* community prospers in the global marketplace. State and federal legislators expect ac-celerated economic growth as one of the returns on the public's investment in research universities. Georgia State is meeting that expectation. *We* are building *our* reputation on the caliber of *our* research, and the increased funding *we* receive is a validation of *our* achievements. *We* are able to ensure the strength and *independence* of *our* research by securing a variety of funding sources, both public and private.[1]

If indeed research (and particularly externally funded research) is what sets Georgia State University *apart*, then the "our," "us," and "we," thrown about so easily in this introductory paragraph should become ambiguous, and, we hope, contentious, as this implies a universality that is not the case: many faculty at the university do not conduct research (and, thus, by extension do not contribute to economic growth), and some will question the logic expressed in this passage, believing that economic growth should not be the mission of the (or any) university. Furthermore, how exactly does an institution's research gain *independence* by securing public and private sources of external funding? Such statements blindly ignore the paradox that Clark Kerr acknowledges with regard to the federal funding of research (we think such a paradox exists for all external funding): the "better and the more individual the university, the greater its chances of succumbing to the federal embrace."[2] Is not that very independence, then, negated by the pursuit and procurement of external funding?

---

1. Carl V. Patton, "Introduction," *Metropolitan: The Magazine of Georgia State University* (Spring 2001): 3. Emphasis added.
2. Clark Kerr, *The Uses of the University*, 5th ed. (Cambridge: Harvard University Press, 2001, c. 1963), 38.

More problematically, the givenness of presumptions such as that reputation and achievement are tied to external funding (particularly that which furthers economic growth) should be carefully considered. Perhaps the economic reality in higher education is such that external funding is essential for pursuing one's research mission, but recognizing this fact need in no way dictate the ways we should affirm it. In other words, as we will show in this chapter, the pursuit of external funding is affirmed in a specific discourse that emphasizes not only economic necessity, but a moral imperative that ensures professional and institutional autonomy and freedom, promotes individual and institutional prestige, guarantees quality instruction, furthers the essential mission of the university, and produces benefits to society. We are suggesting, therefore, that the "necessity" of external funding is true in an important sense only because *one can say that it is.*

We analyze the discourse on grants in order to question the very foundations upon which academic practices are based. This chapter does not seek to provide answers to the perplexing "problems" of decreased public funding for research. If our premises are correct, the discourse on grants significantly structures what we can see and thus do in higher education; we believe, therefore, that it is by questioning this logic that we can open up this discourse to different interpretations, different ways of seeing, and thus different ways of being. Our analysis of the discourse on grants, therefore, is like much of our other chapters and follows generally what Fredric Jameson indicates is the point of deconstruction: to explain both what a discourse *means* and how it *works* to support political arrangements.[3]

This chapter raises questions about the boundaries and limitations of a nonreflective understanding of research done in the name of grants and sponsored research, a task made more pressing by the current manifestations of the discourse on an education science.[4] Much of the angst over the federal government's attempts to define a science of education is due to the fact that its funding mechanisms will change as a result. SRE, as we noted before, was very concerned with establishing a culture of science in a federal funding agency; ASRE was similarly concerned with ensuring that doctoral programs and funding agencies establish a culture of science and grants activity; and when Margaret Eisenhart and Robert DeHaan offered justification for why they think restructuring doctoral study is important, they said it was because federal funding agencies are requiring it.[5] Inculcating a

---

3. See Fredric Jameson, *The Political Unconscious: Narrative as a Socially Symbolic Act* (Ithaca: Cornell University Press, 1981).

4. By sponsored research we mean projects (research and otherwise) funded by external private and public agencies. We do not ignore the commonly believed distinction between public and private funding, as the motives of the former have the possibility of being less *interested* than the latter. We show, however, that distinction now may be more ideological than material, since public entities further the imperatives of privatization, and, indeed, may be essential to them.

5. Margaret Eisenhart and Robert L. DeHaan, "Doctoral Preparation of Scientifically Based Education Researchers," *Educational Researcher* 34, no. 4 (2005): 3–13, 8.

culture of science in education, then, is not simply for itself, or even for the individuals and institutions that will constitute its objects, but for the establishment of an enterprise governed by sponsored research, which is already what has happened in the sciences.

We do not argue, however, that sponsored research is inherently bad. Viewing us as doing so fails to understand our argument, which is directed not at any particular grant per se—except for any that utilizes the experimental design in education—but at the establishment of an *enterprise* of external funding. Sponsored research as such is not the problem. In an era of increased competition for what seems a smaller amount public funding, such research becomes very important in producing knowledge—knowledge that often has societal benefits. It is difficult to question, for example, the advances made in medicine as a result of sponsored research. We do question whether institutional and professional rewards should be tied so rigidly to sponsored-research activities, as we believe is increasingly happening, and whether the unfettered pursuit of such activities deflects attention from the institutional and professional practices that continue to require them. Economic forces, as well as the ideological imperatives of privatization, have led institutions to exert pressure on faculty members to seek external funding for research.[6] And for some time now, sponsored research, especially that coming from federal agencies, has enhanced the reputation of institutions, programs, and faculty.[7] But none of this should be taken to mean that professors should abdicate their responsibility to ask questions about sponsored research.

We argue in this chapter that the idea of sponsored research is as problematic as it is taken for granted in the academy. We situate this discourse within the material and ideological forces of privatization and entrepreneurship and try to account for how traditional academic values obscure the effects of these forces. Furthermore, the presupposition of sponsored research impacts academic freedom in ways that may not fully be clear. Accordingly, we explore the issue of academic freedom in this postindustrial era, teasing out the role that sponsored research plays in modifying and limiting such freedom. We also explore why sponsored research has come to be viewed as not only important but imperative, and what institutional and professional practices continue to ensure that it is. We further examine the implications for the profession when professors begin to act (and thus to see) themselves

---

6. Sheila Slaughter and Larry L. Leslie, *Academic Capitalism: Politics, Policies, and the Entrepreneurial University* (Baltimore: The Johns Hopkins University Press, 1997); and Charles W. Smith, *Market Values in American Higher Education: The Pitfalls and Promises* (Lanham: Rowman and Littlefield, 2000).

7. Roger Geiger, "The Ten Generations of American Higher Education," in *American Higher Education in the Twenty-first Century: Social, Political, and Economic Challenges*, 2nd ed., ed. Philip G. Altbach, Robert O. Berdahl, and Patricia J. Gumport (Baltimore: The Johns Hopkins University Press, 2005), 38–70.

as inevitably, and necessarily, grant getters. We suggest that external pressures for sponsored research, and individual reasons for engaging in sponsored research, present problematic implications for professional autonomy and academic freedom.

Before we proceed farther with our analyses, we wish to say something about the tone of this chapter. In the previous chapters we addressed the issues associated with the science of education and explained its effects on professionalism, inquiry, doctoral education, and the government of individuals. These are in many ways "academic" concerns for us; we are concerned with them as scholars typically are. In this chapter our concern is much more personal, since the "grants culture" that is fortified and intensified by the movement toward "scientific" research in education affected us very directly at Georgia State University and Florida International University. We focus on the economic forces of this movement, but will readily admit a personal stake in this discourse. We know that at least some other faculty members at Georgia State University, Florida International University, and elsewhere have affinity for our arguments here—which are likely to be controversial and perhaps audacious—even if these faculty members do not or cannot readily admit to this affinity in public. At any rate, some of the examples we use here are personal, that is, experienced by or told to us. Yet, we will make our arguments here and offer no apologies for them or for the ways in which we make them.

There can be no question also that we further a rhetoric of "crisis" that characterizes critiques of American higher education.[8] Our critique, however, is not directed entirely at state and federal institutions, funding agencies, corporations and industry, or even institutions of higher education themselves; it is directed at faculty members, too. Our critique signifies an unsettling ambivalence about the future of the academic profession, and a serious concern that faculty are internalizing or incorporating institutional and "corporate" norms, causing them, following Michel Foucault, to discipline themselves.[9] This chapter reflects not only our resentment about what happens to faculty when external forces constrain their behavior, but more fundamentally it laments what faculty do to themselves and to each other in their quest to maintain some control over their work and professional lives, a quest whose goal, as currently pursued, will remain hopelessly elusive.

---

8. For two different but critical perspectives on the "crisis" rhetoric, see Robert Birnbaum and Frank Shushok Jr., "The 'Crisis' Crisis in Higher Education: Is that a Wolf or a Pussycat at the Academy's Door," in *In Defense of American Higher Education*, ed. Philip G. Altbach, Patricia Gumport, and D. Bruce Johnstone (Baltimore: The Johns Hopkins University Press, 2001), 59–84; Joan W. Scott, "The Rhetoric of Crisis in Higher Education," in *Higher Education Under Fire: Politics, Economics, and the Crisis of the Humanities*, ed. Michael Bérubé and Cary Nelson (London and New York: Routledge, 1995), 293–304.

9. See, generally, Michel Foucault, *Discipline and Punish: The Birth of the Prison*, trans. Alan Sheridan (New York: Vintage Books, 1977).

THE "GRANTS CULTURE"

We have heard or seen variations of these comments from administrators and colleagues at Georgia State University, Florida International University, and elsewhere:[10]

1. In order to continue our contributions to economic growth and ensure quality education, we must collaborate with corporate, government, and private agencies to promote research and innovation.

2. We need to ensure our strength and independence by securing a variety of funding sources, both public and private.

3. Last year, we exceeded the ten million dollar level in funded research; we now rank second to XYZ University in the state in funded research.

4. We have the highest quality faculty in our department; this year, our faculty has attracted ten million dollars in external funding.

5. You can't have a PhD program unless you have external funding to support full-time students.

6. Let's congratulate Jane for getting a one million dollar grant from the Department of Education to conduct research on school-business partnerships.

7. In order to be seriously considered for the promising scholar award, you should call attention to work in progress that has won support from foundations or government agencies.

8. John, to ensure your promotion, you must get a grant.

9. I don't know what I am doing wrong, but I have not been able to secure a large grant.

10. Let us thank Jane and John, whose grants will allow many of you to travel to conferences this year.

What these statements have in common is the importance of sponsored research in, and to, the academy. There seems a difference between comments 1 through 5 above and comments 6 through 10. But what kind of difference is this? Comments 1 through 5 appear to be institutional reasons for sponsored research, while the other comments seem to imply, at first glance, other reasons for pursuing grants—reasons that, we argue, tacitly

---

10. We disguised some of the language to protect the identities of individuals.

structure faculty identities and direct them toward grants for what seem like individual goals. Much that is written about sponsored research in higher education suggests that somehow the thinking underlying comments 1 through 5 leads to the kind of thinking underlying comments 6 through 10. We think, however, that the order of operation, that is, from institution to individual, is not so certain, and that institutional and individual reasons for sponsored research are becoming indistinguishable and conflated. We question the institution/individual dialectic in this discourse in our concluding section, but for now, in teasing out the issues associated with sponsored research, we focus in turn on three phenomena: (1) the establishment of an enterprise of sponsored research, (2) the tension between teaching and research, and (3) the rise of the new "men of power."

An Enterprise of Sponsored Research

The pursuit of grants, whether for institutional or individual reasons (and we will argue against that distinction throughout this chapter), has led to what we refer to as a "grants culture" that now characterizes much of what happens in the name of research at universities. Institutions are pressuring faculty to obtain external funds to subsidize their research, to be sure, but it is not clear to us why this is the case. Conventional wisdom suggests that universities pressure faculty to engage in sponsored research because of decreasing public funds for research.[11] But we question the totalizing account of such logic, especially since it is clear that prestige, reputation, and worth are based on the amount of external funding received by institutions,[12] and, similarly, faculty gain prestige and institutional and professional rewards on the basis of their ability to secure grants.[13] Research is, as Sheila Slaughter and Larry Leslie explain, what differentiates among and within institutions.[14]

11. It may be more informative to substitute the phrase "shifting public funds" for "decreased public funding" with regard to revenues coming from state and federal governments. It appears that there has been a shift in government funding away from higher education and toward other social institutions (such as public schools), but concurrently there has been considerable public "investment" in higher education, particularly for solidifying economic growth. So, it is difficult to gauge the claims made about public funding, except to say that there has been a shift.
12. For example, the *U.S. News and World Report* rankings of the top graduate education schools weigh peer school assessments, superintendent assessments, mean GRE scores, acceptance rates, doctorate-granting rates, student/faculty ratio, and *total funded research* and *funded research per faculty members*. See *2006 Graduate School Rankings*, U.S. News and World Report (2006). Available at http://www.usnews.com/usnews/edu/grad/rankings/edu/brief/edurank_brief. php (Retrieved January 27, 2006).
13. Indeed, the richest universities and faculty are the most entrepreneurial. Harvard University, for example, is not poor or dependent on state funding by any stretch of the imagination, and yet it is the entrepreneur par excellence. Despite an endowment of close to $25 billion, at last count, it still refuses to release its faculty from grant writing. For a ranking of endowments, see *The Chronicle of Higher Education*, "Almanac Issue 2006–7" (August 25, 2006): 32–33.
14. Slaughter and Leslie, *Academic Capitalism*, 17.

And it is not at all certain that faculty and institutions would change if public funding practices changed in their favor.

Remarkably, many in higher education take as given the grants culture, and when we have heard any questioning at all, it has been about particular practices associated with grants (e.g., a reduction in basic research, a lack of disinterested research, a lack of adequate funding, shifting governmental and foundation priorities, narrow views of science by the Institute for Education Sciences, little institutional support for the management of grants, extensive reporting requirements associated with grants, and so forth). But the logic of the culture itself is rarely questioned. The logic of the grants culture is such that faculty who secure grants become in a large sense more "independent" from their institutions, as those with grants are relieved from their duties (such as teaching and service) and can move more easily to other institutions (or threaten to do so), where they can negotiate better working conditions (that is, more freedom to pursue grants). But this point suggests a paradox: faculty gain a measure of independence from their universities but only by increasing their dependence on grants. Such a dependence on grants seems to be one of the hidden consequences of the grants culture: the pursuit of grants requires something like a Faustian bargain, offering a kind of independence from institutions but only by requiring dependence on grants.

It might seem appropriate to some to discount our critique of the grants culture as critiquing the practices of just a few select institutions, particularly the elite public and private research universities. Indeed, such universities and their faculty do spend (and receive) the bulk of the money available for sponsored research. Much of federal funding for university re-search goes to 125 universities.[15] Thus, only a small minority of researchers working at the top research-oriented universities produce the bulk of research and receive the majority of external funding (perhaps only 19 percent of academics).[16] This dominance by so few institutions leads to resentment and intense competition, but it also sheds doubt on the integrity of peer review, which supposedly reviews grant proposals on the basis of the merits of the proposal.

Nevertheless, while only a small number of universities and faculty do research and secure external funds, all faculty are affected. As Robert Blackburn and Janet Lawrence explain, where the production of scholarly publications was once the almost exclusive domain of research and doctoral

---

15. Indeed, the National Institutes of Health disproportionately funds research in a few states that house the largest and most prestigious universities. In the early 2000s, one-third of all NIH grant money went to researchers in three states (California, New York, and Pennsylvania), and ten states received a combined 1 percent of the NIH grant money; see Jeffrey Brainard, " 'Have-Nots' See More Funds from the NIH," *The Chronicle of Higher Education* (March 29, 2002): A23–A24.

16. See Philip G. Altbach, "The American Academic Model in Comparative Perspective," in *In Defense of American Higher Education*, ed. Philip G. Altbach, Patricia Gumport, and D. Bruce Johnstone (Baltimore: The Johns Hopkins University Press, 2001), 11–37, 26–27.

universities, today faculty nearly everywhere perceive pressure to obtain external funding, conduct research, and publish their findings.[17] Furthermore, the elite universities and their faculty exert a powerful influence on other institutions and their faculty, as Christopher Jencks and David Riesman noted almost forty years ago.[18] Thus, faculty everywhere wish they could spend more time on research, and colleges and universities are increasingly asking faculty to subsidize their own research through external funding.

Blackburn and Lawrence fail to question this "pressure" to procure grants, recommending instead that "institutions that want to increase this kind of output need to consider ways they can assist faculty members prepare acceptable [grant] proposals."[19] Furthermore, they argue that faculty need relief from assignments such as teaching, help from advanced students who can help them locate key sources, and seed money to start up the research for which they will ultimately seek external funding. This logic is all the more remarkable because it has gone unquestioned so far. It is not just the individual seeking grants whom this affects, but everyone else as well: Other faculty must pick up the "slack" created by relieving the grant writer from institutional assignments; students' work can be exploited for the faculty's and institution's benefit; and money is shifted from elsewhere (because the logic of accounting makes everything a zero-sum game). Such an impact on others is obscured because the logic of grants is such that they can be framed at the level of an abstraction that brackets off the impact their pursuit and securement will have on others, on the production of knowledge, and even on the subject of the research itself: It is not important what the grant is for—the amount is the primary focus; the research itself is irrelevant, or, more accurately, of secondary importance.

The grants culture, it is worth noting, was not caused by the "crisis" associated with decreasing public funding since the 1980s. State and federal entities have indeed dramatically curtailed the rate of funding and have required extensive accounting for the money they now give.[20] But, as

---

17. Robert T. Blackburn and Janet H. Lawrence, *Faculty at Work: Motivation, Expectation, Satisfaction* (Baltimore: The Johns Hopkins University Press, 1995), 144.

18. Christopher Jencks and David Riesman, *The Academic Revolution* (New York: Doubleday, 1968).

19. Blackburn and Lawrence, *Faculty at Work*, 149.

20. We prefer to use the term *accounting* rather than the popular *accountability*, as the former best exemplifies what is now required of institutions of higher education: that they account for how the money is spent and to ensure that such spending matches the purposes for which the money was allocated. While *accountability* incorporates accounting, it also connotes something more ethical or moral: institutions of higher education, incorporated for the purposes of serving the public, should justify their practices—and, indeed, their very existence—to the public, and not just inform the public of what they do and how they do it, but also of how they are serving the public. Thus, we should be leery of using *accountability* when we in fact mean *accounting*, as the former carries moral connotations that the latter does not. We will have occasion to return to the logic of accounting in this chapter.

Lawrence Gladieux, Jaqueline King, and Melanie Corrigan assert, federal support of science at universities pre-dates federal support for student aid, the former traceable to the late 1800s. And while federal funding for research constitutes less than 10 percent of the total revenues for higher education, it can make up about 25 percent of the revenues at research universities.[21] Indeed, federal support of the sciences has so defined the sciences to the point that scientists find it inconceivable to think of their work without external funding.[22]

Yet, we want to pause before attributing the grants culture solely to the federal government or to any one source. Since the 1920s, as Roger Geiger argues, additional wealth was invested in more and better faculty, especially those researchers actively engaged in the advancement of knowledge. This was sparked by philanthropic foundations, particularly the Rockefeller trusts, and such participation in turn increased the prestige of the institution and the faculty member.[23] This phenomenon was exacerbated by the flood of federally sponsored research since after World War II—and especially after Sputnik, which skewed research toward the physical sciences, engineering, and medicine—as a result of the numerous and enormous grants from the National Science Foundation, the National Aeronautical and Space Administration, and the National Institutes of Health.[24] This money essentially "made" the premier research universities, faculty, and even disciplines. Princeton University, for example, was transformed from a university known for its emphasis on humanities-centered undergraduate education to one that is known for its graduate school, science and engineering programs, large-scale sponsored research, and industrial consulting—all because of the securement of extensive federal research funds since World War II.[25] Princeton's supposed core values of focusing on the humanities and separating classified research

---

21. See Lawrence E. Gladieux, Jacqueline E. King, and Melanie E. Corrigan, "The Federal Government and Higher Education," in *American Higher Education in the Twenty-First Century: Social, Political, and Economic Challenges*, 2nd ed., ed. Philip G. Altbach, Robert O. Berdahl, and Patricia J. Gumport (Baltimore: The Johns Hopkins University Press, 2005), 163–97, 168, 173.

22. See Loren R. Graham, "Concerns About Science and Attempts to Regulate Inquiry," *Daedalus: Journal of the American Academy of Arts and Sciences* 107, no. 2 (1978): 1–21, 7–8; Rodney W. Nichols, "Federal Science Policy and Universities: Consequences of Success," *Daedalus: Journal of the Academy of Arts and Sciences* 122, no. 4 (1993): 197–224.

23. See Geiger, "The Ten Generations of American Higher Education," 60.

24. Ibid., 62–63.

25. See Amy Sue Bix, " 'Backing into Sponsored Research': Physics and Engineering at Princeton University," *History of Higher Education Annual* 13 (1993): 9–52. This article explains that the bulk of the research funds came from the Department of Defense, implicating Princeton University, perhaps unintentionally, in American imperialism.

Some scholars refused federal grants to promote language training in Arabic languages (among others) because of their links to the Pentagon; see Anne Marie Borrego, "Scholars Revive Boycott of U.S. Grants to Promote Language Training," *The Chronicle of Higher Education* (August 16, 2002): A25–A26.

from the main campus went by the wayside in its (and its researchers') pursuit of money. It is clear to us that the amount of money from external sources, and the prestige it confers, creates the "need" for it—universities did not "need" this money until they took it and got used to it.

Elaborating upon a point we made earlier, while there seems to be a shift in current patterns of public funding of higher education, we are not sure whether this shift necessarily entails a decrease in such funding, at least for research at the federal level. Thus, while it might be the case that federal investment in higher education has diminished, its logic for investing in science has not changed. It may be that the amount of public funding for research has not diminished all that much, but that its purposes have. Previous patterns of federal funding emphasized basic research and directed grants to individual professors. Current funding patterns suggest that grants are being reallocated to (1) applied (or functional) projects that benefit the American economy as opposed to basic research, (2) earmarked projects rather than those that go through the peer review process,[26] and (3) research institutes and centers rather than individual professors.[27] Furthermore, one may say that traditional public funding for national objectives has been replaced by another kind of "public funding," which (1) furthers privatization and which comes from private and public corporations, subsidized by governments either directly or through tax breaks, and (2) are supported by pro-competitive policies that make knowledge a commodity that is saleable. Indeed, the power of science as a profession is intricately tied to the capitalist forces reshaping the economy and restructuring social institutions accordingly. Capitalists saw science as useful for their interests and so they ensured a heavy public investment in science.[28] All this is done for the sake of "economic growth" and for the benefit of the increasingly large, multinational corporations. These policies are also given the "force of law," since courts uphold them, and by doing so support and extend the imperatives of entrepreneurship and privatization.[29]

Again, focusing on governmental bodies tells only part of the story, for the grants culture has other major players. Private foundations and corporations (which also fund research through the foundations they create) have taken on significance in sponsored research. This is likely the result of shifting patterns of public funding. The critiques of corporate funding,

26. Gladieux, King, and Corrigan, "The Federal Government and Higher Education," 171–72.
27. See Jeffrey Brainard, "U.S. Agencies Look to Interdisciplinary Science," *The Chronicle of Higher Education* (June 14, 2002): A20–A21.
28. John J. Beer and W. David Lewis, "Aspects of the Professionalization of Science," in *The Professions in America*, ed. Kenneth S. Lynn (Boston: Houghton Mifflin, 1965), 110–30.
29. See Benjamin Baez and Sheila Slaughter, "Academic Freedom and Federal Courts in the 1990s: The Legitimation of the Conservative Entrepreneurial State," in *Higher Education: Handbook of Theory and Research, Volume 16* (Bronx: Agathon Press, 2001), 73–118.

as we discuss later, are prevalent, but the critiques of foundation grants are less so. Yet, private foundations affect institutions, faculty, and their research through the choices of areas they support. Foundations certainly have different purposes than governmental entities, but nevertheless shape research and institutional practice in more or less direct ways.[30] These foundations can be community-based foundations (e.g., Neighborhood Associations), family or personal foundations, special-purpose foundations (e.g., Harvard Glee Club), company or corporate foundations, and the more commonly recognized national, independent foundations (e.g., Ford, Kellogg, Carnegie, etc.). Foundations award between $32–35 billion annually,[31] and thus are key players in the movement toward an enterprise of sponsored research.

Is it any wonder, then, that the grants culture has taken hold? Given that external funds went to very few institutions, and that these institutions gained considerable prestige and power as a result, others have emulated them, leading to an intense competition for public and private funds. The logic of the grants culture is that colleges and universities can, technically, refuse external funding. But why would they, when so much revenue can be gained from it, and when institutional and professional identity and prestige are directly tied to grants? Grants exert a real if indirect control over institutions and faculty members, even putting into question their supposed *raison d'etre*: teaching.

Teaching and Grants

At a symposium on higher education at Georgia State University in 2001, Ellen Condliffe Lagemann, former president of the Spencer Foundation and former dean of the Graduate School of Education at Harvard University, spoke about the role of research foundations in colleges and universities. As a historian, she shared her thoughts regarding the development of foundations from the late nineteenth century to the present. She indicated that the twentieth century witnessed a remarkable growth in both the number and influence of foundations, that foundations represent varied political agendas, and that most of the money to start foundations came from wealthy industrialists. Importantly, she also indicated a distinction between research and teaching in universities and argued against equating scholarship and teaching, as Ernest Boyer attempted to do in *Scholarship Reconsidered*.[32] Part

---

30. See Ellen Condliffe Lagemann, *Politics of Knowledge: The Carnegie Corporation, Philanthropy, and Public Policy* (Middletown: Wesleyan University Press, 1989).

31. Fred F. Harcleroad and Judith S. Eaton, "The Hidden Hand: External Constituencies and their Impact," in *American Higher Education in the Twenty-First Century: Social, Political, and Economic Challenges*, 2nd ed., ed. Philip G. Altbach, Robert O. Berdahl, and Patricia J. Gumport (Baltimore: The Johns Hopkins University Press, 2005), 253–83, 256.

32. Ernest L. Boyer, *Scholarship Reconsidered: Priorities of the Professoriate* (Princeton: Carnegie Foundation for the Advancement of Teaching, 1990).

of her point was that research and teaching are fundamentally different enterprises and each should be seen as valuable, especially in terms of faculty promotion and tenure at institutions of higher education.

During the question and answer portion of her talk, one of us asked Lagemann about the effect of foundation-supported research on teaching. Specifically, she was asked if teaching was the first casualty of sponsored research, given that faculty who obtain grants usually "buy" themselves out of teaching in order to fulfill their sponsored research obligations. Lagemann acknowledged the issue as a problem but suggested that the question needed to be answered at the "local level." Foundations should not, she claimed, set policy regarding teaching load reduction at sponsored institutions.

This response was very surprising to us, given what she stated in her talk and in her books. Indeed, she has illustrated before how private foundations directly and indirectly shape the course of research at universities and the direction of government spending on universities, and so they dictate in a very important sense the politics of knowledge and how such politics influences institutional practices. She states,

> But within a society where a politics of knowledge was emerging and intensifying, a foundation so chartered could exercise power beyond that inherent in its extraordinary wealth. The [Carnegie] Corporation's self-imposed mandate to define, develop, and distribute knowledge was, in a sense, a franchise to govern, in important indirect ways.[33]

She also explains that the Carnegie Corporation's "funds have often made a significant difference in a scholarly career, in the development of a field of knowledge, or in the life of a college, research institution, or library."[34] This "power" and influence, she indicates, are

> not unique to one foundation. Other foundations have participated in the politics of knowledge. . . . And other foundations, think tanks, and professional associations have taken advantage of immediate opportunities to advance one or another reform, sometimes in the process giving insufficient attention to the associated long-range, unanticipated, and even undesirable consequences of their actions and achievements.[35]

Thus, to claim that the tensions between research and teaching created by sponsored research are a "local" matter is to deny what she has specifically

---

33. Lagemann, *Politics of Knowledge*, 6.
34. Ibid., 253.
35. Ibid., 263.

written. Perhaps she meant to do this, but we do not believe that her response was necessarily a "cop out," as the legitimacy of the belief in local control is central to the matter at hand.

When all is seen as a "local" concern, the system is left intact. The logic of such a statement assumes that institutions pursue or refuse grants independently, and, consequently, faculty members who pursue grants, pursue them independently, and those who refuse grants, refuse them independently. Yet, institutional (and, increasingly, professional) reputation hinges on attaining these grants, and so the foundations are directly complicit in the priorities institutions make. Faculty pursue and refuse grants only within institutional settings and within a system that rewards and punishes accordingly. Furthermore, those who are relieved of teaching responsibilities to pursue grants do not get relieved independently: others must pick up the slack, so to speak. Those who refuse grants do not do so independently: they are ostracized and their complaints labeled "shrill" and "out of touch," as we heard said about us when we have brought up these concerns at meetings. Moreover, those who refuse grants will find it difficult to obtain institutional funding to pursue their scholarship.[36] Such decisions neither take place independently nor locally, and thus funding agencies are implicated in the very system many of them deny.

The current tenor in higher education—indeed, in all of society— champions free market entrepreneurship over teaching, such that teaching becomes the de facto sacrificial lamb on the alter of foundation-, government-, and corporate-subsidized grants. To push decision making "down" to the "local level" of colleges and universities, or even to faculty members themselves, is therefore not to push decision making down at all. The decision has already been made in favor of entrepreneurship and the message to faculty is becoming increasingly clear, if strident: get grants! Bringing in extra funds to one's college adds to institutional coffers (and one's own) and does offer some important opportunities. Among these opportunities is benefiting society through important research and working closely with a select number of students brought into the project by grant money. The opportunity to do the research in the first place is, of course, an opportunity. Furthermore, budgeting systems may make grants the most effective means of getting work done. They may pay for the salaries of secretaries and other staff who take care of the management of grants; they can allow faculty to

---

36. In a memorandum dated September 12, 2002, to all faculty, Charles Louis, then the Georgia State University Vice President for Research, announced the availability of internal grants available to subsidize research. These nine grants include those with titles such as "Research Initiation Grants," "Faculty Mentoring Grant," "Research Team Grant," "Travel Grant," and "Equipment Matching Fund." All but one of the grants, it turns out, explicitly were tied to external funding or encourage its pursuit (the sole grant that does not include the words *external funding* in its description is the "Dissertation Grant," which is allocated to graduate students to help them with their studies).

travel to conferences in order to disseminate the results of research and to receive support from other colleagues; and they can give many faculty some independence from the whims of administrators.

One wonders, however, if faculty are selling out the majority of their students (and some of their colleagues) by seeking grants in the first place. A closer look at this issue may reveal that faculty are hegemonically reproducing a capital market niche that privileges money over meaning and grant seeking over teaching. In this way, blame does not rest ultimately with foundations, government agencies, and corporate oligarchs, but with institutions and faculty themselves. Indeed, Lagemann may be correct in a way she did not intend to be: the problem of sponsored research *may* be looked for at the "local level."

The expectations for scientific methods and topics of research that get funded limit faculty who might otherwise opt to engage in grant seeking. Here, however, is the crux of the point: Why are faculty engaged in sponsored research at all? What social, political, and economic forces have raised expectations in such a way that buying one's self out of, say, teaching, becomes the goal of teachers qua professors? While the push toward grant getting is reaching a fevered pitch, what consequences result? What assumptions are made about the value and quality of the grant getter and his or her role as teacher and researcher? What limitations are there to sponsored research? Sponsored research is sponsored by someone or something else. Lagemann referenced in her talk conservative and liberal foundations as though their numbers were equal, and hence, their agendas balanced, but conservative foundations outspend liberal ones seven to one.[37] What problems does external funding resolve? What problems does such funding raise and create? What solutions might exist to mediate the arguably negative aspects of selling out for grant money?

And yet the logic of the teaching/research rhetoric is that the latter enriches the former, as the president of Georgia State University states in the epigraph of this chapter. Is this true? As we indicated at the start of this chapter, this may not be provable at our universities since faculty do "buy out" of teaching. The insistence upon a distinction, however, obscures how granting agencies are increasing their influence even over teaching. For example, the Howard Hughes Medical Institute recently awarded twenty research scientists $1 million each "to develop programs that will attempt to bridge the gap between the classroom and the laboratory." Darcy Kelley, one of the recipients of a Hughes grant, claims that the grant "will enable [her] to run students through a state-of-the-art training program."[38] Since

---

37. See Philip Kovacs and Deron Boyles, "Institutes, Foundations, and Think Tanks: Conservative Influences on U.S. Public Schools," *Public Resistance* 1, no. 1 (May 1, 2005): 1–18, 3. Available at http://www.publicresistance.org (Retrieved November 12, 2005).
38. Thomas Bartlett, "20 scholars receive $1-million each for new approaches to teaching science," *The Chronicle of Higher Education* (September 27, 2002): A12.

her students already help with some of her research, one wonders whether
the grant money is not simply a way of paying students to do faculty work
for them (even if they get listed as an author). Is the purpose of "running
students through" a program one related to better teaching or simply another way to publish results of the grant-supported research? Of the students
with whom Kelley interacts, how many other students are deprived of time
with her? That is, when faculty tout the value of a grant as being a way
to support students, they really mean *some* or *a few* students. At the same
time that the amount of interaction among a few students and the professor
increases, other students are left out in the cold since the professor likely
bought herself out of a class of twenty or more in order to work closely
with a few research assistants.

Some studies also shed doubt on the professed link between teaching and research, suggesting that research will sacrifice teaching.[39] Perhaps
this sacrifice is necessary in particular contexts (and, frankly, we know of
professors who should not teach), but one should not pretend otherwise
by believing that there can be a "proper" balance, or that teaching is as
important as research in the university and in the professorate.[40] We do not
intend to claim here that teaching should be sacrificed. We argue only that
it currently is being sacrificed in favor of research, and especially sponsored
(and increasingly "scientific") research. If universities will claim that teaching is part of their central missions, then one should expect them to honor
their claim.

Yet, the argument for the distinction between teaching and research,
and that each, though different, is compatible with the other may be one
of the ways that the field of higher education masks the ways in which it
reinforces privatization and entrepreneurship. Indeed, the logic of the discourse on research takes on specifically economic terms which are masked
by a "higher ground" kind of rhetoric of making faculty more knowledgeable,
providing the most up-to-date knowledge, and so forth.[41] Patton, president
of Georgia State University, states that "researchers develop intellectually
and become better teachers."[42] To say that undergraduate teaching benefits
from the research activities (and by extension grants) of faculty is to sug-

39. See James S. Fairweather, "The Mythologies of Faculty Productivity: Implications for
Institutional Policy and Decision Making," *The Journal of Higher Education* 73, no. 1 (2002):
26–48, 31–34, 44.
40. See, for example, Jonathan Cole, "Balancing Acts: Dilemmas of Choice Facing Research
Universities," *Daedalus: Journal of the American Academy of Arts and Sciences* 122, no. 4 (1993):
1–36, 23–28.
41. For a discussion of the links made between teaching, research, and reputation, see Stephen D. Grunig, "Research, Reputation, and Resources: The Effect of Research Activity on
Perceptions of Undergraduate Education and Institutional Resources Acquisition," *The Journal
of Higher Education* 68, no. 1 (1997): 17–52.
42. Patton, *Metropolitan*, 3.

gest a kind of "trickle down" effect of research. The rhetoric goes like this: because research enhances reputation, which brings in more revenues, it leads to better teaching, since the institution can obtain high-caliber faculty and provide more resources for teaching.[43] All the while the economic foundations of the drive for grants for universities *and* individual faculty members are obscured by such arguments. We will address in greater detail the economic motives of the university later, but next we discuss the power that prolific grant getters can yield.

The New "Men of Power"

That institutions can profit from sponsored research is a claim with which few will disagree, but the claim that individual faculty members profit may be a bit more troubling for some. How do faculty profit from the grants culture? They profit in economic ways, of course, but it would be a superficial claim if all we say is that those profits relate to salary and wages. They also gain power through prestige, expertise, tenure, and so forth, all of which distinguish faculty from each other.[44] Faculty who garner large grants become "free agents." Few would deny faculty this privilege. Indeed, the ability to move from institution to institution is a privilege few of us enjoy, and it certainly marks one's worth in academe. Yet, it might be fruitful to consider how professional privileges are increasingly tied, and become synonymous with, entrepreneurial activities.[45]

There has developed a system of "haves and have nots" among faculty, and this hierarchy is not merely evident between faculty in the sciences and those in the humanities, but also within academic fields and departments.[46] Indeed, as we have personally experienced ourselves, the faculty who do not procure grants, but who may derive some indirect benefit from the grants

---

43. See Grunig, "Research, Reputation, and Resources."
44. See generally, Gary Rhoades, "Whose Property Is It?" *Academe: Bulletin of the American Association of University Professors* (September–October 2001): 39–43.
45. Sheila Slaughter, "Professional Values and the Allure of the Market," *Academe: Bulletin of the American Association of University Professors* (September/October 2001): 22–26.
46. Such entrepreneurship has also contributed to the ideology of accounting that characterizes much of what we regard as valuable in higher education. "Merit," under accounting principles, becomes justifiable. The quality of scholarship cannot be "counted" as easily as the quantity of research grant dollars, which the grants culture increasingly instrumentalizes and privileges. While publications still count predominantly in determining the quality of the faculty, this has always been contested as unfair and ambiguous, which leads to such questions as: What constitutes a "good" journal? Is one article in a prestigious journal more valuable than two articles in less prestigious ones? How does one consider an article with multiple authors? Grants, however, provide a clean dollar amount which is unambiguous. Indeed, one can see how even contested notions such as quality and productivity become seductively subject to accounting. One must then "count" what faculty do in order to make claims about their worth. We will address the implications of such accounting for academic freedom later in the chapter.

others obtain, may be told to express gratitude to the grant getters and are resented when they refuse to do so. This is attributable to the fact that research is the differentiating characteristic among faculty, and they will likely not pursue other activities, even if they were better rewarded for them. And why should they when they become powerful within their institutions and in their fields on the basis of the grants they obtain?

Over thirty-five years ago, Robert Nisbet wrote a stinging critique of the "higher capitalism" and "new men of power" that result from sponsored (predominantly federal) research, a phenomenon he compared with how the gold bullion of the sixteenth century altered the social structure of Western Europe.[47] Similarly, he argues, it is not the amount of wealth gained by universities as a result of the federal investment in the sciences since the 1940s, but the structure of wealth and the means by which it is transferred differently that presents the most powerful agent of change in higher education.[48] And while the pursuit of wealth in this manner originally characterized the physical sciences, the social sciences and the humanities were soon after seduced. The new "men of power," or "academic capitalists," gained significant independence from institutional control. These "men of power" are able to pay scant attention, if any, to institutional concerns, looking instead to external funding sources, and through their centers, bureaus, and institutes, they could run their operations without any institutional assistance. They could obtain their own technicians, graduate students, secretaries, and junior faculty, such that, Nisbet argues, they could rival traditional departments (and even colleges) in size and revenues.[49] He could have added that these capitalists could create their own avenues for publications, bypassing, even, the traditional peer review publication processes. Many of these "men of power" do not even teach, becoming, as Kerr indicates, the "un-faculty," having the title of faculty but not teaching at all, some not even appointed on the tenure track, being, in essence, solely researchers (and managers of grants) and having no other responsibility to the institution, students, colleagues, or the public.[50]

Nisbet and Kerr raise important, if only theoretical questions, about the grants culture. They both seem correct, and Nisbet, in particular, displays the kind of angst that should be associated with sponsored research. Yet, Nisbet also appears to treat the matter simply as one of choice. He claims that the academy could turn its back on wealth and focus its research on what is compatible with teaching in the university. But his account fails to grasp adequately the imperatives of entrepreneurship and privatization that

47. Robert Nisbet, *The Degradation of the Academic Dogma: The University in America 1945–1970* (New York: Basic Books, 1971).

48. Ibid., 72–73.

49. Ibid., 75–76.

50. Kerr, *The Uses of the University*, 49–50.

characterize much of American society, and, thus, institutional and individual behavior, a point we move to next.

THE IMPERATIVES OF ENTREPRENEURSHIP
AND PRIVATIZATION IN HIGHER EDUCATION

Shifting economic priorities (especially of state and federal agencies) have exacerbated the grants culture, which, we will argue, is ensured by the forces of privatization. Privatization encompasses not only the transfer of resources between public and private sectors, but also the movement from state providers to large, corporate providers, the purchase of services from the private sector, and the conversion of state services to market principles.[51] Privatization is deemed to reflect a reduction of the state's role in the management of a country, and an imposition of market forces in the management of public services. We will say more about this later, but for now, the undermining of the nation-state as a result of global cultural and economic exchanges facilitates the forces of privatization. These exchanges shed doubt on the traditional role of universities and their faculty as producing and disseminating knowledge in the interests of national culture.[52] The priorities of nation-states have given way to those of global institutions, especially the transnational corporations, which have redirected national priorities toward their own private interests. Public and private funding of higher education, if in the past focusing on altruistic or "national" concerns, now seems tied to economic prosperity, especially in the so-called global marketplace.[53]

Institutions of higher education, including public ones, have increasingly sought revenues from the private sector. Federal support still dominates the grants and contracts "portfolio" of universities, of course.[54] (And federal research funds for university science alone exceed $57 billion.[55]) Indeed, the federal government accounts substantially for the total revenues for higher education as a whole through student aid and research and development.[56] State governments still provide the greatest amount of revenues for higher education, although we have seen a move toward having students shoulder

---

51. See Paul Spicker, *The Welfare State: A General Theory* (Thousand Oaks: Sage Publications, 2000), 140.
52. See Bill Readings, *The University in Ruins* (Cambridge: Harvard University Press, 1996).
53. See Sheila Slaughter and Gary Rhoades, *Academic Capitalism and the New Economy: Markets, State, and Higher Education* (Baltimore: The Johns Hopkins University Press, 2004).
54. See Gary Rhoades and Sheila Slaughter, "Academic Capitalism, Managed Professionals, and Supply-Side Higher Education," *Social Text* 51, no. 2 (1997): 9–38, 12–13.
55. This number has exceeded the amount the federal government has spent on student aid ($54.9 billion). See *The Chronicle of Higher Education*, "Higher Education and Science" (February 15, 2002): A33.
56. See Gladieux, King, and Corrigan, "The Federal Government and Higher Education," 163.

a greater burden of college expenses through tuition hikes and other fees.[57] For public universities, in particular, grants and contracts revenues have increased, with the greatest share increases coming from the private sector and from the institution itself.[58]

Many universities have moved to "entrepreneurial science" in order to generate revenues, establishing research parks and technology transfer offices.[59] Public universities, especially since the 1980s, have also aggressively turned to fund raising to generate revenues.[60] Long the purview of private institutions, public universities also have established development offices, foundations, and campaigns to raise money, where just twenty-five years ago fund raising was simply a matter of alumni contributions.[61] Indeed, for the prestigious colleges and universities, public and private, billion-dollar campaigns are no longer even noteworthy.

Sheila Slaughter and Gary Rhoades's study of entrepreneurial practices in higher education illustrates that decreases in public funding have required institutions to engage in market-like behavior, including raising tuition, resorting to marketing, utilizing enrollment management, and deferring costs of services to students, fund raising, and intellectual property.[62] Although this is correct, we also might want to ask whether decreased public funding completely explains the move toward privatization. Certainly, some institutions have suffered seriously from shifting state priorities towards health care, K-12 education, corrections, and other social institutions, and so public universities' research budgets, and especially their state-funded research projects, are in jeopardy when states face financial difficulties.[63] Given these constraints, some of the wealthiest public institutions have sought to be released from government constraints on their ability to raise revenues.[64] (Even wealthy private institutions can claim financial difficulties without a hint of shame.[65])

---

57. See Don Hossler, Jon P. Lund, Jackie Ramin, Sarah Westfall, and Steve Irish, "State Funding for Higher Education; The Sisyphean Task," Journal of Higher Education 68, no. 2 (1997): 160–90, 161–62.

58. In 2002, of the top twenty universities in corporate support, thirteen were public universities, with Michigan State University leading the way (revenue exceeding $116 million, surpassing the nearest university, Case Western Reserve University, by more than $26 million). See The Chronicle of Higher Education, "Almanac 2002–3," 33.

59. In education, "entrepreneurial science" will likely become that which will be funded by the IES and reported in the What Works Clearinghouse.

60. Of the top twenty universities in fund raising in 2004–05, nine were public universities. See The Chronicle of Higher Education, "Almanac Issue 2006–7," 30.

61. See David W. Breneman, "For Colleges, This is Not Just Another Recession," The Chronicle Review (June 14, 2002): B7–B9.

62. See Slaughter and Rhoades, Academic Capitalism and the New Economy.

63. See Jeffrey Selingo, "States with the Biggest Deficits Take Aim at Higher Education," The Chronicle of Higher Education (April 19, 2002): A24–A26.

64. Ben Gose, "The Fall of the Flagships: Do the Best State Universities Need to Privatize to Thrive?" The Chronicle of Higher Education (July 5, 2002): A19–A21.

65. John L. Pulley, "Well-Off and Wary," The Chronicle of Higher Education (June 21, 2002): A27–A29.

Nevertheless, there is evidence that economic conditions spark "academic capitalism." Slaughter and Leslie, who studied universities' market-like behavior in a number of countries, argue that as public support for higher education decreases (or shifts in purpose), institutions and their faculty seek to replace that funding with funds from alternative sources.[66] When state support declines, universities will pursue only investments in short- and long-term projects that will garner support from federal government and private industry.[67] Indeed, those projects with the most potential for profits are privileged and rewarded not only by the market but by institutional and professional reward systems.[68] This means, of course, that programs such as engineering, computer sciences, but also the physical sciences more generally, will receive institutional privileges over and against the humanities and the social sciences, including education, which, if they are to survive (or thrive) must similarly model themselves like entrepreneurial programs and achieve "scientific rigor." Indeed, this profit motive is now concentrated on "scientific" research, particularly of the applied kind, as this has the most potential for establishing and increasing market share. So the discourse on science in education, for all the talk about rigor and expertise, is rooted in "economics."

Profit-oriented research means, of course, more university-industry relationships, and these warrant more detailed discussion. American higher education has always been attentive to industry concerns, but the increasing emphasis on vocationalism in colleges and universities since the 1980s makes the university-industry connection much more salient than before. This salience has implications for research, since many university-industry relations are focused largely on research, with industries forming partnerships with universities to obtain help with research of interest to them.[69] These partnerships have led universities to engage heavily in programs to patent

66. Slaughter and Leslie, *Academic Capitalism*, 11. See also, John G. Francis and Mark C. Hampton, "Resourceful Responses: The Adaptive Research University and the Drive to Market," *The Journal of Higher Education* 70, no. 6 (1999): 625–41.

67. Michael Bérubé and Cary Nelson, "Introduction: A Report from the Front," in *Higher Education Under Fire: Politics, Economics, and the Crisis of the Humanities*, ed. Michael Bérubé and Cary Nelson (London and New York: Routledge, 1995), 1–32, 12.

68. One should note here that "success" in entrepreneurial activities is not the important factor—the promise of profits alone allows universities to invest vast amounts of money in such activities, even if such profits fail to materialize. Very few universities generate revenues from commercially sponsored research. See Eyal Press and Jennifer Washburn, "The Kept University," *Atlantic Monthly* (March 2000): 39–54. Ironically, in light of the "free market" ideology supporting commercially sponsored research, few faculty members incur penalties when their "ventures" fail to yield profits or even when they cost their universities great amounts of money. See Slaughter and Leslie, *Academic Capitalism*, 203.

69. See Philip G. Altbach, "Patterns in Higher Education Development," in *American Higher Education in the Twenty-first Century: Social, Political, and Economic Challenges*, 2nd ed., ed. Philip G. Altbach, Robert O. Berdahl, and Patricia J. Gumport (Baltimore: The Johns Hopkins University Press, 2005), 15–37, 26–27.

faculty and student ideas, form confidentiality agreements, and make faculty and students more entrepreneurial. Faculty are encouraged to attract external grants, do consulting, and the like.[70] This, of course, gives the private sector extensive control over university research, ensuring that universities will serve the private sector and overlook or ignore public or altruistic goals.[71] Furthermore, university-industry partnerships may stifle critique within the university, as one is not likely to "bite the hand that feeds you."[72]

The connection between higher education and industry is powerful, but it is not seen necessarily as problematic by many within the university.[73] Indeed, in the epigraph in this chapter, we noted the comments of Patton, president of Georgia State University, who tied university research to economic growth. Similarly, government agencies and foundations see their support of university research much like Patton does. For example, in 1993, the president of the Rockefeller Foundation could state that

> [p]robably no single constituency is as well-placed as are industrial leaders to judge the quality of what is produced by research universities. If graduates have been poorly taught and the research is worthless, America's industrial and corporate leadership would, presumably, begin to disengage. . . . The opposite is the case. The expansion of university-industrial partnerships in recent years is unprecedented. In less than a decade, industry-sponsored research and development at America's universities and colleges quadrupled, reaching $1.2 million in 1991.[74]

---

70. Ibid., 30–31.
71. See the special edition of *Academe* titled "Selling Out? Corporations on Campus," *Academe: Bulletin of the American Association of University Professors* (September–October 2001). See also Teresa Isabelle Daza Campbell, "Public Policy for the 21st Century: Addressing Potential Conflicts in University-Industry Collaboration," *The Review of Higher Education* 20, no. 4 (1997): 357–79; Teresa Isabelle Daza Campbell and Sheila Slaughter, "Faculty and Administrator Attitudes Toward Potential Conflicts of Interest, Commitment, and Equity in University-Industry Relationships," *The Journal of Higher Education* 70, no. 3 (1999): 309–52.
72. David M. Boje, "Corporate Writing in the Web of Postmodern Culture and Postindustrial Capitalism," *Management Communication Quarterly* 14, no. 3 (2001): 507–16.
73. We note here an interesting critique of university-business partnerships: university partnerships with corporations erode the local business community's ties and control over local civic resources, thus hurting local communities by drawing businesses away from their needs to the more private (and national and global) needs of universities; see Leonard Nevarez, "Corporate Philanthropy in the New Urban Economy: The Role of Business-Nonprofit Realignment in Regime Politics," *Urban Affairs Review*, 36, no. 2 (2000): 197–227. The impact of such partnerships on the universities and their faculty (and students) has been well studied, but what about those partnerships' impact on the local communities in which universities reside? How does corporate (and even public) funding alter the relationships between corporations, state agencies, universities, and the communities they inhabit?
74. Kenneth Prewitt, "America's Research Universities Under Public Scrutiny," *Daedalus: Journal of the American Academy of Arts and Sciences* 122, no. 4 (1993): 85–99, 95.

That a president of a public university can claim that its goal of ensuring economic growth is "validated" by the external funds the university receives, or that a president of a major foundation can claim that industry leaders are "well-placed . . . to judge the quality of what is produced by research universities," seems to us very telling of how the notion of public service has been transformed with very little debate. The idea of public service that provided the grounding for the American university, especially since the federal land grants of the 1800s, has been transformed from the practice of university service to local communities, specifically, and society, generally, to that of service to industry. Indeed, the latter has become the "public service" that higher education now provides.

The grants culture, in short, must be understood within the larger economic and political forces of privatization, which were made possible by, but now make possible the: (1) major shifts in federal spending, which have pushed faculty to pursue alternative sources of revenue for their research and to pursue grants more competitively; (2) globalization of the economy, which has put a premium on products and processes derived from scientific innovation; and (3) evolution of government policies, which have enabled the capitalization of knowledge, and which has led to commercialism in faculty and student research.[75] This, as we have been saying, is a global phenomenon, to be sure. National policy makers in advanced industrial countries are moving discretionary research and training funds into programs focused on production aspects of higher education, innovation in multinational corporations (especially in high technology and, we would add, biotechnology), development of intellectual property, and producer services (non-life insurance, accounting, legal services, tax consultation, information services, international securities dealing, etc.), all the while reducing money targeted for education and social welfare functions.[76] Although the commercialization of research is not an American phenomenon by any means, the American research university model, with its mutually constitutive relationship with science, has become predominant in the global marketplace. Because such a model is intricately tied to business and industry, American universities are implicated in, and are crucial parts of, the current forms of imperialism.

It seems rather simplistic, however, to focus so narrowly on university-industry partnerships, when a focus on university-government relationships will illustrate similar problems and tensions. The latter relationships are not treated as problematic as they should be, as federal and state governments have similarly succumbed to the imperatives of entrepreneurship and privatization.[77] Indeed, entrepreneurship and privatization, and the resultant

75. See Melissa Anderson, "The Complex Relations Between the Academy and Industry: Views from the Literature," *The Journal of Higher Education* 72, no. 2 (2001): 226–46.

76. Slaughter and Leslie, *Academic Capitalism*, 14.

77. Slaughter and Leslie in *Academic Capitalism* highlight how government policies in the United States, Canada, the United Kingdom, and Australia further the privatization of higher education.

corporatization of the university, as we discuss later, has hit government agencies perhaps most directly, so that they now not only act like (and on behalf of) corporations, they now look like them as well.[78] The needs of industry may now in effect be the needs of federal and state governments, so much so that industry leaders ask for and get tax credits to "encourage greater support by industry of university research."[79]

Universities, as publicly subsidized institutions, are active and competitive players in the marketplace.[80] Interestingly, as Rhoades and Slaughter point out, the irony of universities' courtship of business is that they are playing supplicant to an industry with an inferior performance record—and the recent scandals illustrate this most compellingly—while, unlike other private corporations, American colleges and universities have an excellent record in terms of their global competitiveness; indeed, they are globally dominant. Furthermore, they engage the marketplace but are protected from its risks, as institutions of higher education rarely go "belly-up."[81]

Given the pervasiveness of entrepreneurial behavior in higher education, and its mutually supportive relationship to privatization, we are rather shocked by not why it happens but why it is questioned at all. Why is all this questioned in the ways it is, including, and especially, by us in this chapter? Why do so many believe that universities should not act in these ways? We would like to pinpoint the origin of this belief. Our theory is that such belief originates from the "idea of the university," an idea that is still strong enough to mask how the public interest is undermined by the imperatives of privatization in higher education. It is to the idea of the university that we turn next.

THE IDEA OF THE UNIVERSITY

The reliance on sponsored research, as Eisenberg suggests, raises serious questions about the reliability and ethics of studies and those who conduct them.[82] The literature has been bombarded with discussions about researchers "on the take"; that is, those with financial interests in the companies (or industries) that fund their research.[83] Researchers themselves are deemed

---

78. For an explanation of how the federal government is modeled like a business, see David E. Sanger, "Trying to Run a Country Like a Corporation," *The New York Times* (July 8, 2001): Section 4, 1, 3.

79. Government-University-Industry Research Roundtable, *Stresses on Research and Education at Colleges and Universities: Institutional and Sponsoring Agency Responses* (Washington, DC: Author, 1994), 12.

80. Slaughter, "Professional Values."

81. Rhoades and Slaughter, "Academic Capitalism, Managed Professionals, and Supply-Side Higher Education," 14, 15.

82. Rebecca S. Eisenberg, "Academic Freedom and Academic Values in Sponsored Research," *Texas Law Review* 66 (1988): 1363–404.

83. See, for example, "Experts on the Take," *Multinational Monitor* (November 2000): 29.

to need protection from the corporations that fund research.[84] Many of us are familiar with the problems faced by David Noble, who was offered an endowed chair in the humanities at Simon Fraser University in Canada, only to have the offer revoked because of his critiques of corporatization and distance education.[85] In addition, there have been critiques about the failure or refusal of scientists to criticize the companies that fund them (and some companies have even punished those who do).[86] The unfettered push for external funding has thus led to serious scientific misconduct.[87] More fundamentally, some question whether external funding drives research priorities, thus altering the scientific norm of pursing basic research (as opposed to applied) and promoting easy dissemination of its results.[88]

It is the concern with the "improper pressure on the design and outcome of research" that forms the basis for the American Association of University Professors' (AAUP) report, "Statement on Corporate Funding of Academic Research."[89] The report, while illustrating correctly the problem of corporate funding, merely recommends that faculty have input in the design of institutional policies on such funding.[90] Certain editorial boards of journals were a bit bolder than the AAUP and instituted policies refusing to publish studies from scientists who have financial interests in the corporation whose products are the subject of research, and other such boards asked for clear disclaimers before publishing those kinds of studies.[91] Some journals have had to modify their policies because scientists' financial interest in

---

84. See, for example, Paul M. Fischer, "Fischer v. The Medical College of Georgia and the R.J. Reynolds Tobacco Company: A Case Study of Constraints on Research," in Academic Freedom: An Everyday Concern, ed. Ernst Benjamin and Donald R. Wagner. New Directions for Faculty Research, no. 88 (San Francisco: Jossey-Bass, 1994), 33–43.

85. See "Heavy Vetting," Lingua Franca (July/August 2001): 9–12.

86. Karen Charman, "Spinning Science into Gold," Sierra (July/August 2001): 40–44/72–73.

87. See Thomas Bartlett, "Blind Trust," The Chronicle of Higher Education (August 16, 2002): A12–A15; Richard Monastersky, "Atomic Lies," The Chronicle of Higher Education (August 16, 2002): A16–A21; Scott Smallwood, "Bitter Aftertaste," The Chronicle of Higher Education (April 12, 2002): A10–A12.

88. See Harvey Brooks, "The Problem of Research Priorities," Daedalus: Journal of the American Academy of Arts and Sciences 107, no. 2 (1978): 171–90; Rebecca S. Eisenberg, "Proprietary Rights and the Norms of Science in Biotechnology Research," Yale Law Journal 97 (1987): 177–231.

89. American Association of University Professors, "Statement on Corporate Funding of Academic Research," Academe: Bulletin of the American Association of University Professors (May/June 2001): 68–70.

90. The association did not make more substantive recommendations against corporate funding probably because many faculty count on such funding, and the association likely did not want to alienate those faculty.

91. See Lila Guterman and Martin Van Der Werf, "12 Journals Adopt Joint Policy on Research Supported by Business," The Chronicle of Higher Education (October 5, 2001): A29; Lila Guterman, "Conflicts of Interest Between the Lines," The Chronicle of Higher Education (February 8, 2002): A14–A17.

companies is a pervasive problem, and strong policies would mean that very few studies would be published.[92] These critiques indicate that the integrity of the research process, and more fundamentally, the university itself is seriously undermined by research that has been commercialized.

What we think seems to be undergirding these critiques is the idea that the university and its researcher are supposed to be *disinterested*. Indeed, the defining characteristic of the traditional university may be the belief that it was engaged in disinterested research, an assumption supported by what John Searle calls the "Western Rationalist Tradition, or the scholarly ideal of the disinterested inquirer engaged in the quest for objective knowledge that will have universal validity [and use]."[93] This has always been more ideal than real, but it is an ideal that has influenced the academic profession, becoming a defining call for faculty. The idea of disinterested research has served as a mantra against institutional and external intrusions into a professor's work, even though such an idea cannot in all honesty be said to be believed by most faculty.

But it is an idea that is strong enough to put a stumbling block on rampant entrepreneurial behavior in higher education. Much of the prevailing critique of entrepreneurial activities in higher education takes this idea of disinterested research as the basis for the critique.[94] Such a critique echoes the earlier polemics against external influences on the university, particularly those of Immanuel Kant, John Henry Newman, and Thorstein Veblen, each of whom argued that knowledge, using Newman's words, is its own end.[95] The university is a site for the production and dissemination of disinterested knowledge, we are told, and it should be protected against external influences, such as totalitarian governments (for Kant), antihumanist motives (Newman), or businesses and professions (Veblen). What makes the commercialization of research particularly problematic for many critics is that the researcher is somehow shirking his or her responsibility, a responsibility, it seems to us, *to* the idea of the university.

---

92. Interestingly, the scandal over some of this corporate-funded research led one journal, *The New England Journal of Medicine*, to refuse, at first, to publish studies in which researchers had a financial interest in the results. The problem was so pervasive, however, that it modified its policy from requiring "no 'financial interest in a company (or its competitor) that makes a product discussed in the article'; the new policy says that authors must have no 'significant' interest." see "Hot Type," *The Chronicle of Higher Education* (June 28, 2002): A16.

93. John R. Searle, "Rationality and Realism, What is at Stake?" *Daedalus: Journal of the American Academy of Arts and Sciences* 122, no. 4 (1993): 55–83, 69.

94. See, for example, Frank Newman, "Saving Higher Education's Soul," *Change* (September/ October 2000): 17–23, 23.

95. Immanuel Kant, *The Conflict of the Faculties*, trans. Mary J. Gregor (Lincoln: University of Nebraska Press, 1979, c. 1798); John Henry Newman, *The Idea of the University* (Notre Dame: University of Notre Dame Press, 1982, c. 1852); Thorstein Veblen, *The Higher Learning in America* (New Brunswick: Transaction Publishers, 1993, c. 1918).

Thus, Veblen's logic still rings true for many: the "university is the only accepted institution of the modern culture on which the quest of knowledge unquestionably devolves," (one may say this the university's *authority*) and the keepers of that knowledge are the scientists and scholars of the university (one may say this is the faculty's *responsibility*).[96] Veblen indicates that such authority and responsibility have become secondary in the university to the more functional goals of industrial development and professional gate-keeping, an argument that hinges on whether or not his idea of the university is actually valid. It seems that American universities, at least, must contend with a structural tension between the disinterested pursuit of knowledge and the idea of public service, often defined, as we explained in the previous section, as meeting the needs of industry. But our primary point here is more theoretical. We ask, From where does the authority and responsibility that Veblen presumes come?

We discussed in chapter 4 the historical origins of the conventions that provide performativity to scientific research, and that history similarly grounds the idea of the university. We will not repeat here what we have already stated, but suffice it to say that the origins of the idea, and its continued relevance, came from the conventions that established the university as the primary site for scientific knowledge, and the researcher as the objective producer of such knowledge. American universities were not always the primary sites for the production and dissemination of such knowledge, as this was shared by journalists, freelance scholars, men of wealth, and scientists outside the academy.[97] But, in line with the Enlightenment project of progress through science, and with the installation of the sciences—natural and social—the university became the site for the most powerful kinds of knowledge.

So the critiques of sponsored research are limited when the extent of the critique is that the university and its researchers forget their *raison d'être*, that is, the pursuit of disinterested knowledge. These critiques should also account for the institutional practices that give universities and their researchers the authority to pursue knowledge, as such authority ultimately provides the grounds from which the problems of sponsored research originate. In other words, if the pursuit of knowledge is its own end, then it becomes "obvious" and "inevitable" that universities and their faculty will pursue external funding when governments and institutions do not support that pursuit themselves.

The idea of the university as furthering knowledge for its own sake, or for the Enlightenment project of social progress, makes the grants culture possible. As the former president of Duke University, Nannerl Keohane, states, "The modern university is a company of scholars engaged in discovering

---

96. Veblen, *The Higher Learning in America*, 1, 11.
97. Stanley Aronowitz, *Roll Over Beethoven: The Return of Cultural Strife* (Hanover: Wesleyan University Press, 1993), 205–206.

and sharing knowledge, with a responsibility to see that such knowledge is used to improve the human condition."[98] This allows her to reconcile the pursuit of knowledge with the pursuit of external funds. Indeed, there appears to be nothing in the idea of research per se that makes it inherently incompatible with the idea of disinterestedness. But today that incompatibility must be presumed, at least. Perhaps William Tierney is correct that one should distinguish the scientist from the intellectual, the latter being a social critic who seeks to decode the idea of "pure" research and the implicit power of the state.[99] It seems to us, however, that the distinction itself must be decoded to uncover its institutional bases, as well as how it is implicated in the grants culture, which takes for granted the idea of the university and its researcher as disinterested producers of knowledge, and, indeed, counts on it.

We believe that to become the kinds of intellectuals to which Tierney refers requires that faculty, following Michael Bérubé and Cary Nelson, "defetishize" research, which has been framed in a discourse of accounting and instrumentalism that permits institutions to require that faculty produce more to achieve tenure.[100] Furthermore, given the existence of the "academic ratchet," faculty seek to increase their discretionary time (for pursuing personal and professional goals, such as research, scholarship, graduate teaching, and professional service) over and against teaching and service to the institution.[101] Faculty, therefore, are more likely to engage in those practices that will lead to the most rewards, and, increasingly, that means pursuing grants, especially the "scientific" ones. The institutional and professional rewards that are tied to research prevent any significant consensus on the moral or political responsibility that Tierney suggests should guide intellectual practice.

More on point, we believe that scholars should avoid assuming an "idea of the university" that may be no longer be, if it ever was. To negate that the university serves the ends of transnational capitalism exemplifies willful blindness. That is, while it might be important to argue for the idea of the university, one should not forget that it is just *an idea*, and it should not allow us to displace the imperatives of capitalism to other social institutions. One might start the critique of external funding by acknowledging that the university is an instrument of capitalism and question its practices accordingly. Thus, as with capitalism, one needs to pay attention to how "ordinary" and "obvious" values ensure capitalism (such as the notion of

98. Nannerl O. Keohane, "The Mission of the Research University," *Daedalus: Journal of the American Academy of Arts and Sciences* 122, no. 4 (1993): 101–25, 103.
99. William G. Tierney, "The Autonomy of Knowledge and the Decline of the Subject: Postmodernism and the Reformulation of the University," *Higher Education* 41 (2001): 353–72, 363.
100. Bérubé and Nelson, "Introduction: A Report from the Front," 16.
101. See generally, William Massy and Robert Zemsky, "Faculty Discretionary Time: Departments and the 'Academic Ratchet,' " *The Journal of Higher Education* 66, no. 1 (1994): 1–22.

utility in research, almost always defined in economic terms). We elaborate on this point in the concluding section of this chapter.

Perhaps Bourdieu is correct that the social and economics fields are mutually supportive of each other but deny that relationship.[102] The cultural fields, such as education, are arranged along two axes: the one in which cultural capital is transformed into economic capital, and the other within subfields, where the dominant class establishes what it will value highly and to which it grants high salaries, research grants, consultancies, and so forth. The academy, in particular, attributes primary value precisely to the scientific purity and disinterestedness of intellectual judgment, and so it is a central weapon in the exercise of symbolic power, which reinforces the status quo and was developed historically to fill that role.[103] With research grants, economic capital is at play, as we have explained, but to obscure this, the dominant class within higher education—the researchers—insist upon a notion of *disinterested* research and public service, which only obscures how such research and service are themselves privileges of those with power and are susceptible to the imperatives of new forms of capitalist practices. Many will not argue against us that the idea of disinterested research obscures the movement toward academic capitalism, but our argument that an idea even more fundamental to the academic profession—academic freedom—furthers that imperative is quite another story, an argument with which we conclude the major part of this book.

THE "CORPORATE UNIVERSITY" AND ACADEMIC FREEDOM

The concept of academic freedom is paradoxical. The "freedom" to which it refers is actually a limitation on academic institutions, and sometimes on the larger social institutions that establish them (such as the nation-state). Yet, the qualifier "academic" is also a limitation on the individual's "freedom." In other words, it is not a "general" freedom to which we refer, and it is not just any person who enjoys whatever that freedom is. Academic freedom is a kind of freedom that only academics qua academics can assert. Thus, academic freedom, despite being a kind of freedom for certain individuals, is, fundamentally, an institutional concept. There is, to be sure, an individual who asserts such freedom, but that individual asserts it *because* he or she is a particular institutional being, that is, a being whose existence is possible solely because certain institutions are there to grant and maintain such existence. Academics do not exist outside of the institutions that authorize them. Furthermore, the institutions that grant such status are themselves authorized

---

102. Pierre Bourdieu, *Distinction: A Social Critique of the Judgment of Taste*, trans. Richard Nice (Cambridge: Harvard University Press, 1984), especially 226–56.
103. See also Nicholas Garnham, "Extended Review: Bourdieu's *Distinction*," *Sociological Review* 34, no. 2 (1986): 423–33, 423.

by other social institutions to create academic beings. Academic freedom, therefore, does not, and cannot, exist outside of a particular institutional order, which is situated in a particular cultural/historical context.

We tend to think of academic freedom, however, as an individual concept, that is, as entailing particular rights (and perhaps obligations) that individuals have. It is that, of course, but only in the most superficial sense. The fact is that there must be an institutional order that creates individuals vested with certain rights (and obligations), and it is as institutional actors that academics have such rights (and obligations). We might attend, therefore, to that institutional order and, one can easily say, dispense with the ideas of the individual that might hinder our understanding of what academic freedom actually means. But institutions are not disembodied things; they need the actions of individuals to remain effective as such. Academic freedom, then, for all that we can say about it, is really only the name we give to the dialectical relationship between individuals and institutions. To think of academic freedom requires attention to institutions and to how individuals invest those institutions with the power the latter have. The institution/academic dialectic does provide a significant lens through which to view academic freedom concerns, as Slaughter illustrates.[104] To think of academic freedom today, however, also means reconsidering whether that dialectic is as tenable as we imagine it to be. Specifically, how does such dialectic obscure the complexity of the institution/academic relationship in the grants culture?

We want to argue in this section that the traditional principles of academic freedom no longer make sense because the constitutive relationship between academics and their institutions, and between academic institutions and the social context in which they exist, are undergoing drastic change, and so those principles are no longer intelligible or practicable, at least as currently formulated. Our intent is not to suggest nostalgia for some idyllic period of happy institution/academic relationships; no such period has ever existed, and to suggest that it has is, in its most positive light, to misunderstand willfully the history of academic freedom. Our concluding argument instead takes the form of a challenge—a call for a renewed understanding of our existence as academics and of the institutional order that grants us that existence. We are hoping that we actually give thought to that institutional order, and ask of ourselves whether we might not want to bring it down, even if that means that we threaten our very existence in the process.

As a way of introducing our argument, we mention two incidents that influenced our thinking on this matter. In the first, and as part of our research

---

104. Sheila Slaughter, " 'Dirty Little Secrets': Academic Freedom, Governance, and Professionalism," in *Academic Freedom: An Everyday Concern*, ed. Ernst Benjamin and Donald R. Wagner. New Directions for Higher Education, no. 88 (San Francisco: Jossey-Bass, 1994), 59–75.

for a paper on the grants culture for a conference in 2002,[105] we came across a survey, published in 2000 and sponsored by TIAA-CREF, suggesting that 79 percent of the faculty polled agreed that "intrusions on academic freedom by the administration are rare."[106] This finding was troubling to us because it makes academic freedom thinkable solely in terms of an opposition between the academic and the administration. Indeed, the authors of the survey assumed the opposition to such an extent that it was left unremarked. We wonder about this opposition, since the boundary between the administrative and the academic is often meaningless. Administrators are increasingly becoming involved in teaching (especially as courses become "technologized" and "accountability" expected) and research (especially as external funding becomes essential and intellectual property is mined). Furthermore, academics historically have taken on administrative roles: as presidents, provosts, vice presidents for research, deans, department chairs, program coordinators, managers of research projects, and so on. Academics are also taking on, or helping the administration with, certain administrative activities: recruitment and retention of students, fund raising, public relations, and so forth. And, of course, academics take on administrative functions when they sit on hiring committees, promotion and tenure committees, academic misconduct committees, and so forth. Indeed, principles of shared governance ensure that academics have a say in the administration of their institutions. So, when we say that administrative intrusions on academic freedom are rare, what do we mean exactly? In the absence of explicit actions by administrators, do intrusions on academic freedom not take place?

The second incident influencing our understanding of academic freedom was much more personal to us. In 2004, Georgia State University Provost Ron Henry, purportedly because of budget shortfalls, decided to conduct a campus-wide review of academic and administrative programs to determine whether they would be eliminated. This is a long and sordid story, but the short version is that eleven academic programs, nine in the College of Education, including four in our department, were chosen for further review to determine whether they would be maintained. This whole process had taken place with great speed, with ever-shifting criteria, with very little information to the university community, and without much faculty input, or at least through the formal mechanisms for such input, such as the University Senate. Interestingly, one of us is facing a similar situation at Florida International University, indicating that this phenomenon is not

---

105. See Benjamin Baez and Deron R. Boyles, "Are We Selling Out? Entrepreneurship, Grants, and the Future of the Academic Freedom." Paper presented at the Annual Meeting of the American Educational Studies Association, Pittsburgh, Pennsylvania, October 31, 2002.
106. Allen Sanderson, Voon Chin Phua, and David Herda, The American Faculty Poll (Chicago: National Opinion Research Center, 2000), 31. We did not wind up using this study in our presentation.

limited to one institution. Probably to allay concerns about shared governance, the provost empaneled a committee late in the process to review the programs. This committee was made up of faculty members, although it was never really clear to us why the chosen faculty members were so entrusted with this task, other than that they came mostly from one of the senate's subcommittees, not coincidentally, the senate committee chaired by the provost himself. Regardless, the committee reviewing the programs was divided up into subcommittees of three members each to review each of the eleven programs, to report their findings, and to make recommendations to the full committee about whether or not to maintain, eliminate, or enhance the programs.

We attended the meetings of committees, as well as other subsequent public meetings in which these program reviews were discussed. We were struck by the absurdity of the spectacle in which each program was discussed abstractly in accounting language (e.g., numbers of students, "comparative advantages," academic test scores, the number and amount of grants—probably the dispositive criterion—etc.), thus permitting the provost and the faculty members (many of whom turned out to be his lackeys) to disembody the programs, to talk about them as if they did not involve human lives, lives that would be unintelligible under the logic of accounting that characterized the entire spectacle. The thing that struck us even more was how zealously the faculty members on the committee performed their task. It felt like a bloodbath to us, and it should have, since our programs were "on the block," as we often heard it termed. But what was surprising to us was that the ones overtly drawing blood were our fellow faculty colleagues, not the provost, who displayed throughout a facade of absolute neutrality. Part of the reason for the bloodbath certainly had to do with the atmosphere of competition that characterized this process: the provost promised that eliminating programs would free up money for those that remained. In other words, those faculty deciding the fate of other faculty, via their programs, stood to *gain* from cutting those programs. Our point here, however, is that there did not exist an opposition between the administration and the faculty, despite the fact that the criteria were dubious, and certainly not established by faculty, and that principles of shared governance were not adhered to for much of this process, if at all. We were surprised by how willing the faculty were to do the work of the administration in this case. Does, then, the idea of academic freedom made thinkable via the institution/academic dialectic really work anymore to explain adequately what happens in academe in the grants culture, which is made possible (and in turn makes possible) the imperatives of entrepreneurship and privatization? If not, what does?

Academic freedom, as we have indicated, is premised on a certain relationship between the individual, the academic institution, and the social context in which they exist. This statement appears obvious enough, at least when these concepts (i.e., the individual, the institution, and the social context) are thought of as abstractions, and, particularly with regard to academic freedom, as legal abstractions such as "rights" and "responsibilities." The statement becomes less obvious when these concepts are thought about in material terms. What is the exact relationship between the individual, the institution, and the social context? How does it manifest itself? How do we experience that relationship? Do the language, the principles, and the meanings we have been using for such a relationship still make sense? The idea of academic freedom historically has been one in which professors qua professors are permitted to act in more or less autonomous ways, purportedly because such autonomy, paradoxical as it is in the ways we asserted at the outset of this section, serves the institutions and the social world in which they exist. Given how this understanding still defines academic freedom today, it is important to think further about its origins and assumptions.

Academic Freedom, Historically

The cry for academic freedom in American universities originates, as we indicated in chapter 4, from the early European scholars' cry for the freedom to philosophize, or *libertas philosophandi*, and especially from the German professors' variation of such freedom, particularly their notion of freedom of inquiry characterized by the term *Lehrfreiheit*.[107] The American version of academic freedom was first explicitly given expression in the AAUP's *1915 Declaration of Principles of Academic Freedom and Tenure* ("1915 Principles").[108] These principles addressed three concerns of its authors, all relating to what the authors saw as the primary activities of the academic: freedom of inquiry and research; freedom of teaching; and freedom of extramural utterance and action. The final concern received the greatest attention, since, as the authors of the 1915 Principles indicated, it was much more likely (at the time) that professors would be punished for viewpoints expressed outside of their teaching and scholarly activities. The authors posited these freedoms as being in the public's interest, since boards of trustees, as the legal authority of their institutions, were actually entrusted by the state with providing a crucial service to the public, and trustees could not legitimately assume this public trust without granting professors the freedoms necessary to accomplish the latter's own public duty: to serve society with the knowledge they produce. Walter Metzger points out that by framing higher education as a public trust, and the professors' freedom of inquiry as a public service, the authors of the 1915 Principles got around the fact that in the United

---

107. Robert B. Sutton, "The Phrase *Libertas Philosophandi*," *Journal of the History of Ideas*, 14 (1953): 310–16, 310.

108. American Association of University Professors, "1915 Declaration of Principles of Academic Freedom and Tenure," in *Policy Documents and Reports*, 9th ed. (Washington, DC: American Association of University Professors and The Johns Hopkins University Press, 2001), 291–301.

States, unlike in Germany, higher education took place in private as well as public institutions.[109]

Metzger also argues that the American notions of academic freedom as expressed in the 1915 Principles were unlike the German notions granting freedoms to the professor, the student, and even the institution itself; in the United States, academic freedom came to stand for the freedom of the academic. It did not stand, Metzger argues, for the freedom of the student to learn or for the institution in general, except in cases where a threat to the autonomy of the institution bore directly on the academic (e.g., when states required loyalty oaths of its employees after World War II). Metzger explains that the primary concern of the 1915 Principles was with what happened *in* a university, not with what happened *to* a university.[110] Metzger's reading appears to us to be correct, but only in the most superficial sense, as we explained above. Academics are institutional beings, and in being granted rights, it is for the institution itself that those rights are granted, since academics act on its behalf when they act as academics. This is true even when this means that the institution's own actions will be constrained. To authorize the academic to act is to authorize the institution to act, since they are in a mutually constitutive relationship with each other (note that we do not say the relationship is tensionless, only that it is *constitutive*). The academic exists because the institution exists, and the institution exists because the academic exists, each being the other's *raison d'être*. Thus, what happens *to* the university also happens *in* the university, since neither the university nor its academic exists without the other.

The 1940 Statement of Principles on Academic Freedom and Tenure ("1940 Statement"), the definitive understanding of the AAUP's stance on academic freedom, while imposing some responsibilities on the academic, also accepted the premises of the 1915 Principles, namely that the primary concern of the academic is inquiry and research, teaching, and extramural activities, that the institution assumes a public trust, and that academic freedom is exercised in service of the public, stating that the "free search for truth and its free exposition" is the basis for "the common good."[111] To have received the almost universal acceptance that it has, however, meant that the 1940 Statement had to be more *nuanced* in elaborating upon these freedoms than were the 1915 Principles. Thus, while professors should indeed enjoy the freedom of inquiry, they also should be honest in

---

109. Walter P. Metzger, "Academic Freedom and Scientific Freedom," *Daedalus: Journal of the American Academy of Arts and Sciences* 107, no. 2 (1978): 93–114, 98.

110. Ibid., 97.

111. American Association of University Professors, "1940 Statement of Principles on Academic Freedom and Tenure (with 1970 Interpretive Comments)" in *Policy Documents and Reports*, 9th ed. (Washington, DC: American Association of University Professors and The Johns Hopkins University Press, 2001), 3–10, 3.

conducting research; while professors should have the freedom to teach their courses, they should stick to matters within their expertise; and while professors, also being citizens of the larger public, should be able to express issues important to them, they should be careful to dissociate themselves from their institutions when doing so.[112]

Nevertheless, the core premises of the 1915 Principles were assumed by the latter Statement. Are these premises still valid? Or, more accurately, does the context to which they were to be made applicable still exist and mean the same thing? The first premise is that academic institutions assume a public trust, so that the professors' activities are public services, that is, they serve the common good. Is this still a valid premise? The answer hinges on this understanding: the existence of something "public" that is separate, distinct, and perhaps in opposition, to something "private." The second premise is that the primary activities of the professors (inquiry, teaching, and extramural utterances) require the freedom to perform them, since they are public services. Is this still valid? The answer hinges on these understandings: (1) inquiry is to be *disinterested*; (2) teaching is a primary function of the academic; and (3) the professor is a both a citizen of the institutions and of the public. We will critique the two premises, starting with the first, namely, that institutions assume a public trust.

The University as a Public Trust

The premise that academic institutions assume a public trust, if ever it was justifiable, is highly questionable today, if one assumes that there is something "public" that is in opposition to something "private." The common understanding of a university is best captured by the term coined by Kerr in 1963: The university is a "multiversity."[113] What are the implications of the acceptance of such a term? If it is true, and it is quite difficult to argue against this, that today's American university caters to so many interests and engages in so many divergent activities, then one has to wonder about *the* public trust supposedly assumed by it. If the "multiversity" caters to many things, the question, then, should not be whether the university serves *the* public trust, but *which* public(s) does the university serve? If it serves many publics, does it serve each equitably? And what are the implications of this for academic freedom? Kerr seemed rather untroubled, at least in 1963, by how this "multiversity" redefined its relationship to its professor. He recognizes how external influences were affecting life in the university, to be sure, but he indicates that this means "greater freedom" for the professor, the actual triumph of *Lehrfreiheit*, allowing the professor to "do as he pleases."[114] Of

---

112. Ibid., 3–4.
113. Kerr, *The Uses of the University*, 5.
114. Ibid., 33.

course, a professor who can "do as he pleases" is no longer serving the public but himself, thus shedding doubt on one of the major premises of academic freedom. But what is even more interesting to us is that Kerr sees "greater" rather than lesser freedom in the multiversity, and this warrants some attention to what sort of freedom that is. If we are to situate the university in today's political context of global capitalism, is freedom actually possible? For what uses is the idea of such freedom now deployed?

We might well be served to recognize that any notion of "freedom" is now deployed in a system of transnationally exchanged capital that has transformed the entire world. Masao Miyoshi argues that because of the phenomenal advances in communication and transportation since World War II, capital has circulated with unprecedented ease in search of maximum profit across nations. With the rise of transnational corporations, which are accountable primarily to their shareholders and officers and have little regard for national controls, the nation-state lost much of its power to intervene effectively in the market, allowing the gap between rich and poor to increase drastically. The elimination of the public sector and communitarianism in favor of privatization, individualism, and identitarianism was pervasive, resulting in the intensification of competition and the fragmentation of society.[115] This capital relies less on manufacturing than on knowledge and international finance, and it has exacerbated inequities at the level of individuals (the rich are richer, the poor poorer), groups (racial, gender, ethnic, and class inequalities are reproduced within and across nations), and nations ("developed" nations have relatively greater ability to dominate the global market and dictate the actions of the underdeveloped nations, by, primarily, defining "development" as participating in the global market, which the former control.) The university is a key figure in all this, since transnational capital—global, exploitive, and all-absorbing—uses higher education, not primarily for training workers, since technology makes workers less necessary, but for research and development.[116] In short, the university has been "corporatized" for the global economic exchanges it serves and legitimates.

Indeed, the corporate influence in institutions of higher education has changed the way the university understands itself, so that the logic of accounting redefines the students and the public as "clients," "constituents," and "customers." Such accounting discourse inevitably makes profit the point

115. Masao Miyoshi, "Ivory Tower in Escrow," boundary 2 (2000): 1–50, 15.

116. See generally, Slaughter and Leslie, Academic Capitalism, 25. See, also, Richard S. Ruch, Higher Ed, Inc.: The Rise of the For-Profit University (Baltimore: The Johns Hopkins University Press, 2001); Jennifer Washburn, University, Inc.: The Corporate Corruption of Higher Education (New York: Basic Books, 2005); David Kirp, Shakespeare, Einstein, and the Bottom Line: The Marketing of Higher Education (Cambridge: Harvard University Press, 2003); and Roger L. Geiger, Knowledge and Money: Research Universities and the Paradox of the Marketplace (Stanford: Stanford University Press, 2004).

of it all. The search for profit restructures research and its rewards, so that research with commercial potential is privileged and intellectual property is mined. Profit restructures even teaching itself, so that maximizing enrollments and teaching online become central activities. Economic efficiency now dictates what is deemed worthwhile. At Georgia State University, for example, in considering which programs to eliminate, the question of quality is not to be understood philosophically; it is to be answered using the logic of accounting. How does the program serve its clients? What is the university's "return on its investment"? If these questions cannot be answered quantitatively, then there are "no data" to support the program. That a program's students have had their lives enriched by their interactions with others in the program would make no sense; their enrichment is thinkable only if it can be shown to lead to a job placement, or a pay increase, or things of that sort. That the program's faculty guide the students in asking important questions is not evidence of quality; only the amounts of their grants can be counted as such. Georgia State's status as a public institution is relevant only to the extent that it can use its "public-ness" to blame the state for abandoning public higher education (read as: "It has cut our budget"); its status as public trust is completely bracketed off, incomprehensible to it under the logic of accounting in which it now understands itself. Readings is absolutely correct: universities are not *like* corporations, they *are* corporations.[117] And if the corporation that is Georgia State University wants to join the ranks of the "universities of excellence," as it most certainly does, it will do so by "accounting" for what its "investments" entail.

The university of excellence is a bureaucratic corporation that now serves itself, not the state or the public, Readings argues, and so it has to restructure itself to look like the corporation that it really is. The predominance of the corporate model in higher education, therefore, makes absolute sense, since it reflects what the university *is*. There is something rather ironic about the increasing use of corporate models of governance in higher education, given the increasing number of corporate scandals in the media.[118]

---

117. Readings, *The University in Ruins*, 22.
118. One might be leery of assuming that the corporate scandals are external to the university, that is, something not of its doing. Note that the university is a gatekeeper for the professions, and university business schools socialize, as much as they "train," businessmen and women. In an interesting report in *The Chronicle of Higher Education*, this connection between the university and the corporate scandals, especially Enron's, was made explicitly clear. Corporations endow business schools and programs, *their* faculty members (i.e., the business program's faculty, but one is authorized to read this possessive pronoun ambiguously) collect paychecks for serving on corporate boards and consulting, their faculty members write case studies (which are so common in business programs), and they socialize students into an ethos in which "shareholder value" outweighs other values; see Katherine S. Mangan, "The Ethics of Business Schools," *The Chronicle of Higher Education* (September 20, 2002): A14–A16. In this sense, business schools (and universities) are implicated in corporate scandals, which many now analyze as if this implication was not at all problematic.

But perhaps it is not so ironic, since corporate misbehavior is deemed an anomaly, not a structural condition of corporate greed. Such organizational frameworks, at any rate, as Joan Scott argues, ignore the academic custom of including faculty in governance resting on the acknowledgment of their educational expertise.[119] Yet that is neither here nor there, since such expertise and the values that come with it are hindrances to the corporate university. The corporate models supposedly make colleges and universities more efficient, that is, they will gain the most revenues and incur the least costs. The corporate university now has the answer with which easily to dispense with the fundamental (and historically unresolvable) questions that have characterized academe in the past, such as: What knowledge is most worth knowing; What does merit mean; Whom do we promote? The logic that now forms the basis for answers to such questions: economic efficiency and profit.

The reader may be skeptical and quip, yes, universities today are more corporate-like, but they are not really corporations in the ways real corporations are. This would be a good response, if today's corporations were also corporations in the traditional sense. One of the phenomena that the forces of globalization expose is the increasing number, power, and influence of multinational or transnational corporations; that is, corporations with (divergent) operations in more than one country, the most prominent and powerful having headquarters in a number of countries.[120] Their wealth can exceed that of entire countries. Their actions are less influenced by their home markets than by a unified global corporate strategy. Given that global forces have restructured nation-states, which are now able to exert less and less control of these corporations, the culture of their managers and workers also begins to have less and less to do with the countries in which they reside than with the corporate culture.[121] These corporations have become, in a significant sense, "sovereigns."[122]

The corporatization of the university, therefore, means its globalization, since the crucial corporations are typically transnational. Simon Marginson and Mark Considine explain that universities are being remade in many ways by globalism, especially through countless international engagements.[123]

119. Joan Wallach Scott, "The Critical State of Shared Governance," *Academe: Bulletin of the American Association of University Professors* (July–August 2002): 41–48.
120. For a more extensive discussion of multinational corporations and the legal dilemmas they present for nation-states, see Linda A. Mabry, "Multinational Corporations and U.S. Technology Policy: Rethinking the Concept of Corporate Nationality," *Georgetown Law Journal* 87 (1999): 563–673.
121. Ibid., 575.
122. See Lawrence E. Mitchell, "American Corporations: The New Sovereigns," *The Chronicle of Higher Education* (January 18, 2002): B13–B14.
123. Simon Marginson and Mark Considine, *The Enterprise University: Power, Governance, and Reinvention in Australia* (Cambridge: Cambridge University Press, 2000), 47–49.

Many of us have heard about the support of research projects by multinational corporations, such as Norvatis at the University of California at Berkeley, since these arrangements are controversial. Other international engagements are more subtle but no less important. Some of these other engagements include: visit exchanges and conferences; transnational collaborations; transnational circulation of publications; internationally funded projects, endowed chairs, grants, and fellowships.[124] Many institutions offer programs or degrees to people in other countries, and, not just always online but physically in those other countries as well. One also cannot ignore the international-academic industry that traffics in human beings. It is not just academic knowledge that is being exchanged globally, the recruitment of international students and programs for students to study abroad amounts to the transnational exchange of students. Thus, the global exchanges of knowledge, information, and bodies lead to the "internationalization" of the university.[125] And if the university is a corporation, then these international engagements makes it a transnational corporation.

Given this "global academic industry," to quote Miyoshi, involving knowledge and bodies, we now need a global corporate strategy for it. Thus, we now have "experts" in the global exchange of higher education who emerge around these international engagements, advising universities on how they might "export" higher education.[126] Education and training, we are told, ranks among the country's top service exports, totaling approximately $10 billion dollars in 1999.[127] This phenomenon, requiring such technical expertise, takes the functions of research and teaching away from the faculty and puts them into the hands of the technicians of the "international education business." It is now clear to us that the "freedom" we invest in those with control over knowledge and learning is not of the academic but of the corporate university and its "staff," although the privileged academics will be those who, for all intents and purposes, really are "staff."

The transnational capitalism that has contributed to what we call "globalization" has restructured universities as much as it has corporations, shedding doubt on the traditional understanding of university as a public trust, and of academics as public servants. Indeed, any notion of a public trust can be questioned as untenable today, since the "trust creator," or the state, which supposedly holds goods in common, is being privatized, among other things, by transnationally exchanged capitalist interests (one

124. Miyoshi, "Ivory Tower in Escrow," 36–37.

125. Eugene B. Skolnikoff, "Knowledge Without Borders? Internationalization of the Research Universities," *Daedalus: Journal of the American Academy of Arts and Sciences* 122, no. 4 (1993): 225–52.

126. See Marjorie Peace Lenn, "The Right Way to Export Higher Education," *The Chronicle of Higher Education* (March 1, 2002): B24.

127. Ibid., B24.

need only think of the Edison schools and privatized prisons as examples of traditional state functions that have been privatized). The priorities of the nation-state, therefore, have given way to those of transnational corporations, including universities, which have redirected national priorities toward their own interests. "Public goods" seem now tied to economic prosperity and to the scientific innovation that is deemed to lead to it, especially in the global marketplace.

Furthermore, the "responsibility" for, and the "risks" of, such prosperity are being shifted downward to the individual. The state is less and less involved in the welfare of the populace, and that populace bears more and more of the costs and risks for its subsistence, such as when federal financial aid shifts toward loans and away from grants. Consequently, entrepreneurship has become a virtue arising out of necessity, and this is no less so in the university. Entrepreneurship in the university has now become synonymous with merit, prestige, and reputation. Faculty, whatever the level of professional autonomy they had before, now are increasingly "managed" by their institutions and asked to fund their own work by securing grants from external agencies (of course, universities will capture the products of that work if it leads to profits, whether or not they put up the money for it). If there is to be any "investment" in research, there must be a "return," and thus it is research with commercial potential that warrants any significant institutional expenditure.

Moreover, the transnational economy's primary effect on the university is technology transfer from the university to industry.[128] And to ensure their "fair share" in such an economy, universities convert that research into intellectual property. There can be no question that technology transfer has benefits to the society at large, but the conversion of knowledge into intellectual property means that "the public" is excluded from using that knowledge *as a matter of right*. The corporate university is a major player in the intellectual property scene, and it competes very well with multinational corporations.[129] The first premise of the traditional notion of academic freedom, that universities assume a public trust, therefore, no longer makes sense. Not only is the corporate university furthering its own interests, but the idea of a public trust itself should be reconsidered in light of the global age and the privatization of public services that characterizes it.

The claim that the university plays a prominent role in global capitalism, as we have argued, probably will not surprise many, and so our questioning of the tenability of the premise of academic freedom of a university in the public trust may not seem all that problematic for some. But is the other

---

128. Miyoshi, "Ivory Tower in Escrow," 18.
129. See Benjamin Baez, "Private Knowledge, Public Domain: The Politics of Intellectual Property in Higher Education," in *Schools or Markets? Commercialism, Privatization, and School-Business Partnerships*, ed. Deron R. Boyles (Mahwah: Lawrence Erlbaum Associates, 2005), 119–48.

premise for academic freedom also questionable? That is, are the primary activities of the academic (inquiry, teaching, and extramural activities) in the service of the public? The answer, as we indicated before, hinges on these presumptions: (1) inquiry is to be *disinterested*; (2) teaching is a primary function of the academic; and (3) the professor is a both a citizen of the institution and of the public. We now discuss these presumptions in turn.

The Primary Activities of the Academic

Freedom of Inquiry. We have already critiqued the presumption underlying this notion in our critique of the idea of the university. As universities lose their traditional providers of funds for their research, state and federal agencies now promote global capital. We can say without pausing that research—at least the research *that matters*, to those individuals *who matter* (e.g., university administrators, policy makers, and corporate officials)—is *not* disinterested. To be sure, the authors of the 1940 Statement recognized that researchers can have pecuniary motives, but they assumed those motives were anomalies, since the Statement only requires that the researcher disclose his or her motives in such cases. The idea that research is to be disinterested was still very much a part of why the freedom of inquiry was to be protected; one cannot serve the public through such inquiry if one does so only for pecuniary gain—such gain is tolerable only if it is merely a byproduct of, or an exception to, disinterested inquiry. Much of the prevailing critique of entrepreneurial research in higher education, as we have said, takes this idea of disinterested research as the basis for critique, but it may well be better for the profession to assume that the research serves the ends of transnational capitalism. And for the academic, now an entrepreneur in a transnational capitalist exchange system, to be granted the freedom of inquiry is to give legitimacy and license to the imperatives of transnational capitalism and the exploitation that it brings. Ours is not an argument for having institutions and state agencies constrain the academic's choice, however, but an argument against assuming that the idea of disinterested inquiry actually counters the movements co-opting research for private gain.

Freedom of Teaching. We have already discussed how the grants culture has undermined teaching. Here want to attend to the presumption underlying the idea of freedom of teaching in our notions of academic freedom. Is it the case that teaching is all that important to the academic? This question requires, we think, an understanding of the role of teaching in the corporate university. Teaching has become a form of masquerade for the corporate university, allowing it to justify itself to the external world as *not* like the other corporations, and thus still warranting public support. Yet, whereas formerly, and arguably, there existed an uneasy balance between teaching and research, it has now become more typical for most prestigious institutions—and these corporations do dictate what others do—to focus on research. As Nelly Stromquist points out, as teaching becomes less central to a university's reputation, particularly at the undergraduate level, it is increasingly relegated to nontenured and non–tenure track faculty members. In colleges where job training prevails, "teaching" is deemed more important than research, but then these are the institutions that are especially overly populated by part-time and temporary faculty who are less likely to develop any significant institutional engagement.[130]

The teaching that does take place is increasingly subjected to the logic of accounting, so that teachers must now worry about "learning outcomes," "assessment," "infusion of technology," and so forth. The professor is expected to "package" instruction, and conformity of curricular and instructional activities is the name of the game. This applies as much to traditional classroom instruction as it does to the online and distance learning courses that are being reproduced rapaciously. David Noble's work on online and distance learning instruction highlighted how technology has reshaped teaching, how it has commodified it.[131] Universities are also increasingly attempting to convert the products of teaching (e.g., syllabi, course notes, etc.) into intellectual property.[132]

Technology in teaching, as Slaughter and Rhoades argue, unbundles the faculty role, so that instead of professors involved in developing and delivering the course (or curriculum), the process is broken up and handled by managerial professionals into various tasks, ranging from designing and delivering the class, evaluation, assessment of students, technical advising, academic advising, and more.[133] The logic of entrepreneurship also affects teaching and it is used to generate new streams of resources, by developing occupational programs meant to attract new students (such as programs to create electronic games), to increase and maximize classroom space,[134] or to maximize enrollments per class so as to make the professor's time more efficient. Slaughter and Rhoades also point to a number of entrepreneurial strategies involving teaching, including increasing credit-hour production by developing new programs, expanding summer programs for that reason, creating professional master's programs (often thesis-free, targeting business employees who can pay full tuition), fundraising, and placing students in

130. Nelly P. Stromquist, *Education in a Globalized World: The Connectivity of Economic Power, Technology, and Knowledge* (Lanham: Rowman and Littlefield, 2002), 105.
131. David F. Noble, *Digital Diploma Mills: The Automation of Higher Education* (New York: Monthly Review Press, 2002).
132. See Slaughter and Rhoades, *Academic Capitalism and the New Economy*, 28–29.
133. Ibid., 169.
134. Florida International University recently changed its schedule of day classes by requiring that classes be taught three days a week (instead of one), maximizing classroom space throughout the week. The point of this was to generate revenue, as the state's funding policies required full maximization of classroom facilities. This was instituted with little regard for pedagogy. In the College of Education, for example, where student interns must be in the schools during the day, this scheduling proves very problematic.

industry.[135] So teaching, like research, has been "corporatized," and so granting academics the freedom of teaching means also that it is the imperatives of transnational capitalism which gain, not the student and certainly not the "public."

Freedom for Extramural Speech. The third presumption about the primary functions of the academic, that associated with freedom of extramural utterances, also warrants questioning. We think that this freedom is based on the understanding that the professor is a both a citizen of the institution and of the public, for which the professor has a duty to speak to on important matters. There is no question that professors are members of both their institutions and the larger society in which those institutions exist. But, as we have been discussing, these institutions and the larger society are undergoing drastic change in the face of global capital exchanges. And thus the *privileged* citizens and institutions will be those who are effective in furthering those exchanges. These will be the ones with the protection; the others are dispensable.

The new "men of power"—some are women now, of course, though not as many yet—or the academic capitalists, are the privileged citizens in the academy, and their extramural utterances are protected because they do not have any. They speak only the language of transnational capitalism and are unlikely to question its tenets, since to do so is to eviscerate their existence. There are still others, however, who do question the tenets of transnational capitalism through their words or actions. And some of these are tenured, thus protected from being dismissed for this questioning. To the corporate university, however, these "holdouts" are hindrances, and future holdouts must be prevented. So the academic capitalism that characterizes academe now requires that the tenure process be restructured so as to ensure that these people are excluded from the ranks with protected utterances, utterances that are protected because they are nonexistent. It is no coincidence that the ratcheting up of tenure requirements and the reward structures coincide with the conversion of the university into a corporation. It is no surprise that grant activities are now part and parcel of what one must submit for tenure and promotion. It is the capitalists who will attain tenure, if such a thing does not itself become a hindrance to transnational capitalism. The faculty who do the bulk of the teaching—the "mere" teachers—are increasingly those with no tenure, and thus no assurances that their extramural utterances will be protected. The understanding that the freedom of extramural utterances protects the "citizens of the university" is now questionable.

Yet academics are citizens of a larger public, and they do speak on matters relating to that public, and so they should have the freedom to do so. No? Well, is there really such a public anymore, if there ever was? Globalism is increasingly making any idea of the public obsolete, since it assumes

---

135. Slaughter and Rhoades, *Academic Capitalism and the New Economy*, 189.

a boundary between the public and the private, which global exchanges eviscerate. Globalization reflects a new world order in which there are no fixed boundaries or barriers, which is dominated by a series of national and supranational entities that manage hybrid identities, flexible hierarchies, and plural exchanges. This world order is replacing industrial labor with communicative, cooperative, and affective labor, and its central concern is the bio-political production of social life itself, a production that combines and invests in all that is economic, political, and cultural.[136] There is little that is "public" anymore, that is, little that is understood outside the notion of private ownership. Everything is subject to be turned into transnational capital, including knowledge, culture, and human bodies themselves. Global corporate operations now subordinate state functions, and in the name of competition, productivity, and freedom, public spaces are being markedly reduced. The function of the university, in this context, then, according to Miyoshi, is being transformed from state apologetics to industrial management, an unmistakably radical reduction of its public and critical role.[137]

Slaughter and Rhoades argue that colleges and universities are shifting from a "public good knowledge/learning regime" to an "academic capitalist knowledge/learning regime." The public good regime was characterized by valuing knowledge as a public good to which the citizenry has claims, and which paid heed to academic freedom honoring professors' right to follow research where it leads and to share their knowledge freely. The academic capitalist regime, however, values knowledge privatization and profit taking in which institutions, inventor faculty members, and corporations have claims that come before the public's. Knowledge is construed as a private good, valued for creating streams of high technology products that generate profit as they flow through global markets, and which requires that professors disclose their knowledge to their institutions, which then determine how the knowledge will be used.[138]

We think Slaughter and Rhoades are correct. They might disagree, but we think they took too moderate, and perhaps meliorist, a stance with regard to this phenomenon, arguing that something of the public good regime remains. We are not as sanguine about this as they are. Our polemic situating the university within transnational capitalism was meant to challenge us to reimagine what we now mean to our institutions and to our societies.

---

136. Michael Hardt and Antonio Negri, *Empire* (Cambridge: Harvard University Press, 2000), xi–xiii.
137. Masao Miyoshi, " 'Globalization,' Culture, and the University," in *The Cultures of Globalization*, ed. Fredric Jameson and Masao Miyoshi (Durham: Duke University Press, 1998), 247–70, 263.
138. Slaughter and Rhoades, *Academic Capitalism and the New Economy*, 28–29. Our position runs counter to others who appear to see the university as "sanctuaries of nonrepression." See Amy Gutman, *Democratic Education* (Princeton: Princeton University Press, 1998), 172–231.

Academic freedom, premised on the notions of university as public trust and our work as public service, no longer makes sense, and, indeed, to insist upon such premises is detrimental to the very public the premises are posited as protecting. The university is now a corporation, and a transnational one at that. The academic is now in the service of such a corporation. Tenure still protects a few holdouts, of course, but the tenure system is now serving the imperatives of the corporate culture of the university, and soon those holdouts will be gone. The remaining ones will be the academic capitalists, and actually we may dispense with the qualifier "academic" here, since it will soon have very little meaning inside the system of transnationally exchanged capital.

It is tempting to argue for some reconciliation of the traditional principles of academic freedom with the new economy. Since the traditional principles of academic freedom have for so long and in so many ways defined how we speak of ourselves to ourselves, the temptation is understandable. So we can forgive those who seek redemption in those traditional principles. We can forgive them, yes, but we prefer not to encourage them. It behooves us to reconsider what, if anything, holds academics and academic institutions above the critiques we level so freely on the capitalists who look like capitalists are thought to look.

Returning to the issue with which we started this chapter, we fear that the grants culture—supported by, and supportive of, transnational capitalist exchanges—has significantly altered what it means to be a professor. Indeed, in the sciences, which are supposed to provide the model for education research, professors have become accustomed to working for pay, so to speak.[139] What happens to the traditional idea of academic freedom when faculty begin to act as obviously and inevitably grant getters? Getting a grant becomes the driving force, if a double-edged sword, in the struggle for tenure and other professional rewards. The future is not looking bright, either, since graduate students are being socialized into the grant culture in order to secure an academic job. They are being encouraged to work with faculty on grant projects so that they can develop research and collaborative "skills," which also "introduces [them] to the world of sponsored research."[140]

Of course, not everyone seeks grants, and certainly not everyone gets them. But, if one "needs" to live in an environment in which universities pressure faculty to pursue grants, faculty "need" not make it easier for those universities to exert such pressure by blindly (or clairvoyantly) buying into the grants culture. A more critical role is necessary, if academics

---

139. See generally, Karen Seashore Louis, Melissa S. Anderson, Lisa Jones, and David Blumenthal, "Entrepreneurs in Academe Redux." Paper presented at the 1999 Annual Meeting of the American Research Association, Montreal, Canada, April 19–23, 1999.

140. See Elizabeth A. Stasny, "How to Get a Job in Academics," *The American Statistician* 55, no. 1 (2001): 35–40.

are to maintain a relative sense of difference from those they disparage for their *interestedness*. Perhaps Henry Giroux is correct that educators need to reconsider their current roles and assume that of the "public intellectual," who challenges rather than reinscribes societal (and professional) norms.[141] We are not certain about the use of that term, *public intellectuals*, since that implies a distinction between the public and private spheres that the age of privatization has exposed as a fiction. But faculty need more rather than less reflection and criticism, not just about their institutions but also their profession and society. Scott argues that the marriage of business and academe has made instrumentalism a reigning ethos, and faculty should promote more critical work, work that challenges the categories that organize their existence.[142] We agree. And we propose that such challenge should begin with current professional ideas about the university, research, and the academic itself. Faculty must ask themselves how these ideas originated and what effects they produce (and obscure) at the individual, institutional, and societal levels, which may now all be one and the same.

In particular, any notion of academic freedom that is premised on a social reality that no longer exists is useful only to the extent that it masks the emergence of new realities. The "public good" has been co-opted by neoliberal rationalities, and so it can no longer serve to explain our existence as academics. The institutional order that supports transnational capitalism should be brought down, because it is exploitive and destroys the possibility of something public ever forming itself again, or perhaps for the first time. If there is something left that is public, and if we wish to serve it, then that means that we will have to question the institutional order that gives us life, as it were. Bringing down that order must start with questioning the assumptions that support it.

In this questioning, we must dispense with the idea that there are common values and traditions that bind academics to each other. We must recognize that traditional values can no longer legitimate us, so to speak, and try to create a new discourse for understanding and rationalizing our existence. There is a risk to doing this, to be sure, and we may find ourselves in an abyss. But this is a risk that arises from being put at risk, by the practices and rationalities of transnational capitalism and the institutional order that creates and sustains them. Academic freedom, understood as a public good served by the autonomy of the professor, must be dispensed with and recast in light of the imperatives of transnational capitalism and the scientific practices that sustain them. If we are even remotely correct about anything we have said in this book, we will leave readers with two disconcerting questions: How might we redefine our existence? What can we become?

---

141. Henry Giroux, *Pedagogy and the Politics of Hope: Theory, Culture, and Schooling* (Boulder: Westview Press, 1997), 257–69.
142. Scott, "The Rhetoric of Crisis in Higher Education," 303.

EPILOGUE

It may seem odd to have an epilogue in a book such as this, but we feel compelled to provide one because this project is actually not new for us, and many things have happened between when we started thinking about it and when we actually put it all together to send out for publication. This book, while perhaps "academic" in nature, is also, as our last chapter in particular illustrates, very personal. And so, we felt compelled to bring a sense of closure to this entire project. It was more than five years ago that we wrote a paper on the grants culture, which is the basis for what became our last chapter. You could say, then, that we started to write the end of this book first. It took us over five years to write the book largely because of the vicissitudes of our working and personal lives, but also because at every turn something happened that moved us in different directions in our thoughts on education research and the forces that shape and are shaped by it.

Of the things that happened, among the most important were our conference experiences when we presented some of the ideas in this book. We experienced a range of opinions. Most of the people who heard or read aspects of this work (and who took the time to say something to us) expressed being moved to think differently. This makes us happy, as it is the reason we wanted to write the book in the first place. Some people were probably only curious; they asked us for copies of our presentations but we heard nothing more from them. A few others have been resistant to one or more of our arguments. The latter view bothered us the most. No one likes not to be believed, of course, but, in fact, what bothered us was not simply their resistance to our ideas, but its nature.

The logic of this resistance we could summarize as follows: "You are being unrealistic; things are not going to change." "You should offer readers something more concrete." "What is the point of this?" We think some readers of this book will also have similar concerns, and so we would like to address here what we think underlies the most significant—and perhaps most damning—challenge to our book: its utility. In closing this book, then, we discuss briefly one other force shaping the politics of inquiry in education: the discourse of utility.

In some ways, we have addressed this already, more or less explicitly, especially in our last chapter where we indicate that utility is being defined solely in economic terms, and also in our first chapter where we critique the "what works" logic of the federal government's attempts at defining a science of education research. We have derided this logic as a "gutter utilitarianism." Perhaps we should not have done that, for the question of something's usefulness is not to be derided or dismissed so hastily. Narrow notions of utility shape the behavior of governmental agencies, of funding agencies, of policy makers, and even of the so-called practitioners of education. But do such notions also shape our work as scholars and readers of education? Do we wonder whether this or that work is useful? It is a question, which appears to us to be also a covered-over admonition, that we put to the work of others and to our own. At some level we all worry about whether our own work is useful. Indeed, to be a researcher, a scholar, a professor, an administrator, a teacher, or a practitioner in education is to want to be useful, if not to specific people, such as students, faculty, employers, or funding agents, then to that abstraction we call the "public." How else can be we entitled to demand the public subsidy of our work?

We are actually less concerned here with utility per se than we are with how it is defined, and increasingly so by external agents, such as funders, and by how such definition in done in advance of scholarship, constituting a kind of prior restraint on how we might think of inquiry and its use. Is it *useless* to want to defer the question of usefulness to some future day? Some might see this question as advancing another version of the basic versus applied distinction so commonly thrown about in the sciences. We hope we have illustrated throughout this book how problematic that distinction is in the age of privatization and the "governmental" practices associated with privatization.

But our concern goes much deeper than whether a work of scholarship is useful now or later. What if instead of always trying to define our work's utility, we think of our work as part of the general movement of energy on the earth? The earth uses up the energy it needs for subsistence and then expels the excess, sometimes violently but always purposelessly. We borrow this logic from the late French critic, Georges Bataille, who offers an interesting perspective on political economy which reposes questions about the utility of our work in a different light. Bataille proposes, audaciously, that the problem of political economy can be posed like this: The "*sexual act is in time what the tiger is in space.*"[1] There is no growth but a luxurious squandering of energy in every form. The tiger represents the immense power of consumption of life. In the general effervescence of life, the tiger is a point of extreme incandescence, as is the sexual act, which is the occasion for a sudden and frantic squandering of energy resources, carried in a moment to the limit of possibility (i.e., it is in time what the tiger is in space).

1. Georges Bataille, *The Accursed Share: An Essay on General Economy, Volume I*, trans. Robert Hurley (New York: Zone Books, 1988), 12. Emphasis in original.

Thus, for Bataille, thinking about political economy "should run counter to ordinary calculations," and, thus, "*it is not necessity but its contrary,"luxury," that presents living matter and mankind with their fundamental problems.*"[2]

If Bataille is even remotely correct that luxury is the root of our problem because energy, physical and political, is almost always in excess, and that excess must always be spent, and often for no purpose, what use is there in worrying about "usefulness"? Does the discourse of utility actually further, but cover over, the imperatives of capitalist production? Utility seems to us to be important only to those who want to accumulate resources, be they economic, political, or social. But such accumulation is always doomed to failure, if excess energy must be spent, and spent purposelessly. We think that releasing ourselves from the discourse of utility is to think of research not as necessity, but, following Bataille, as luxury. And what can be more luxurious than the freedom to think, the freedom to think without having to worry that others will find it useful? Might experiencing something like freedom, then, also mean that we deem our work to be, in this specific sense, "useless?"

We do not really mean to say literally that this book should be deemed "useless," but we do want to offer it as a work of thought, as an essay. In other words, we would like the reader to judge its "utility" as a work of thought—"does it make you think differently?" One of the difficulties some of us in schools of education face today is the constant pressure to produce "research," often restricted by narrow definitions of utility, especially of the kind that must be fundable. We suppose that such utilitarianism has led to important discoveries, programs, social change, and so forth. And in that sense the research experience is, to borrow John Dewey's idea, *educative*, in that it allows for some social problem to be solved. But we think such experience is also *mis-educative*, in this sense: It structures our thought toward a limited understanding of what research might mean.

Indeed, the literature on education research reveals an interesting discursive phenomenon: "Research," as Robert Nisbet wrote more than thirty-five years ago, has become the "research project." That is, we have seen the replacement of research of a degree in size, individuality, and character that was compatible with teaching in the university—of "teaching-in-scholarship, of scholarship-in-teaching"—with another kind of research, the "development" kind, that is huge in size, calling for large managerial staffs, complete with workers and technicians, and which could have been left to government and industry. What has happened, according to Nisbet, is that "the *project system* . . . converted scholars into *managers of research enterprises*—with *research*, as a word, gradually succeeding scholarship in prestige."[3] We are not sure if he was correct then, but we are pretty sure he is now.

---

2. Ibid. Emphasis in original.
3. Robert Nisbet, *The Degradation of the Academic Dogma: The University in America 1945–1970* (New York: Basic Books, 1971), 80–81.

How often do we use the word *project* in our work or in describing others' work? What would happen if we insisted upon putting the term "project" always within quotations to indicate to ourselves and to others that the use of this term is to be made problematic? We would like readers of this book to understand the possibility that the word's ubiquity is much more than semantic. Could it be that the ubiquity of the word illustrates that research is being restructured, particularly into the large-scale, team-oriented, comparative, generalizable, or, in a word, "project"? And, does it redirect us in education away from "thought" as the most salient activity of the individual? With the advent of the "research project," are we losing, if we ever had it, the scholar whose production of knowledge arose entirely from his or her teaching? With the institution of the "research project" in education, are we losing the essay?

BIBLIOGRAPHY

A Brief History of Johns Hopkins University. www.jhu.edu/news_info/jhuinfo/ history.html.

Abbott, Andrew. 1986. "Jurisdictional Conflicts: A New Approach to the Development of the Legal Professions." *American Bar Foundation Research Journal* 11, no. 2: 187–224.

Agnew, Bruce. June 11, 1999. "Scientists Block NIH Plans to Grant Ph.D.'s." *Science*: 1743.

Alcoff, Linda Martin, ed. 1998. *Epistemology: The Big Questions*. Oxford: Blackwell.

Altbach, Philip G., Robert Oliver Berdahl, and Patricia J. Gumport, eds. 2005. *American Higher Education in the Twenty-first Century: Social, Political, and Economic Challenges*. Baltimore: Johns Hopkins University Press.

Altbach, Philip G., Patricia J. Gumport, and D. Bruce Johnstone, eds. 2001. *In Defense of American Higher Education*. Baltimore: Johns Hopkins University Press.

American Association of University Professors. 2001. *Policy Documents & Reports*, 9th ed. Washington, DC: American Association of University Professors and The Johns Hopkins University Press.

———. 2001. Statement on Corporate Funding of Academic Research. *Academe: Bulletin of the American Association of University Professors* (May/June): 68–70.

Anderson, Gary L. 2002. "Reflecting on Research for Doctoral Students in Education." *Educational Researcher* 31, no. 7: 22–25.

Anderson, Lisa. 2003. *Pursuing Truth, Exercising Power: Social Science and Public Policy in the 21st Century*. New York: Columbia University Press.

———. November 26, 2003. "The Global Reach of American Social Science," *The Chronicle Review*: B7.

Anderson, Melissa. 2001. "The Complex Relations Between the Academy and Industry: Views from the Literature." *Journal of Higher Education* 72, no. 2: 226–46.

Aronowitz, Stanley. 1993. *Roll Over Beethoven: The Return of Cultural Strife*. Hanover: Wesleyan University Press.

Audi, Robert, ed. 1995. *The Cambridge Dictionary of Philosophy*. New York: Cambridge University Press.

Austin, J. L. 1975. *How to Do Things with Words*. Cambridge: Harvard University Press.

Azelvandre, John P. 2001. "Constructing Sympathy's Forge: Empiricism, Ethics, and Environmental Education in the Thought of Liberty Hyde, Bailey, and John Dewey." *Philosophy of Education*: 170–78.

Baez, Benjamin. 2004. "The Study of Diversity." *Journal of Higher Education* 75, no. 3: 285–306.

————. 2006. "Merit and Difference." *Teachers College Record* 108, no. 6: 996–1016.

Baker, Bernadette. 2002. "The Hunt for Disability: The New Eugenics and the Normalization of School Children." *Teachers College Record* 104, no. 4: 663–703.

Bannister, Robert C. 1987. *Sociology and Scientism: The American Quest For Objectivity, 1880–1940.* Chapel Hill: University of North Carolina Press.

Barone, Tom. 2001. "Science, Art, and the Predispositions of Educational Researchers." *Educational Researcher* 30, no. 7: 24–28.

Bartelson, Jens. 2001. *The Critique of the State.* Cambridge: Cambridge University Press.

Bartlett, Thomas. August 16, 2002. "Blind Trust." *Chronicle of Higher Education:* A12.

Bataille, Georges. 1988. *The Accursed Share: An Essay on General Economy.* New York: Zone Books.

Beghetto, Ron. 2003. Scientifically Based Research. Eugene: Clearinghouse on Educational Policy Management. http://eric.uoregon.edu/publications/roundup/spring2003.html.

Benjamin, Ernst, and Donald R. Wagner, ed. 1994. *Academic Freedom: An Everyday Concern.* New Directions for Faculty Research, no. 88. San Francisco: Jossey-Bass Publishers.

Benjamin, Walter. 1936. "The Work of Art in the Age of Mechanical Reproduction." http://www.marxist.org/reference/subject/philosophy/works/ge/benjamin.html.

Berger, Peter L., and Thomas Luckmann. 1966. *The Social Construction of Reality: A Treatise in the Sociology of Knowledge.* New York: Anchor Books.

Berliner, David C. 2002. "Educational Research: The Hardest Science of All." *Educational Researcher* 31, no. 8: 18–20.

Bérubé, Michael, and Cary Nelson. 1995. *Higher Education under Fire: Politics, Economics, and the Crisis of the Humanities.* New York: Routledge.

Biesta, Gert. 2007. "Why 'What Works' Won't Work: Evidence-Based Practice and the Democratic Deficit in Educational Research." *Educational Theory* 57, no. 1: 1–22.

Bix, Amy Sue. 1993. " 'Backing into Sponsored Research': Physics and Engineering at Princeton University." *History of Higher Education Annual* 13: 9–52.

Blackburn, Robert T., and Janet H. Lawrence. 1995. *Faculty at Work: Motivation, Expectation, Satisfaction.* Baltimore: Johns Hopkins University Press.

Bloch, Marianne. 2004. "A Discourse that Disciplines, Governs, and Regulates: The National Research Council's Report on Scientific Research in Education." *Qualitative Inquiry* 10, no. 1: 96–110.

Boje, David M. 2001. "Corporate Writing in the Web of Postmodern Culture and Postindustrial Capitalism." *Management Communication Quarterly* 14, no. 3: 507–16.

Borrego, Anne Marie. August 16, 2002. "Scholars Revive Boycott of U.S. Grants to Promote Language Training." *The Chronicle of Higher Education:* A25.

Bourdieu, Pierre. 1977. *Outline of a Theory of Practice.* Cambridge: Cambridge University Press.

————. 1984. *Distinction: A Social Critique of the Judgement of Taste.* Cambridge: Harvard University Press.

———. 1991. *Language and Symbolic Power*. Translated by Gino Raymond and Matthew Adamson. Edited by John B. Thompson. Cambridge: Harvard University Press.

———. 1993. *Sociology in Question*. Thousand Oaks, CA: Sage.

Bourdieu, Pierre, Jean Claude Passeron, and Monique de Saint Martin. 1994. *Academic Discourse: Linguistic Misunderstanding and Professorial Power*. Stanford: Stanford University Press.

Bowen, William G., and Derek Curtis Bok. 1998. *The Shape of the River: Long-Term Consequences of Considering Race in College and University Admissions*. Princeton: Princeton University Press.

Boydson, Jo Ann. 1988. *John Dewey: The Later Works, 1925–1953, Volume 4*. Carbondale: Southern Illinois University.

Boyer, Ernest L. 1990. *Scholarship Reconsidered: Priorities of the Professoriate*. Princeton: Carnegie Foundation for the Advancement of Teaching.

Boyles, Deron. 2000. *American Education and Corporations: The Free Market Goes to School*. New York: Falmer.

———. 2005. *Schools or Markets? Commercialism, Privatization, and School-Business Partnerships*. Mahwah, NJ: Lawrence Erlbaum Associates.

———. 2006. "Dewey's Epistemology: An Argument for Warranted Assertions, Knowing, and Meaningful Classroom Practice." *Educational Theory* 56, no. 1: 57–68.

Brainard, Jeffrey. June 14, 2002. "U.S. Agencies Look to Interdisciplinary Science." *Chronicle of Higher Education*: A20.

———. March 29, 2002. " 'Have-Nots' See More Funds from the NIH." *The Chronicle of Higher Education*: A23.

Breneman, David W. 2002. "For Colleges, This Is Not Just Another Recession." *Chronicle of Higher Education* 48, no. 40: B7.

Brennan, Marie. 1995. "Education Doctorates: Reconstructing Professional Partnerships Around Research?" *Australian Universities' Review* 38, no. 2: 20–22.

Brint, Steven G. 1994. *In an Age of Experts: The Changing Role of Professionals in Politics and Public Life*. Princeton: Princeton University Press.

Brooks, Harvey. 1978. "The Problem of Research Priorities." *Daedalus: Journal of the American Academy of Arts and Sciences* 107, no. 2: 171–90.

Brubacher, John S. 1970. "The Theory of Higher Education." *The Journal of Higher Education* 41, no. 2: 98–115.

Brubacher, John Seiler, and Willis Rudy. 1958. *Higher Education in Transition: An American History, 1636–1956*. New York: Harper.

Burke, Tom. 1994. *Dewey's New Logic: A Reply to Russell*. Chicago: University of Chicago Press.

Bush, Vannevar. 1945. *Science: The Endless Frontier*. Washington, DC: United States Government Printing Office. http://www.nsf.gov/od/lpa/nsf50/vbush1945.htm.

Butler, Judith. 1997. *Excitable Speech: A Politics of the Performative*. New York: Routledge.

Campbell, Teresa Isabelle Daza. 1997. "Public Policy for the 21 Century: Addressing Potential Conflicts in University-Industry Collaboration." *The Review of Higher Education* 20, no. 4: 357–79.

Campbell, Teresa Isabelle Daza, and Sheila Slaughter. 1999. "Faculty and Administrator Attitudes Toward Potential Conflicts of Interest, Commitment, and Equity in University-Industry Relationships." *Journal of Higher Education* 70, no. 3: 309–52.

Cannella, Gaile S., and Yvonna S. Lincoln. 2004. "Dangerous Discourses II: Comprehending and Countering the Redeployment of Discourses (and Resources) in the Generation of Liberatory Inquiry." *Qualitative Inquiry* 10, no. 2: 165–74.

Castells, Manual. 1196. *The Rise of the Network Society*. Oxford: Blackwell Publishers.

Chafetz, Morris E. 1996. *The Tyranny of Experts: Blowing the Whistle on the Cult of Expertise*. Lanham: Madison Books.

Charlton, D. G. 1959. *Positivist Thought in France During the Second Empire, 1852–1870*. Oxford: Oxford University Press.

Charman, Karen. 2001. "Spinning Science Into Gold." *Sierra* 86, no. 4: 40.

Chronicle of Higher Education. August 25, 2006. Almanac Issue 2006–7.

Coalition for Evidence-Based Policy. 2003. *Identifying and Implementing Educational Practices Supported by Rigorous Evidence: A User Friendly Guide*. Washington, DC: Institute for Education Sciences.

Cole, Jonathan. 1993. "Balancing Acts: Dilemmas of Choice Facing Research Universities." *Daedalus: Journal of the American Academy of Arts and Sciences* 122, no. 4: 1–36.

Collins, Randall. 1994. *Four Sociological Traditions*. New York: Oxford University Press.

Constas, Mark A. 1998. "The Changing Nature of Educational Research and a Critique of Postmodernism." *Educational Researcher* 27, no. 2: 26–33.

———. 1998. "Deciphering Postmodern Educational Research." *Educational Researcher* 27, no. 9: 36–42.

Culler, Jonathan. 1997. *Literary Theory: A Very Short Introduction*. Oxford: Oxford University Press.

de Man, Paul. 1982. "The Resistance to Theory." *Yale French Studies* 63: 3–20.

de Marrais, Kathleen. 2004. "Elegant Communications: Sharing Qualitative Research with Communities, Colleagues, and Critics." *Qualitative Inquiry* 10, no. 2: 281–97.

Demos, Raphael. 1953. "Aspects of Positivism." *Philosophy and Phenomenological Research* 13, no. 3: 377–93.

Denzin, Norman K., and Yvonna S. Lincoln. 1994. *Handbook of Qualitative Research*. Thousand Oaks, CA: Sage.

Derber, Charles, William A. Schwartz, and Yale R. Magrass. 1990. *Power in the Highest Degree: Professionals and the Rise of a New Mandarin Order*. New York: Oxford University Press.

Derrida, Jacques. 1984. "The Principle of Reason: The University in the Eyes of Its Pupils." *Graduate Faculty Philosophy Journal* 10, no. 1: 5–29.

———. 1988. "Signature Event Context." In *Limited Inc*. Edited by Gerald Graff, 1–23. Evanston: Northwestern University Press.

Dewey, John. 1896. "The Reflect Arc Concept in Psychology." *Psychological Review* 3: 357–70.

———. 1916. *Democracy and Education: An Introduction to the Philosophy of Education.* Text-book series in education. New York: Macmillan.

———. 1920. *Reconstruction in Philosophy.* Boston: Beacon Press.

———. 1929. *The Sources of a Science of Education.* New York: H. Liveright.

———. April 3, 1937. "Democracy and Educational Administration." *School and Society* 45: 457–62.

———. January 1937. "President Hutchins' Proposals to Remake Higher Education." *The Social Frontier* 3, no. 22: 103–104.

———. 1957. *The Public and Its Problems.* Athens: Swallow Press.

———. 1997. *Experience and Education.* New York: Touchstone.

Dewey, John, and Arthur Fisher Bentley. 1949. *Knowing and the Known.* New York: Beacon Press.

Education Sciences Reform Act of 2002, Pub. L. No. 107-279.

Edwards, Paul. 1967. *The Encyclopedia of Philosophy.* New York: Macmillan.

"Experts on the Take." November 2000. *Multinational Monitor*: 29.

Eisenberg, Rebecca S. 1987. "Proprietary Rights and the Norms of Science in Biotechnology Research." *Yale Law Journal* 97: 177–231.

———. 1988. "Academic Freedom and Academic Values in Sponsored Research." *Texas Law Review* 66: 1363–404.

Eisenhart, Margaret. 2005. "Science Plus: A Response to the Responses to Scientific Research in Education." *Teachers College Record* 107, no. 1: 52–58.

Eisenhart, Margaret, and Robert L. DeHaan. 2005. "Doctoral Preparation of Scientifically Based Education Researchers." *Educational Researcher* 34, no. 4: 3–13.

Eisenhart, Margaret, and Lisa Towne. 2003. "Contestation and Change in National Policy on 'Scientifically Based' Education Research." *Educational Researcher* 32, no. 7: 31–38.

Eisner, Elliot W. 1997. "The Promise and Perils of Alternative Forms of Data Representation." *Educational Researcher* 26, no. 6: 4–10.

Erickson, Frederick, and Kris Gutierrez. 2002. "Culture, Rigor, and Science in Educational Research." *Educational Researcher* 31, no. 8: 21–24.

Fairweather, James S. 2002. "The Mythologies of Faculty Productivity: Implications for Institutional Policy and Decision Making." *The Journal of Higher Education* 73, no. 1: 26–48.

Feshbach, Herman. 1975. "Graduate Education and Federal Support of Research." *Daedalus: Journal of the American Academy of Arts and Sciences* 104, no. 1: 248–50.

Feuer, Michael J., Lisa Towne, and Richard J. Shavelson. 2002. "Scientific Culture and Educational Research." *Educational Researcher* 31, no. 8: 4–14.

Feyerabend, Paul. 1975. *Against Method.* New York: Verso.

Foucault, Michel. 1970. *The Order of Things: An Archaeology of the Human Sciences.* London: Tavistock Publications.

———. 1972. *The Archaeology of Knowledge.* Translated by A. M. Sheridan Smith. New York: Pantheon Books.

———. 1977. *Discipline and Punish: The Birth of the Prison.* New York: Vintage Books.

———. 1978. *The History of Sexuality: An Introduction Volume I.* Translated by Robert Hurley. New York: Vintage Books.

————. 1980. *Power/Knowledge: Selected Interviews and Other Writings 1972–1977*. Edited and translated by Colin Gordon. New York: Pantheon Books.

————. 1984. *The History of Sexuality: The Use of Pleasure, Volume 2*. Translated by R. Hurley. New York: Pantheon.

————. 1993. "About the Beginning of the Hermeneutics of the Self: Two Lectures at Dartmouth." *Political Theory* 21, no. 2: 198–227.

————. 1997. *"Society Must Be Defended:" Lectures at the Collège de France*. Edited by Mauro Bertani and Alessandro Fontana. Translated by David Macey. New York: Picador.

Francis John G., and Mark C. Hampton. 1999. "Resourceful Responses: The Adaptive Research University and the Drive to Market." *The Journal of Higher Education* 70, no. 6: 625–41.

Fraser, Nancy. 1989. "Talking About Needs: Interpretive Contests as Political Conflicts in Welfare State Societies." *Ethics* 99, no. 2: 291–313.

Freidson, Eliot. 2001. *Professionalism: The Third Logic*. Chicago: The University of Chicago Press.

Freud, Sigmund. 1957. *The Future of an Illusion*. Translated by W. D. Robson-Scott. Edited by James Strachey. New York: Anchor Books.

Fuller, Steve. 2002. *Social Epistemology*. Bloomington: Indiana University Press.

Graham, Loren R. 1978. "Concerns About Science and Attempts to Regulate Inquiry." *Daedalus: Journal of the American Academy of Arts and Sciences* 107, no. 2: 1–21.

Garnham, Nicholas. 1986. "Extended Review: Bourdieu's *Distinction*." *Sociological Review* 34, no. 2: 423–33.

Garrison, James. 2001. "An Introduction to Dewey's Theory of Functional 'Trans-Action': An Alternative Paradigm for Activity Theory." *Mind, Culture, and Activity* 8: 275–96.

Gartman, David. 1991. "Culture as Class Symbolization or Mass Reification? A Critique of Bourdieu's *Distinction*." *American Journal of Sociology* 97, no. 2: 421–47.

Gee, James Paul. 2005. "It's Theories All the Way Down: A Response to Scientific Research in Education." *Teachers College Record* 107, no. 1: 10–18.

Geiger, Roger L. 2004. *Knowledge and Money: Research Universities and the Paradox of the Marketplace*. Stanford: Stanford University Press.

Giroux, Henry A. 1997. *Pedagogy and the Politics of Hope: Theory, Culture, and Schooling: A Critical Reader*. Boulder: WestviewPress.

Godfrey-Smith, Peter. September 2002. "Dewey on Naturalism, Realism, and Science." *Philosophy of Science* 69: 1–11.

Gose, Ben. 2002. "The Fall of the Flagships: Do the Best State Universities Need to Privatize to Thrive?" *Chronicle of Higher Education* 48, no. 43: A19.

Gould, Stephen Jay. 1981. *The Mismeasure of Man*. New York: Norton.

Gregory, Stephen, and Roger Sanjek, ed. 1996. *Race*. New Brunswick: Rutgers University Press.

Grenfell, Michael. 1996. "Bourdieu and Initial Teacher Education: A Post Structuralist Approach." *British Educational Research Journal* 22, no. 3: 287–306.

Grunig, Stephen D. 1997. "Research, Reputation, and Resources: The Effect of Research Activity on Perceptions of Undergraduate Education and Instituttional Resources Acquisition." *Journal of Higher Education* 68, no. 1: 17–52.

Guterman, Lila. February 8, 2002. "Conflicts of Interest Between the Lines." *Chronicle of Higher Education*: A14.

Guterman, Lila, and Martin Van Der Werf. October 5, 2001. "12 Journals Adopt Joint Policy on Research Supported by Business." *Chronicle of Higher Education*: A29.

Haack, Susan. 2003. *Defending Science—Within Reason: Between Scientism and Cynicism*. Amherst, NY: Prometheus Books.

Hacking, Ian. 1979. "Michel Foucault's Immature Science." *Nous* 13, no. 1: 39–51.

———. 1990. *The Taming of Chance*. Cambridge: Cambridge University Press.

Hardt, Michael, and Antonio Negri. 2000. *Empire*. Cambridge: Harvard University Press.

Hatch, Nathan O. 1988. *The Professions in American History*. Notre Dame: University of Notre Dame Press.

"Heavy Vetting." July/August 2001. *Lingua Franca*: 9–12.

Heller, Thomas C., Morton Sosna, and David E. Wellbery. 1986. *Reconstructing Individualism: Autonomy, Individuality, and the Self in Western Thought*. Stanford: Stanford University Press.

"Higher Education and Science." February 15, 2002. *Chronicle of Higher Education*: A33.

Hildebrand, David L. 2003. *Beyond Realism and Antirealism: John Dewey and the Neopragmatists*. Nashville: Vanderbilt University Press.

Holton, Robert. 1997. "Bourdieu and Common Sense." *SubStance* 84: 38–52.

Hossler, Don, Jon P. Lund, Jackie Ramin, Sarah Westfall, and Steve Irish. 1997. "State Funding for Higher Education; The Sisyphean Task." *Journal of Higher Education* 68, no. 2: 160–190.

Hostetler, Karl. 2005. "What is 'Good' Education Research?" *Educational Researcher* 34, no. 5: 16–21.

"Hot Type." June 28, 2002. *Chronicle of Higher Education*: A16.

Howe, Kenneth R. 2004. "A Critique of Experimentalism." *Qualitative Inquiry* 10, no. 1: 42–61.

———. 2005. "The Question of Education Science: Experimentism Versus Experimentalism." *Educational Theory* 55, no. 3: 307–21.

Hume, David. 1974. "An Enquiry Concerning Human Understanding." In *The Empiricists: Locke, Berkeley, Hume*, 307–430. New York: Anchor Books.

Hutchins, Robert Maynard. 1978. *The Higher Learning in America*. New Haven: Yale University Press.

Iannone, Ron. 1992. "A Critical Perspective Reform Paradigm for Ed.D. Programs." *Education* 112, no. 4: 612–17.

Institute of Education Sciences. "About the Institute of Education Sciences." http://www.ed.gov/about/offices/list/ies/index.html.

Jackson, John A. 1970. *Professions and Professionalization*. London: Cambridge University Press.

Jaeger, Richard M. 1988. *Complementary Methods for Research in Education*. Washington, DC: American Educational Research Association.

Jameson, Fredric. 1981. *The Political Unconscious: Narrative as a Socially Symbolic Act*. Ithaca: Cornell University Press.

Jameson, Fredric, and Masao Miyoshi.1998. *The Cultures of Globalization (Post-Contemporary Interventions)*. Durham: Duke University Press.

Jencks, Christopher, and David Riesman. 1968. *The Academic Revolution*. Garden City, NY: Doubleday.

Kant, Immanuel. 1979. *The Conflict of the Faculties*. Translated by Mary J. Gregor. Lincoln: University of Nebraska Press.

Keller, George. 1998. "Does Higher Education Research Need Revisions?" *The Review of Higher Education* 21, no. 3: 267–78.

Kelly, Michael, ed. 1994. *Critique and Power: Recasting the Foucault/Habermas Debate*. Cambridge: MIT Press.

Keohane, Nannerl O. 1993. "The Mission of the Research University." *Daedalus: The Journal of the American Academy of Arts and Sciences* 122, no. 4: 101–25.

Kerr, Clark. 2001. *The Uses of the University*. Cambridge: Harvard University Press.

Kirp, David L. 2003. *Shakespeare, Einstein, and the Bottom Line: The Marketing of Higher Education*. Cambridge: Harvard University Press.

Klemke, E. D., Robert Hollinger, David Wÿss Rudge, and A. David Kline. 1998. *Introductory Readings in the Philosophy of Science*. Amherst, NY: Prometheus Books.

Kolbert, Jered B., and Johnston M. Brendel. 1997. "Current Perceptions of the Doctor of Philosophy and Doctor of Education in Counselor Preparation." *Counselor Education and Supervision* 36, no. 3: 207–15.

Kovacs, Philip, and Deron Boyles. 2005. "Institutes, Foundations, and Think Tanks: Conservative Influences on U.S. Public Schools." *Public Resistance* 1, no. 1: 1–18. http://www.publicresistance.org.

Krathwohl, David R. 1993. *Methods of Educational and Social Science Research: An Integrated Approach*. New York: Longman.

Kuhn, Thomas S. 1970. *The Structure of Scientific Revolutions*. 2nd ed. Chicago: University of Chicago Press.

———. 1977. *The Essential Tension: Selected Studies in Scientific Traditions and Change*. Chicago: University of Chicago Press.

Kuklick, Bruce. 1977. *The Rise of American Philosophy, Cambridge, Massachusetts, 1860–1930*. New Haven: Yale University Press.

Kulp, Christopher B. 1992. *The End of Epistemology: Dewey and His Current Allies on the Spectator Theory of Knowledge*. Westport, CT: Greenwood Press.

Labaree, David F. 2003. "The Peculiar Problems of Preparing Educational Researchers." *Educational Researcher* 32, no. 4: 13–22.

Lacan, Jacques. 1977. *Écrits: A Selection*. Translated by Alan Sheridan. New York: W. W. Norton.

Lagemann, Ellen Condliffe. 1997. "Contested Terrain: A History of Education Research in the United States, 1890–1990." *Educational Researcher* 26, no. 9: 5–17.

———. 2000. *An Elusive Science: The Troubling History of Education Research*. Chicago: University of Chicago Press.

Lagowski, J. L. 1996. "Rethinking the Ph.D.: A New Social Contract." *Journal of Chemical Education* 73, no. 1: 1.

Larson, Magali Sarfatti. 1977. *The Rise of Professionalism: A Sociological Analysis*. Berkeley: University of California Press.

Lather, Patti. 2004. "This IS Your Father's Paradigm: Government Intrusion and the Case of Qualitative Research in Education." *Qualitative Inquiry* 10, no. 1: 15–34.

Lather, Patti, and Pamela Moss. 2005. "Introduction: Implications of the Scientific Research in Education Report for Qualitative Inquiry." *Teachers College Record* 107, no. 1: 1–3.

Leary, Lewis. 1960. *American Literary Essays*. New York: Crowell.

Lechte, John. 1994. *Fifty Key Contemporary Thinkers: From Structuralism to Postmodernity*. London and New York: Routledge.

Lemert, Charles C. 1993. *Social Theory: The Multicultural and Classic Readings*. Boulder: Westview Press.

Lenn, Marjorie Peace. 2002. "The Right Way to Export Higher Education." *Chronicle of Higher Education* 48, no. 25: B24.

Levine, Arthur. 2005. *Educating School Leaders*. Washington, DC: The Education Schools Project.

Lincoln, Yvonna S. 1995. "Emerging Criteria for Quality in Qualitative and Interpretive Research." *Qualitative Inquiry* 1, no. 3: 275–89.

Lincoln, Yvonna S., and Gaile S. Cannella. 2004. "Dangerous Discourses: Methodological Conservatism and Governmental Regimes of Truth." *Qualitative Inquiry* 10, no. 1: 5–14.

———. 2004. "Qualitative Research, Power, and the Radical Right." *Qualitative Inquiry* 10, no. 2: 175–201.

Littlefield, Alice, Leonard Lieberman, and Larry T. Reynolds. 1982. "Redefining Race: The Potential Demise of a Concept in Physical Anthropology." *Current Anthropology* 23, no. 6: 641–55.

Louis, Karen Seashore, Melissa S. Anderson, Lisa Jones, and David Blumenthal. April 19–23, 1999. "Entrepreneurs in Academe Redux." Montreal: American Educational Research Association.

Lundberg, George A. 1939. "Contemporary Positivism in Sociology." *American Sociological Review* 4, no. 1: 42–55.

Lynn, Kenneth S. 1965. *The Professions in America*. Boston: Houghton Mifflin.

Lyotard, Jean François. 1984. *The Postmodern Condition: A Report on Knowledge*. Translated by Geoff Bennington and Brian Massumi. Minneapolis: University of Minnesota Press.

Mangan, Katherine S. September 20, 2002. "The Ethics of Business Schools." *Chronicle of Higher Education*: A14.

Manicas, Peter T. 1988. "Pragmatic Philosophy of Science and the Charge of Scientism." *Transactions of the Charles S. Peirce Society* 24, no. 4: 179–222.

Mannheim, Karl. 1936. *Ideology and Utopia: An Introduction to the Sociology of Knowledge*. Translated by Louis Wirth and Edward Shils. San Diego: Harcourt.

Mabry, Linda A. 1999. "Multinational Corporations and U.S. Technology Policy: Rethinking the Concept of Corporate Nationality." *Georgetown Law Journal* 87: 563–673.

Marginson, Simon, and Mark Considine. 2000. *The Enterprise University: Power, Governance, and Reinvention in Australia*. Cambridge: Cambridge University Press.

Margolis, Joseph. 2003. *The Unraveling of Scientism: American Philosophy at the End of the Twentieth Century*. Ithaca: Cornell University Press.

226 BIBLIOGRAPHY

Martinson, Brian C., Melissa S. Anderson, and Raymond de Vries. June 9, 2005. "Scientists Behaving Badly." *Nature* 435, no. 7043: 737–38.

Marx, Leo. 1978. "Reflections on the Neo-Romantic Critique of Science." *Daedalus: Journal of the American Academy of Arts and Sciences* 107, no. 2: 61–73.

Massy, William, and Robert Zemsky. 1994. "Faculty Discretionary Time: Departments and the 'Academic Ratchet.'" *Journal of Higher Education* 66, no. 1: 1–22.

Maxwell, Joseph A. 2004. "Causal Explanation, Qualitative Research, and Scientific Inquiry in Education." *Educational Researcher* 33, no. 4: 3–11.

———. 2004. "Reemergent Scientism, Postmodernism, and Dialogue Across Differences." *Qualitative Inquiry* 10, no. 1: 35–41.

Mayer, Richard E. 2000. "What Is the Place of Science in Educational Research?" *Educational Researcher* 29, no. 6: 38–39.

McCarthy, E. Doyle. 1996. *Knowledge as Culture: The New Sociology of Knowledge.* New York: Routledge.

McDonald, Hugh J. 1943. "The Doctorate in America." *Journal of Higher Education* 14, no. 4: 189–94.

McLaren, Peter, and James M. Giarelli. 1995. *Critical Theory and Educational Research.* Albany: State University of New York Press.

Merton, Robert K. 1968. *Social Theory and Social Structure.* New York: The Free Press.

———. 1972. "Insiders and Outsiders: A Chapter in the Sociology of Knowledge." *The American Journal of Sociology* 78, no. 1: 9–47.

Merton, Robert King, and Elinor G. Barber. 2004. *The Travels and Adventures of Serendipity: A Study in Historical Semantics and the Sociology of Science.* Princeton: Princeton University Press.

Metz, Mary Haywood. 2001. "Intellectual Border Crossing in Graduate Education: A Report from the Field." *Educational Researcher* 30, no. 5: 12–18.

Metz, Mary Haywood, and Reba N. Page. 2002. "The Uses of Practitioner Research and Status Issues in Educational Research: Reply to Gary Anderson." *Educational Researcher* 31, no. 7: 26–27.

Metzger, Walter P. 1978. "Academic Freedom and Scientific Freedom." *Daedalus: Journal of the American Academy of Arts and Sciences* 107, no. 2: 93–114.

Miller, David L. 1947. "Science, Technology, and Value Judgments." *Ethics* 58, no. 1: 63–69.

Mitchell, Lawrence E. 2002. "American Corporations: The New Sovereigns." *Chronicle of Higher Education* 48, no. 19: B13.

Miyoshi, Masao. 2000. "Ivory Tower in Escrow." *boundary* 2: 1–50.

Monastersky, Richard. August 16, 2002. "Atomic Lies." *Chronicle of Higher Education*: A16.

Moss, Pamela A. 2005. "Toward 'Epistemic Reflexivity' in Educational Research: A Response to Scientific Research in Education." *Teachers College Record* 107, no. 1: 19–29.

———. 2005. "Understanding the Other/Understanding Ourselves: Toward a Constructive Dialogue about 'Principles' in Educational Research." *Educational Theory* 55, no. 3: 263–83.

Nash, Roy. 1999. "Bourdieu, 'Habitus,' and Educational Research: Is it All Worth the Candle?" *British Journal of Sociology of Education* 20, no. 2: 175–87.

National Academy of Sciences. "The National Research Council." http://www.nationalacademies.org/nrc/.

National Academy of Sciences. "About the National Academy of the Sciences." http://www.nasonline.org/site/PageServer?pagename=ABOUT_main_page.

National Research Council. 1999. *Improving Student Learning: A Strategic Plan for Educational Research and its Utilization.* Washington, DC: National Academy Press.

National Research Council. 2002. *Scientific Research in Education,* ed. Richard J. Shavelson and Lisa Towne. Washington, DC: National Academy Press.

National Research Council (U.S.). Committee on Research in Education. 2004. "Implementing Randomized Field Trials in Education: Report of a Workshop." Washington, DC: National Academies Press.

———. 2004. "Strengthening Peer Review in Federal Agencies That Support Education Research." Washington, DC: National Academies Press.

National Research Council. 2005. *Advancing Scientific Research in Education,* ed. Lisa Towne, Lauress L. Wise, and Tina M. Winters. Washington, DC: National Academies Press.

Nelkin, Dorothy. 1975. "The Political Impact of Technical Expertise." *Social Studies of Science* 5, no. 1: 35–54.

Nelson, Jack K., and Calleen Coorough. 1994. "Content Analysis of the Ph.D. Versus Ed.D. Dissertations." *Journal of Experimental Education* 62, no. 2: 158–68.

Nietzsche, Friedrich Wilhelm. 1967. *The Will to Power.* Translated by Walter Arnold Kaufmann and R. J. Hollingdale. Edited by Walter Arnold Kaufmann. New York: Vintage Books.

Newman, John Henry. 1982. *The Idea of the University.* Notre Dame: University of Notre Dame Press.

Newman, Frank. September/October 2000. "Saving Higher Education's Soul." *Change:* 17–23.

Nichols, Rodney W. 1993. "Federal Science Policy and Universities: Consequences of Success." *Daedalus: Journal of the American Academy of Arts and Sciences* 122, no. 4: 197–224.

Nisbet, Robert A. 1971. *The Degradation of the Academic Dogma: The University in America, 1945–1970.* New York: Basic Books.

No Child Left Behind Act of 2001, Pub. L. No. 107-110.

Noble, David F. 2001. *Digital Diploma Mills: The Automation of Higher Education.* New York: Monthly Review Press.

Olafson, Frederick A. 2001. *Naturalism and the Human Condition: Against Scientism.* New York: Routledge.

Olson, David R. 2004. "The Triumph of Hope Over Experience in the Search for 'What Works': A Response to Slavin." *Educational Researcher* 33, no. 1: 24–26.

Omi, Michael, and Howard Winant. 1994. *Racial Formation in the United States: From the 1960s to the 1990s,* 2nd ed. New York: Routledge.

Osguthorpe, Russell T., and Mei J. Wong. 1993. "The Ph.D. Versus the Ed.D.: Time for a Decision." *Innovative Higher Education* 18: 47–63.

Page, Reba N. 2001. "Reshaping Graduate Preparation in Educational Research Methods: One School's Experience." *Educational Researcher* 30, no. 5: 19–25.

Pallas, Aaron M. 2001. "Preparing Education Doctoral Students for Epistemological Diversity." *Educational Researcher* 30, no. 5: 6–11.

Patton, Carl V. Spring 2001. "Introduction." *Metropolitan: The Magazine of Georgia State University*, 3.

Peirce, Charles S. November 1877. "The Fixation of Belief." *Popular Science Monthly* 12: 1–15.

Pellegrino, James W., and Susan R. Goldman. 2002. "Be Careful What You Wish For: You May Get It: Educational Research in the Spotlight." *Educational Researcher* 31, no. 8: 15–17.

Petress, Kenneth C. 1993. "Are Doctorates Really Needed for Non-Research Positions?" *Journal of Instructional Psychology* 20, no. 4: 321–22.

Phillips, D. C. 1987. *Philosophy, Science, and Social Inquiry: Contemporary Methodological Controversies in Social Science and Related Applied Fields of Research*. New York: Pergamon Press.

———. 2000. *The Expanded Social Scientist's Bestiary: A Guide to Fabled Threats to, and Defenses of, Naturalistic Social Science*. Lanham, MD: Rowman and Littlefield.

Popkewitz, Thomas S. 1997. "A Changing Terrain of Knowledge and Power: A Social Epistemology of Educational Research." *Educational Researcher* 26, no. 9: 18–29.

———. 2004. "Is the National Research Council Committee's Report on Scientific Research in Education Scientific? On Trusting the Manifesto." *Qualitative Inquiry* 10, no. 1: 62–78.

Popkewitz, Thomas S., and Marie Brennan, eds. 1998. *Foucault's Challenge: Discourse, Knowledge, and Power in Education*. New York: Teacher's College Press.

Popper, Karl R. 1940. "What is Dialectic?" *Mind* 49, no. 196: 403–26.

———. 1962. *The Open Society and its Enemies, Volume I: The Spell of Plato*. Princeton: Princeton University Press.

———. 1962. *The Open Society and Its Enemies: The High Tide of Prophecy: Hegel, Marx, and the Aftermath, Volume 2*. Princeton: Princeton University Press.

Press, Eyal, and Jennifer Washburn. March 2000. "The Kept University," *Atlantic Monthly*: 39–54.

Prewitt, Kenneth 1993. "America's Research Universities Under Public Scrutiny." *Daedalus: Journal of the American Academy of Arts and Sciences* 122, no. 4: 85–99.

Pritchett, H. S. 1900. "The Relation of Educated Men to the State." *Science* 12, no. 305: 657–66.

Pulley, John L. 2002. "Well-off and Wary." *Chronicle of Higher Education* 48, no. 41: A27.

Quine, W. V. O. 1977. *Ontological Relativity*. New York: Columbia University Press.

Radford, John. 2001. "Doctor of What?" *Teaching in Higher Education* 6, no. 4: 527–29.

Randall, E. Vance, Bruce S. Cooper, and Steven J. Hite. 1999. "Understanding the Politics of Research in Education." *Educational Policy* 13, no. 1: 7–22.

Reading Excellence Act of 1999, Pub. L. 105-277.

Readings, Bill. 1996. *The University in Ruins*. Cambridge: Harvard University Press.

Reinsmith, William A. 1992. *Archetypal Forms in Teaching: A Continuum.* Westport: Greenwood Press.

Rhoades, Gary. September–October 2001. "Whose Property Is It?" *Academe:* 39–43.

Rhoades, Gary, and Sheila Slaughter. 1997. "Academic Capitalism, Managed Professionals, and Supply-Side Higher Education." *Social Text* 51, no. 2: 9–38.

Robbins, Derek. 1993. "The Practical Importance of Bourdieu's Analyses of Higher Education." *Studies in Higher Education* 18, no. 2: 151 63.

Rorty, Richard. 1979. *Philosophy and the Mirror of Nature.* Princeton: Princeton University Press.

Rosenau, Pauline Marie. 1992. *Post-Modernism and the Social Sciences: Insights, Inroads, and Intrusions.* Princeton: Princeton University Press.

Rosenberg, Alexander. 1988. *Philosophy of Science,* 2nd ed. Boulder: Westview Press.

Rossides, Daniel W. 1998. *Professions and Disciplines: Functional and Conflict Perspectives.* Upper Saddle River, NJ: Prentice-Hall.

Ruch, Richard S. 2001. *Higher Ed,Inc.: The Rise of the For-profit University.* Baltimore: Johns Hopkins University Press.

Rudolph, Frederick. 1962. *The American College and University: A History.* Athens: The University of Georgia Press.

Said, Edward W. 1978. *Orientalism.* New York: Pantheon Books.

————. 1983. *The World, the Text, and the Critic.* Cambridge: Harvard University Press.

Sanderson, Allen, Voon Chin Phua, David Herda. 2000. The American Faculty Poll. Chicago: National Opinion Research Center.

Sanger, David E. July 8, 2001. "Trying to Run a Country Like a Corporation." *The New York Times:* Section 4.

Sarat, Austin, and Thomas R. Kearns, eds. 1996. *Legal Rights: Historical and Philosophical Perspectives.* Ann Arbor: The University of Michigan Press.

Scheurich, James J. and Michelle D. Young. 1997. "Coloring Epistemologies: Are Our Research Epistemologies Racially Biased? *Educational Researcher* 26, no. 4: 4–16.

Schilpp, Paul Arthur, and John Dewey. 1939. *The Philosophy of John Dewey.* New York: Tudor.

Schmitt, Frederick F. 1997. *Socializing Epistemology: The Social Dimensions of Knowledge.* Lanham: University Press of America.

Scott, David, and Robin Usher. 1996. *Understanding Educational Research.* New York: Routledge.

Scott, Joan Wallach. 2002. "The Critical State of Shared Governance." *Academe* 88, no. 4: 41.

Searle, John R. 1993. "Rationality and Realism, What Is at Stake?" *Daedalus: Journal of the American Academy of Arts and Sciences* 122, no. 4: 55–83.

Seidman, Steven. 1994. *The Postmodern Turn: New Perspectives on Social Theory.* Cambridge: Cambridge University Press.

Selingo, Jeffrey. 2002. "States with the Biggest Deficits Take Aim at Higher Education." *Chronicle of Higher Education* 48, no. 32: A24.

Shelley, Mary Wollstonecraft. 1993. *Frankenstein, or, the Modern Prometheus.* New York: Barnes and Noble Classics.

Silva, Edward T., and Sheila Slaughter. 1980. "Prometheus Bound: The Limits of Social Science Professionalization in the Progressive Period." *Theory and Society* 9, no. 6: 781–819.

Simon, W. M. 1963. *European Positivism in the Nineteenth Century*. Ithaca: Cornell University Press.

Skolnikoff, Eugene B. 1993. "Knowledge Without Borders? Internationalization of the Research Universities." *Daedalus: Journal of the American Academy of Arts and Sciences* 122, no. 4: 225–52.

Slaughter, Sheila. 2001 September/October. "Professional Values and the Allure of the Market." *Academe*: 22–26.

Slaughter, Sheila, and Gary Rhoades. 2004. *Academic Capitalism and the New Economy: Markets, State, and Higher Education*. Baltimore: Johns Hopkins University Press.

Slavin, Robert E. 2002. "Evidence-based Education Policies: Transforming Educational Practice and Research." *Educational Researcher* 31, no. 7: 15–21.

———. 2004. "Education Research Can and Must Address 'What Works' Questions." *Educational Researcher* 33, no. 1: 27–28.

Smallwood, Scott. April 12, 2002. "Bitter Aftertaste." *Chronicle of Higher Education*: A10–A12.

Smith, Charles W. 2000. *Market Values in American Higher Education: The Pitfalls and Promises*. Lanham, MD: Rowman and Littlefield.

Smith, Linda Tuhiwai. 1999. *Decolonizing Methodologies: Research and Indigenous Peoples*. London: Zed Books.

Smith, Paul R. 2000. "A Meeting of Cultures: Part-time Students in an Ed.D. Program." *International Journal of Leadership in Education* 3, no. 4: 359–80.

Snow, C. P. 1993. *The Two Cultures*. London: Cambridge University Press.

Sommer, Toby J. 2001. "Suppresion of Scientific Research: *Bahramdipity* and *Nulltiple* Scientific Discoveries." *Science and Engineering Ethics* 7, no. 1: 77–104.

Spicker, Paul. 2000. *The Welfare State: A General Theory*. Thousand Oaks: Sage.

Spring, Joel. 1997. *Political Agendas for Education: From the Christian Coalition to the Green Party*. Mahwah, NJ: Lawrence Erlbaum Associates.

St. Pierre, Elizabeth Adams. 2002. " 'Science' Rejects Postmodernism." *Educational Researcher* 31, no. 8: 25–27.

St. Pierre, Elizabeth, and Wanda S. Pillow. 2000. *Working the Ruins: Feminist Poststructural Theory and Methods in Education*. New York: Routledge.

———. 2004. "Refusing Alternatives: A Science of Contestation." *Qualitative Inquiry* 10, no. 1: 130–39.

Stasny, E. A. 2001. "How to Get a Job in Academics." *The American Statistician* 55: 35–40.

Stromquist, Nelly P. 2002. *Education in a Globalized World: The Connectivity of Economic Power, Technology, and Knowledge*. Lanham, MD: Rowman and Littlefield.

Sutton, Robert B. 1953. "The Phrase *Libertas Philosophandi*." *Journal of the History of Ideas* 14, no. 2: 310–16.

Talburt, Susan. 2004. "Ethnographic Responsibility without the 'Real.' " *Journal of Higher Education* 75, no. 1: 80–103.

Tierney, William G. 2000. "On Translation: From Research Findings to Public Utility." *Theory into Practice* 39, no. 3: 185–90.

————. 2001. "The Autonomy of Knowledge and the Decline of the Subject: Postmodernism and the Reformulation of the University." *Higher Education* 41, no. 4: 353–72.

Thrift, Nigel. 2004. "Movement-Space: The Changing Domain of Thinking Resulting from the Development of New Kinds of Spatial Awareness." *Economy and Society* 33, no. 4: 582–604.

Topper, Keith. 2001. "Not So Trifling Nuances: Pierre Bourdieu, Symbolic Violence, and the Perversions of Democracy." *Constellations* 8, no. 1: 30–56.

Torstendahl, Rolf, and Michael Burrage. 1990. *The Formation of Professions: Knowledge, State, and Strategy.* Newbury Park, CA: Sage.

Travers, Robert M. 1983. *How Research Has Changed American Schools: A History from 1840 to the Present.* Kalamazoo: Mythos Press.

Trigg, Roger. 1985. *Understanding Social Science: A Philosophical Introduction to the Social Sciences.* New York: Basil Blackwell.

Turner, James, and Paul Bernard. 1993. "The 'German Model' and the Graduate School: The University of Michigan and the Origin Myth of the American University." *History of Higher Education Annual* 13: 69–98.

U.S. Department of Education. 2002. *Strategic Plan 2002–2007.* Washington, DC: U.S. Department of Education.

U.S. News and World Report. 2006. *2006 Graduate School Rankings.* http://www.usnews.com/usnews/edu/grad/rankings/edu/brief/edurank_brief.php.

Van Alstyne, William W. ed. 1993. *Freedom and Tenure in the Academy.* Durham: Duke University Press.

Veblen, Thorstein. 1996. *The Higher Learning in America.* New Brunswick, NJ: Transaction Publishers.

Veysey, Laurence R. 1965. *The Emergence of the American University.* Chicago: University of Chicago Press.

Vierra, Andrea, and Judith Pollock. 1992. *Reading Educational Research,* 2nd ed. Scottsdale, AZ: Gorsuch Scarisbrick Publishers.

Vinovskis, Maris A. 1996. "The Changing Role of the Federal Government in Educational Research and Statistics." *History of Education Quarterly* 36, no. 2: 111–28.

Walls, Laura Dassow. 1997. "Textbooks and Texts from the Brooks: Inventing Scientific Authority in America." *American Quarterly* 49, no. 1: 1–25.

Washburn, Jennifer. 2005. *University, Inc.: The Corporate Corruption of American Higher Education.* New York: Basic Books.

Webster's New World Dictionary of the American Language. 1989. New York: Simon and Schuster.

Weinstein, Matthew. 2004. "Randomized Design and the Myth of Certain Knowledge: Guinea Pig Narratives and Cultural Critique." *Qualitative Inquiry* 10, no. 2: 246–60.

Wells, Susan. 1996. *Sweet Reason: Rhetoric and the Discourses of Modernity.* Chicago: University of Chicago Press.

What Works Clearinghouse. "Review Process." http://www.whatworks.ed.gov/review-process/standards.html.

————. "Topics." http:www.whatworks.ed.gov/topics/current_topics.html.

————. "Who We Are." http:www.whatworks.ed.gov/whoweare/overview.html.

Whitehead, Alfred North. 1925. *Science and the Modern World*. New York: The New American Library.

Whitehurst, Grover J. n.d. *Statement on Research Methods*. Washington, DC: Institute of Education Sciences.

Williams, Raymond. 1983. *Keywords: A Vocabulary of Culture and Society*. Oxford: Oxford University Press.

Willinsky, John. 1998. *Learning to Divide the World: Education at Empire's End*. Minneapolis: University of Minnesota Press.

————. 2001. "The Strategic Education Research Program and the Public Value of Research." *Educational Researcher* 30, no. 1: 5–14.

————. 2005. "Scientific Research in a Democratic Culture: Or What's a Social Science For?" *Teachers College Record* 107, no. 1: 35–51.

Wimer, Jeffrey W., and Debra S. Vredenburg. November 1, 2003. "When Ideology Sabotages the Truth: The Politics of Privately-funded Educational Vouchers in One Urban School District." Mexico City, Mexico: American Educational Studies Association.

Winter, Richard, Morwenna Griffiths, and Kath Green 1992. "The 'Academic' Qualities of Practice: What Are the Criteria for a Practice-based Ph.D.?" *Studies in Higher Education* 25, no. 1: 25–37.

Young, Lauren Jones. 2001. "Border Crossings and Other Journeys: Re-envisioning the Doctoral Preparation of Education Researchers." *Educational Researcher* 30, no. 5: 3–5.

Young, Michael D. 1961. *The Rise of the Meritocracy, 1870–2033: An Essay on Education and Equality*. New York: Penguin Books.

INDEX